Book

Sixth Edition

The Humanistic Tradition

Faith, Reason, and Power in the
Early Modern World

Book

4

Sixth Edition

The Humanistic Tradition

Faith, Reason, and Power
in the Early Modern World

Gloria K. Fiero

Boston   Burr Ridge, IL   Dubuque, IA   New York   San Francisco   St. Louis
Bangkok   Bogotá   Caracas   Kuala Lumpur   Lisbon   London   Madrid   Mexico City
Milan   Montreal   New Delhi   Santiago   Seoul   Singapore   Sydney   Taipei   Toronto

THE HUMANISTIC TRADITION, BOOK 4
FAITH, REASON, AND POWER IN THE EARLY MODERN WORLD

Published by McGraw-Hill, an imprint of The McGraw-Hill Companies, Inc.,
1221 Avenue of the Americas, New York, NY, 10020.

This book is printed on acid-free paper.

3 4 5 6 7 8 9 0 / 0

Library of Congress Cataloging-in-Publication Data

Fiero, Gloria K.
    The humanistic tradition / Gloria K. Fiero.– 6th ed.
        p. cm.
    Includes bibliographical references and index.
    ISBN-13: 978-0-07-352397-2 (bk. 1 : alk. paper)
    ISBN-10: 0-07-352397-6 (bk. 1 : alk. paper)
        1. Civilization, Western–History–Textbooks.
        2. Humanism–History–Textbooks.
        I. Title.

CB245.F47 2009
909'.09821–dc22

2009027018

Permissions Acknowledgments appear on page 170,
and on this page by reference.

Publisher: *Chris Freitag*
Director of Development: *Rhona Robbin*
Associate Sponsoring Editor: *Betty Chen*
Editorial Coordinator: *Sarah Remington*
Marketing Manager: *Pamela Cooper*
Managing Editor: *David Staloch*
Senior Production Supervisor: *Tandra Jorgensen*
Typeface: *10/12 Goudy*
Printer: *Phoenix Offset, Hong Kong*

http://www.mhhe.com

 This book was designed and produced by
Laurence King Publishing Ltd., London
www.laurenceking.com

Commissioning Editor: *Kara Hattersley-Smith*
Senior Editor: *Melissa Danny*
Production Controller: *Simon Walsh*
Picture researcher: *Emma Brown*
Designer: *Robin Farrow*

Front cover
Jacques-Louis David, *The Death of Marat*
(detail), 1793. Oil on canvas, 65 x 50½ in.
© Musées Royaux des Beaux-Arts de
Belgique, Bruxelles.

Back cover
Unknown artist, portrait of Emperor Kangxi
reading. Imperial Palace Museum, Beijing.

Frontispiece
Jan Steen, *The Drawing Lesson*, 1665. Oil
on canvas, 19⅜ x 16¼ in. The J. Paul Getty
Museum, Los Angeles. Credit: © The J. Paul
Getty Museum.

Series Contents

Book 4 Contents

Preface

Each generation leaves a creative legacy, the sum of its ideas and achievements. This legacy represents the response to our effort to ensure our individual and collective survival, our need to establish ways of living in harmony with others, and our desire to understand our place in the universe. Meeting the challenges of *survival, communality,* and *self-knowledge,* we have created and transmitted the tools of science and technology, social and political institutions, religious and philosophic systems, and various forms of personal expression—the totality of which we call *culture.* Handed down from generation to generation, this legacy constitutes the humanistic tradition, the study of which is called *humanities.*

The Humanistic Tradition originated more than two decades ago out of a desire to bring a global perspective to my humanities courses. My fellow humanities teachers and I recognized that a western-only perspective was no longer adequate to understanding the cultural foundations of our global world, yet none of the existing texts addressed our needs. At the time, the challenge was daunting—covering the history of western poetry and prose, art, music, and dance was already an ambitious undertaking for a survey course; how could we broaden the scope to include Asia, Africa, and the Americas without over-packing the course? What evolved was a thematic approach to humanities, not as a collection of disciplines, but as a discipline in itself. This thematic approach considers the interrelatedness of various forms of expression as they work to create, define, and reflect the unique culture of a given time and place. It offers a conceptual framework for students to begin a study of the humanistic tradition that will serve them throughout their lives. I am gratified that others have found this approach to be highly workable for their courses, so much so that *The Humanistic Tradition* has become a widely adopted book for the humanities course.

The Humanistic Tradition pioneered a flexible six-book format in recognition of the varying chronological range of humanities courses. Each slim volume was also convenient for students to bring to classes, the library, and other study areas. The sixth edition continues to be available in this six-book format, as well as in a two-volume set for the most common two-term course configuration.

The Sixth Edition of
The Humanistic Tradition

While the sixth edition of *The Humanistic Tradition* contains a number of new topics, images, and selections, it remains true to my original goal of offering a manageable and memorable introduction to global cultures. At the same time, I have worked to develop new features that are specifically designed to help students master the material and critically engage with the text's primary source readings, art reproductions, and music recordings. The integration of literary, visual, and aural primary sources is a hallmark of the text, and every effort has been made to provide the most engaging translations, the clearest color images, and the liveliest recorded performances, as well as the most representative selections for every period. The book and companion supplements are designed to offer all of the resources a student and teacher will need for the course.

New Features that Promote Critical Thinking

New to the sixth edition are special features that emphasize connections between time periods, styles, and cultures, and specific issues of universal significance. These have been added to encourage critical thinking and classroom discussion.

- **Exploring Issues** focuses on controversial ideas and current debates, such as the battle over the ownership of antiquities, the role of the non-canonical Christian gospels, the use of optical devices in Renaissance art, the dating of African wood sculptures, and creationism versus evolution.
- **Making Connections** brings attention to contrasts and continuities ibetween past and present ideas, values, and styles. Examples include feudalism East and West, Classical antiquities as models for Renaissance artists, and African culture as inspiration for African-American artists.

New Features that Facilitate Learning and Understanding

The sixth edition provides chapter introductions and summaries that enhance the student's grasp of the materials, and a number of features designed to make the materials more accessible to students:

- **Looking Ahead** offers a brief, preliminary overview that introduces students to the main theme of the chapter.
- **Looking Back** closes each chapter with summary study points that encourage students to review key ideas.
- **Iconographic "keys"** to the meaning of images have been inset alongside selected artworks.
- **Extended captions** to illustrations throughout the text provide additional information about artworks and artists.
- **Chronology boxes** in individual chapters place the arts and ideas in historical background.
- **Before We Begin** precedes the Introduction with a useful guide to understanding and studying humanities.

Organizational Improvements and Updated Content

The sixth edition responds to teachers' requests that the coverage of Mesopotamia precede Egypt and other ancient African cultures in the opening chapters. The global coverage has been refined with revised coverage of the early Americas, new content on archeological discoveries in ancient Peru, a segment on the role of the West in the Islamic Middle East, and a discussion of China's global ascendance. Chapters 36 through 38 have been updated and reorganized: Ethnicity and ethnic identity have been moved to chapter 38 (Globalism and the Contemporary World), which brings emphasis to recent developments in digital technology, environmentalism, and global terrorism. Other revisions throughout the text also respond to teacher feedback; for example, a description of the *bel canto* style in music has been added; Jan van Eyck's paintings appear in both chapters 17 and 19 (in different contexts); and T. S. Eliot's works are discussed in both chapters 32 and 35.

Among the notable writers added to the sixth edition are William Blake, Jorge Luis Borges, Seamus Heaney, and John Ashbury. New additions to the art program include works by Benozzo Gozzoli, Buckminster Fuller, Kara Walker, Jeff Wall, Damien Hirst, El Anatsui, and Norman Foster.

Beyond *The Humanistic Tradition*

Connect Humanities

Connect Humanities is a learning and assessment tool designed and developed to improve students' performance by making the learning process more efficient and more focused through the use of engaging, assignable content, which is text-specific and mapped to learning objectives, and integrated tools. Using this platform, instructors can deliver assignments easily online, and save time through an intuitive and easy to use interface and through modifiable pre-built assignments.

Connect provides instructors with the Image Bank, a way to easily browse and search for images and to download them for use in class presentations.

Visit mcgrawhillconnect.com

Traditions: Humanities Readings through the Ages

Traditions is a new database conceived as both a stand-alone product as well as a companion source to McGraw-Hill's humanities titles. The collection is broad in nature, containing both western and non-western readings from ancient and contemporary eras, hand-picked from such disciplines as literature, philosophy, and science. The flexibility of Primis Online's database allows the readings to be arranged both chronologically and by author.

Visit www.primisonline.com/traditions

Music Listening Compact Discs

Two audio compact discs have been designed exclusively for use with *The Humanistic Tradition*. CD One corresponds to the music listening selections discussed in Books 1–3 (Volume I), and CD Two contains the music in Books 4–6 (Volume II). Music logos (right) that appear in the margins of the text refer to the Music Listening Selections found on the audio compact discs. The compact discs can be packaged with any or all of the six books or two-volume versions of the text.

Online Learning Center

A complete set of web-based resources for *The Humanistic Tradition* can be found at

www.mhhe.com/fierotht6e

Materials for students include an audio pronunciation guide, a timeline, research and writing tools, links to select readings, and suggested readings and Web sites. The instructor side of the Online Learning Center includes discussion and lecture suggestions, music listening guides, key themes and topics, and study questions for student discussion and review and written assignments.

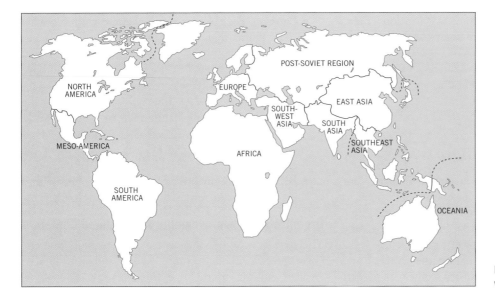

Key map indicating areas shown as white highlights on the locator maps

Acknowledgments

Personal thanks go to my discerning editor, Betty Chen (McGraw-Hill), and to the editorial and production staff of Laurence King Publishing. As with former editions, my colleague and husband, James H. Dormon, read all parts of the manuscript and made substantive editorial suggestions. This edition is dedicated to him. I am also grateful to Eric C. Shiner (curator and art historian) for his assistance in contemporary Asian art.

In the preparation of the sixth edition, I have benefited from the suggestions and comments generously offered by Donald F. Andrews (Chattanooga State Technical Community College), Samuel Barnett (University of Maryland), Bobbie Bell (Seminole Community College), Marjorie Berman (Red Rocks Community College), Terri Birch (Harper College), Pat Bivin (International Academy of Design and Technology), Casey Blanton (Daytona Beach Community College), Diane Boze (Northeastern State University), Nellie Brannan (Brevard Community College), Diane S. Brown (Valencia Community College, Osceola), Joyce Caldwell Smith (University of Tennessee at Chattanooga), Cynthia Clegg (Pepperdine University), Harry S. Coverston (University of Central Florida), Julie deGraffenried (Baylor University), Ann Dunn (University of North Carolina, Asheville), Renae Edge (Norwalk Community College), Monika Fleming (Edgecombe Community College), A. Flowers (College of Alameda), Rod Freeman (Estrella Mountain College), Arby L. Frost (Roanoke College), Samuel Garren (North Carolina A&T University), Caryl Gibbs (Rose State College), Robin Hardee (Santa Fe College), Melissa T. Hause (Belhaven College), Barbara A. Hergianto (South Florida Community College), Dale Hoover (Edison College), Ron Israel (San Diego Mesa College), Marian Jacobson (Albany College of Pharmacy), Theresa James (South Florida Community College), Judith Jamieson (Providence College), Keith W. Jensen (William Rainey Harper College), Jerry Jerman (University of Oklahoma), Patrick Kiley (Marian College), Donald Koke (Butler County College), Jayson Larremore (Oral Roberts University), Bonnie Loss (Glendale Community College), Diana Lurz (Rogers State University), Eldonna Loraine May (Wayne State University), Barbara J. Mayo (Northeast Lakeview College), Susan McClung (Hillsborough Community College), Trudy McNair (Valencia Community College), Richard Middleton-Kaplan (Harper College), Yvonne J. Milspaw (Harrisburg Area Community College), Maureen Moore (Cosumnes River College), Sean P. Murphy (College of Lake County), Judy Navas (Sonoma State University), Jack L. Nawrocik (St. Philip's College), James Norwood (University of Minnesota), Craig Payne (Indian Hills College), Randall M. Payne (South Florida Community College), Laurel S. Peterson (Norwalk Community College), Richard W. Peyton (Florida Agricultural and Mechanical University), Anne L. Pierce (Hampton University), William H. Porterfield (West Virginia State Community & Technical College), Judith Poxon (Sacramento City College), Robin Poynor (University of Florida), Verbie Lovorn Prevost (University of Tennessee at Chattanooga), Andreas W. Reif (Southern New Hampshire University), Denise M. Rogers (University of Louisiana at Lafayette), Karen Rumbley (Valencia Community College), Maria Rybakova (San Diego State University), John Scolaro (Valencia Community College), Vanessa Sheldon (College of the Desert), Mary Slater (Missouri Valley College), Linda Spain (Linn-Benton Community College), Hartley S. Spatt (SUNY Maritime College), Lisa Stokes (Seminole Community College), Alice Taylor (West Los Angeles College), Andreia Thaxton (Florida Community College at Jacksonville), Randall K. Van Schepen (Roger Williams University), Andrew Vassar (Northeastern State University), John Michael Vohlidka (Gannon University), Laura Wadenpfuhl (New Jersey City College), John R. Webb (Highland Community College), Jason Whitmarsh (Florida State College at Jacksonville), and Linda Woodward (Lone Star Montgomery College).

—Gloria K. Fiero

BEFORE WE BEGIN

Studying humanities engages us in a dialogue with *primary sources*: works original to the age in which they were produced. Whether literary, visual, or aural, a primary source is a text; the time, place, and circumstances in which it was created constitute the context; and its various underlying meanings provide the subtext. Studying humanities from the perspective of text, context, and subtext helps us understand our cultural legacy and our place in the larger world.

Text

The *text* of a primary source refers to its medium (that is, what it is made of), its form (its outward shape), and its content (the subject it describes).

Literature: Literary form varies according to the manner in which words are arranged. So, *poetry*, which shares rhythmic organization with music and dance, is distinguished from *prose*, which normally lacks regular rhythmic patterns. Poetry, by its freedom from conventional grammar, provides unique opportunities for the expression of intense emotions. Prose usually functions to convey information, to narrate, and to describe.

Philosophy, (the search for truth through reasoned analysis), and *history* (the record of the past) make use of prose to analyze and communicate ideas and information.

In literature, as in most forms of expression, content and form are usually interrelated. The subject matter or form of a literary work determines its *genre*. For instance, a long narrative poem recounting the adventures of a hero constitutes an *epic*, while a formal, dignified speech in praise of a person or thing constitutes a *eulogy*.

The Visual Arts: The visual arts employ a wide variety of media, ranging from the traditional colored pigments used in painting, to wood, clay, marble, and (more recently) plastic and neon used in sculpture, to a wide variety of digital media, including photography and film. The form or outward shape of a work of art depends on the manner in which the artist manipulates the elements of color, line, texture, and space. Unlike words, these formal elements lack denotative meaning.

The visual arts are dominantly spatial, that is, they operate and are apprehended in space. Artists manipulate form to describe or interpret the visible world (as in the genres of portraiture and landscape), or to create worlds of fantasy and imagination. They may also fabricate texts that are non-representational, that is, without identifiable subject matter.

Music and Dance: The medium of music is sound. Like literature, music is durational: it unfolds over the period of time in which it occurs. The major elements of music are melody, rhythm, harmony, and tone color—formal elements that also characterize the oral life of literature.

However, while literary and visual texts are usually descriptive, music is almost always nonrepresentational: it rarely has meaning beyond sound itself. For that reason, music is the most difficult of the arts to describe in words.

Dance, the artform that makes the human body itself the medium of expression, resembles music in that it is temporal and performance-oriented. Like music, dance exploits rhythm as a formal tool, and like painting and sculpture, it unfolds in space as well as in time.

Studying the text, we discover the ways in which the artist manipulates medium and form to achieve a characteristic manner of execution or expression that we call *style*. Comparing the styles of various texts from a single era, we discover that they usually share certain defining features and characteristics. Similarities between, for instance, ancient Greek temples and Greek tragedies, or between Chinese lyric poems and landscape paintings, reveal the unifying moral and aesthetic values of their respective cultures.

Context

The *context* describes the historical and cultural environment of a text. Understanding the relationship between text and context is one of the principal concerns of any inquiry into the humanistic tradition. To determine the context, we ask: In what time and place did our primary source originate? How did it function within the society in which it was created? Was it primarily decorative, didactic, magical, or propagandistic? Did it serve the religious or political needs of the community? Sometimes our answers to these questions are mere guesses. For instance, the paintings on the walls of Paleolithic caves were probably not "artworks" in the modern sense of the term, but, rather, magical signs associated with religious rituals performed in the interest of communal survival.

Determining the function of the text often serves to clarify the nature of its form, and vice-versa. For instance, in that the Hebrew Bible, the *Song of Roland*, and many other early literary works were spoken or sung, rather than read, such literature tends to feature repetition and rhyme, devices that facilitate memorization and oral delivery.

Subtext

The *subtext* of a primary source refers to its secondary or implied meanings. The subtext discloses conceptual messages embedded in or implied by the text. The epic poems of the ancient Greeks, for instance, which glorify prowess and physical courage, suggest an exclusively male perception of virtue. The state portraits of the seventeenth-century French king Louis XIV bear the subtext of unassailable and absolute power. In our own time, Andy Warhol's serial adaptations of Coca-Cola bottles offer wry commentary on the commercial mentality of American society. Examining the implicit message of the text helps us determine the values of the age in which it was produced, and offers insights into our own.

Summary of the Renaissance and the Reformation

The following paragraphs provide an overview of the Renaissance and Reformation, the two movements that ushered in the modern era in the West. This summary of fifteenth- and sixteenth-century culture (dealt with in detail in Book 3) offers some background to the materials contained in Books 4, 5, and 6, which deal with the modern era in a global context.

Classical Humanism

The effort to recover, edit, and study ancient Greek and Latin manuscripts, a movement known as Classical humanism, first occurred in fourteenth-century Italy, where it marked the beginnings of the Renaissance. This revival of Greco-Roman culture was to spread throughout Western Europe over the following 300 years. Petrarch, the father of humanism, provided the model for Renaissance scholarship and education. He promoted the study of the classic Greek and Latin writers, especially Cicero, encouraged textual criticism, and wrote introspective and passionate sonnets that were revered and imitated for centuries to come.

The city of Florence was the unrivaled center of Classical humanism in the first 150 years of the Renaissance. A thriving commercial and financial center dominated by a well-to-do middle class, Florence found political and cultural leadership in such wealthy and sophisticated families as the Medici. Classical humanism helped to cultivate a sense of civic pride, a new respect for oral and written eloquence, and a set of personal values that sustained the ambitions of the rising merchant class.

Fifteenth-century humanists carried on Petrarch's quest to recover the Classical past. Ficino translated the entire body of Plato's writings, while Pico's investigations in Hebrew and Arabic led him to believe that the world's great minds shared a single, universal truth. Pico's *Oration on the Dignity of Man* proclaimed the centrality of humankind and defended the unlimited freedom of the individual within the universal scheme.

Renaissance humanists cultivated the idea of the good life. Following Alberti's maxim, "A man can do anything he wants," they applied the moral precepts of the Classical past to such contemporary pursuits as diplomacy, politics, and the arts. While Petrarch and his peers were concerned primarily with the recovery of Classical manuscripts and the production of critical editions, Alberti, Castiglione, and Machiavelli infused scholarship with action. Allying their scrutiny of the past with an empirical study of the present, they fostered a heroic ideal of the individual that surpassed all Classical models. For Alberti, wealth and authority proceeded from the exercise of *virtù*; for Castiglione, the superior breed of human being was *l'uomo universale*, the well-rounded person; for Machiavelli, only a ruthless master of power politics could ensure the survival of the state. Alberti, Castiglione, and Machiavelli were representative of the larger group of Renaissance humanists who envisioned self-knowledge and individualism as crucial to success in the secular world. Their views shaped the modern character of the humanistic tradition in the European West.

Renaissance Artists

The artists of the Renaissance brought a scientific curiosity to the study of the natural world and untiringly investigated its operations. Such Early Renaissance artists as Donatello, Pollaiuolo, Masaccio, and Brunelleschi studied the mechanics of the human body, the effects of light on material substances, and the physical appearance of objects in three-dimensional space. At the same time, Renaissance artists were masters of invention: they perfected the technique of oil painting, formulated the laws of perspective, and applied the principles of Classical art to the representation of Christian and contemporary subjects. Patronized by a wealthy middle class, they revived such this-worldly genres as portraiture and gave new attention to the nude body as an object of natural beauty.

The art of the High Renaissance marks the culmination of a hundred-year effort to wed the techniques of naturalistic representation to Classical ideals of proportion and order. Leonardo da Vinci, the quintessential artist–scientist, tried to reconcile empirical experience with abstract principles of design. The compositions of Raphael, with their monumental scale and unity of design, became standards by which Western paintings would be judged for centuries. The multitalented Michelangelo brought a heroic idealism to the treatment of traditional Christian and Classical themes. In Venice, Titian's painterly handling of the reclining female nude represented a new and more sensuous naturalism. The centrally planned buildings of Bramante and Palladio realized the architectural ideals of harmony, balance, and clarity pursued in the Early Renaissance by Brunelleschi and Alberti.

The Renaissance produced an equally splendid flowering in music, especially among Franco-Flemish composers. Secular compositions began to outnumber religious ones. The techniques of imitation and word painting infused both religious and secular music with homogeneity and increased expressiveness. Printed sheet music helped to popularize the madrigal and other secular, vernacular song forms. Instrumental music and dance now emerged as independent genres. Like their Classical predecessors, Renaissance artists placed human concerns and feelings at the center of their creative efforts. A spirit of optimism, combined with intellectual curiosity and increasing worldliness, fueled the early modern era in the West.

Shattering the Old Order: Protest and Reform

The sixteenth century was a time of rapid change marked by growing secularism, advancing technology, and European overseas expansion. It was also an age of profound religious and social upheaval. Northern humanists led by Erasmus of Rotterdam studied early Christian literature and urged a return to the teachings of Jesus and the early church fathers. Demands for Church reform went hand in hand with the revival of early Christian writings to culminate in the Protestant Reformation.

Aided by Gutenberg's printing press, Martin Luther challenged the authority of the Church of Rome. He held that Scripture was the sole basis for religious interpretation and emphasized the idea of salvation through faith in God's grace rather than through good works. As Lutheranism and other Protestant sects proliferated throughout Europe, the unity of medieval Christendom was shattered.

The music and the art of the Northern Renaissance reflect the mood of religious reform. In music, the Lutheran chorale became the vehicle of Protestant piety. In art, the increasing demand for illustrated devotional literature and private devotional art stimulated the production of woodcuts and metal engravings. The works of Dürer and Grünewald exhibit the Northern Renaissance passion for realistic detail and graphic expression, while the fantastic imagery of Hieronymus Bosch suggests a pessimistic and typically Northern concern with sin and death. Bosch's preoccupation with the palpable forces of evil found its counterpart in the witch hunts of the sixteenth century. In painting, too, such secular subjects as portraiture, landscapes, and scenes of everyday life mirrored the tastes of a growing middle-class audience for an unidealized record of the visual world.

Northern Renaissance writers took a generally skeptical and pessimistic view of human nature. Erasmus, More, and Rabelais lampooned individual and societal failings and described the ruling influence of folly in all aspects of human conduct. In France, Montaigne devised the essay as an intimate form of rational reflection. In Spain, Cervantes' novel, *Don Quixote*, wittily attacked outmoded feudal values and ideals. The most powerful form of literary expression to evolve in the late sixteenth century, however, was secular drama. In the hands of William Shakespeare, the play became the ideal vehicle for reconciling personality and circumstance. Shakespeare's tragedies (as opposed, for instance, to Montaigne's essays) reveal the human condition through overt action, rather than through private reflection.

By the end of the sixteenth century, national loyalties, religious fanaticism, and commercial rivalries for control of trade with Africa, Asia, and the Americas had splintered the European community. These conditions rendered ever more complex the society of the West. And yet, on the threshold of modernity, the challenges to the human condition—economic survival, communality, self-knowledge, and the inevitability of death—were no less pressing than they had been 2000 years earlier. If the technology of the sixteenth century offered greater control over nature than ever before, it also provided more devastating weapons of war and mass destruction. In the centuries to come, the humanistic tradition would be shaped and reshaped by changing historical circumstances that would put the West in a position of increasing world dominance.

Chapter

20

The Catholic Reformation and the Baroque Style

ca. 1550–1750

"So sweet are the colloquies of love which pass between the soul and God …"
Saint Teresa of Avila

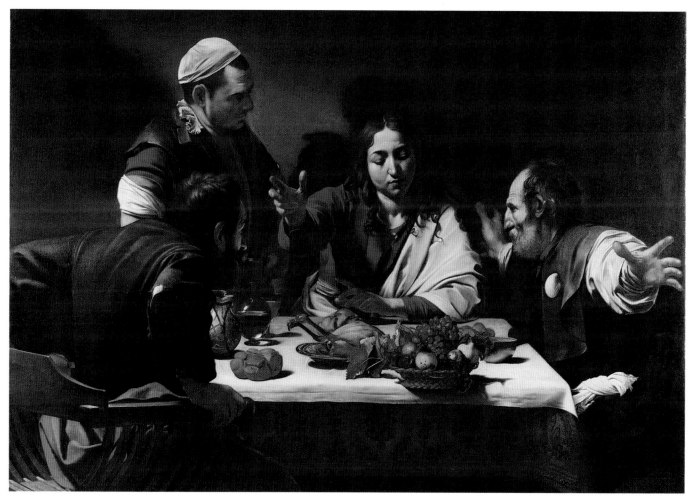

Figure 20.1 CARAVAGGIO, *The Supper at Emmaus*, ca. 1600. Oil on canvas, 4 ft. 7 in. × 6 ft. 5½ in. As Jesus raises his hand to bless the bread and wine, his two disciples recognize him as the Christ. Caravaggio dispenses with the traditional halo, but enshrouds Jesus with a dark shadow. Bread, fowl, and fruit are recreated in vivid realistic detail.

LOOKING AHEAD

The early modern era, often called the Age of the Baroque, was a time of deep contradictions. In the West, fervent, even mystical, religious sentiment vied with dramatic advances in science and scientific methods of investigation. Newly developed theories of constitutional government contended with firmly entrenched claims to monarchy. The rising wealth of a small segment of the population came to contrast with widespread poverty and old aristocratic privilege. Overseas exploration and travel produced a broader and more accurate geographic perception of the planet. All of these phenomena provided the context for the emergence of the style known as "the Baroque." Characterized by theatrical expressiveness and spatial grandeur, the Baroque became the hallmark of an age of vigorous expansion, fueled by the human ambition to master nature on a colossal scale. In Italy, it mirrored the religious fervor of the Catholic Reformation. In France and elsewhere among authoritarian regimes, it worked to glorify royal wealth and majesty. In Northern Europe, it conveyed the self-reflective spirit of Protestant devotionalism. Throughout the West, it embraced the new, dynamic view of the universe as set forth by proponents of the Scientific Revolution. Each of these aspects of the Baroque will be examined in the following chapters, beginning with its earliest phase during the advent of the Catholic Reformation.

The Catholic Reformation

The Protestant Reformation created a religious upheaval unlike any other in the history of Western Christendom. Luther's criticism of the Roman Catholic Church had encouraged religious devotion free of papal authority and had prepared the way for the rise of other Protestant sects (see chapter 19). The rival religious beliefs that fragmented Western Europe quickly accelerated into armed combat. The Thirty Years' War (1618–1648), which ended with the establishment of Protestantism throughout most of Northern Europe, caused the death of some five million Christians. During the sixteenth century, as Protestant sects began to lure increasing numbers of Christians away from Roman Catholicism, the Church launched an evangelical campaign to win back to Catholicism those who had strayed to Protestantism, a movement known as the Counter-Reformation. Even earlier, however, the Church had begun an internal program of papal and monastic reform, known as the Catholic Reformation. These two interdependent movements ultimately produced a renewed Catholicism that emphasized a return to the original ideals of the Church, ensuring its survival in the modern world.

Loyola and the Jesuits

The impetus for renewal came largely from fervent Spanish Catholics, the most notable of whom was Ignatius Loyola (1491–1556). A soldier in the army of King Charles I of Spain (the Holy Roman emperor Charles V; 1500–1558), Loyola brought to Catholicism the same iron will he had exercised on the battlefield. After his right leg was fractured by a French cannonball at the siege of Pamplona, Loyola became a religious teacher and a hermit, traveling lame and barefoot to Jerusalem in an effort to convert Muslims to Christianity. In the 1530s he founded the Society of Jesus, the most important of the many new monastic orders associated with the Catholic Reformation. The Society of Jesus, or Jesuits, followed Loyola in calling for a militant return to fundamental Catholic dogma and the strict enforcement of traditional church teachings. In addition to the monastic vows of celibacy, poverty, and obedience, the Jesuits took an oath of allegiance to the pope, whom they served as soldiers of Christ.

Under Loyola's leadership, the Jesuit order became the most influential missionary society of early modern times. Rigorously trained, its members acted as preachers, confessors, and teachers—leaders in educational reform and moral discipline. Throughout Europe, members of the newly formed order worked as missionaries to win back those who had strayed from "Mother Church." The Jesuits were fairly successful in stamping out Protestantism in much of France, southern Germany, and other parts of Europe. But their reach extended further: as pioneers in learning the languages and customs of India, China, and Japan, the Jesuits were the prime intermediaries between Europe and Asia from the sixteenth through the nineteenth century. In the Americas, which became prime targets for Jesuit activity, missionaries mastered Native American tribal languages and proceeded to convert thousands to Roman Catholicism. Their success in Mexico and Central and South America stamped these parts of the world with a distinctive cultural character.

The Jesuit order was a fascinating amalgam of two elements: mysticism and militant religious zeal. The first emphasized the personal and intuitive experience of God, while the second involved an attitude of unquestioned submission to the Church as the absolute source of truth. These two aspects of Jesuit training—mysticism and militancy—are reflected in Loyola's influential handbook, the *Spiritual Exercises*. In his introductory observations, Loyola explains that the spiritual exercises should do for the soul what physical exercise does for the body. As aids to the development of perfect spiritual discipline, these devotional exercises—each of which should occupy a full hour's time—engage the body in perfecting the soul. In the Fifth Exercise, a meditation on Hell, each of the five senses is summoned to heighten the mystical experience:

FIRST POINT: This will be to *see* in imagination the vast fires, and the souls enclosed, as it were, in bodies of fire.

SECOND POINT: To *hear* the wailing, the howling, cries, and blasphemies against Christ our Lord and against His saints.

THIRD POINT: With the sense of *smell* to perceive the smoke, the sulphur, the filth, and corruption.

FOURTH POINT: To *taste* the bitterness of tears, sadness, and remorse of conscience.

FIFTH POINT: With the sense of *touch* to feel the flames which envelop and burn the souls.

Loyola also insists on an unswerving commitment to traditional church teachings. Among his "rules for thinking with the Church" is the admonition that Christians put aside all judgments of their own and remain obedient to the "holy Mother, the hierarchical Church."

READING 20.1 From Loyola's *Spiritual Exercises* (1548)

The following rules should be observed to foster the true attitude of mind we ought to have in the church militant.

1 We must put aside all judgment of our own, and keep the mind ever ready and prompt to obey in all things the true Spouse of Christ our Lord, our holy Mother, the hierarchical Church.

2 We should praise sacramental confession, the yearly reception of the Most Blessed Sacrament, and praise more highly monthly reception, and still more weekly Communion, provided requisite and proper dispositions are present.

3 We ought to praise the frequent hearing of Mass, the singing of hymns, psalmody, and long prayers whether in the church or outside; likewise, the hours arranged at fixed times for the whole Divine Office, for every kind of prayer, and for the canonical hours.[1]

5 We must praise highly religious life, virginity, and continency; and matrimony ought not be praised as much as any of these.

5 We should praise vows of religion, obedience, poverty, chastity, and vows to perform other works . . . conducive to perfection. . . .

6 We should show our esteem for the relics of the saints by venerating them and praying to the saints. We should praise visits to the Station Churches,[2] pilgrimages, indulgences, jubilees,[3] crusade indults,[4] and the lighting of candles in churches.

7 We must praise the regulations of the Church with regard to

---

[1] The eight times of the day appointed for special devotions; see chapters 9 and 15.

[2] Churches with images representing the stages of Christ's Passion.

[3] A time of special solemnity, ordinarily every twenty-five years, proclaimed by the pope; also, special indulgences granted during that time. The jubilee principle is based on a biblical injunction to free slaves, return land to its original owners, and leave fields untilled once every fifty years (Leviticus 25).

[4] Church indulgences granted to Christian crusaders.

fast and abstinence. . . . We should praise works of penance, not only those that are interior but also those that are exterior.

8 We ought to praise not only the building and adornment of churches, but also images and veneration of them according to the subject they represent.

9 Finally, we must praise all the commandments of the Church, and be on the alert to find reasons to defend them, and by no means in order to criticize them. . . .

13 If we wish to proceed securely in all things, we must hold fast to the following principle: What seems to me white, I will believe black if the hierarchical Church so defines. For I must be convinced that in Christ our Lord, the bridegroom, and in His spouse the Church, only one Spirit holds sway, which governs and rules for the salvation of souls. For it is by the same Spirit and Lord who gave the Ten Commandments that our holy Mother Church is ruled and governed.

Q What is meant by "the true attitude of mind?" What by "the church militant?"

The Council of Trent

Loyola's affirmation of Roman Catholic doctrine anticipated the actions of the Council of Trent, the general church council that met between 1545 and 1563 to make doctrinal, ecclesiastical, and spiritual reforms. The Council of Trent reconfirmed all seven of the sacraments. It reasserted the basic tenets of Catholicism, including all theological matters that had been challenged by the Protestants. It set clear guidelines for the elimination of abuses among members of the clergy, emphasized preaching to the uneducated laity, and encouraged the regeneration of intellectual life within Catholic monasteries. Church leaders revived the activities of the Inquisition—the special court authorized to try and convict heretics (see chapter 12) and established the *Index Expurgatorius*, a list of books judged heretical and therefore forbidden to Catholic readers. Finally, the council approved a number of new religious orders, including the Jesuits, the Capuchins (an offshoot of the Franciscans notable as preachers and ministers to the poor), and the Ursulines (an order of females devoted to educating girls).

Over the course of more than ten years, Church reformers supported a broadly based Catholicism that emphasized the return to a personal relationship with Christ. At the same time, they encouraged an intuitive, even mystical, embrace of Mother Church. Although the Church of Rome would never again reassume the universal authority it had enjoyed during the Middle Ages, both its internal reforms and its efforts to rekindle the faith restored its dignity in the minds and hearts of its followers.

Catholicism's Global Reach

The evangelical activities of the Jesuits and other religious orders were widespread, but not uniformly successful. In China, where European traders were regarded as "ocean devils," the Catholic missionaries developed a cordial relationship with the intellectual classes and succeeded in converting a number of Chinese scholars. By the eighteenth century, however, disputes between the Jesuits and the Dominicans over the veneration of Confucius (aggravated by papal condemnation of Confucian rites in 1744) weakened Catholic influence.

In Japan, the first Jesuit missionaries, admirers of Tokugawa culture (see chapter 21), diligently mastered the Japanese language and culture. While the Jesuits introduced the Japanese to European styles of painting and music, the Portuguese (and thereafter, Dutch and English) merchants brought commercial interests to Japan (see chapter 18), thus clouding the evangelical aims of the Jesuits with European material ambitions. The Jesuit efforts at conversion were also frustrated by rival Franciscan missionaries. Over time, the Jesuits fell into disfavor with Japanese Buddhists, who came to view all Christians as potentially subversive to the traditional social order. By 1606, following decades of disruption caused by European efforts to win trading privileges in Japan, the Japanese outlawed Christianity. In 1624, following a wave of brutal persecutions of both European Christians and Japanese converts to Catholicism, the country expelled almost all Western foreigners from Japanese soil.

Christian evangelism in the Americas proved to be far more successful. In sixteenth-century Mexico, where Spanish political authority went largely unchallenged, Catholicism went hand in hand with colonization. The arrival of the Jesuits in 1571 followed that of the Augustinians, the Dominicans, and the Franciscans in a vast program of Christianization. Just as the convergence of Europeans and Native Americans came to produce a unique new "Latin American" population, so the blend of European Catholic and native religious traditions produced a creolized Mexican culture. A formidable example of this phenomenon, and one that testifies to the powerful religious impact of Catholicism, is the Miracle of the Virgin of Guadalupe. In 1531, ten years after the conquest of Mexico by Cortés, on the site of a former shrine to the Aztec mother-goddess, the Virgin Mary appeared before a simple Mexican peasant named Juan Diego. Speaking in the native Aztec tongue, she asked that a church honoring her be built on that site. When the local bishop asked for a sign to prove the truth of Juan's story, the Virgin instructed the peasant to gather roses (blooming miraculously in winter) and deliver them to the bishop. As the roses were unloaded from Juan's cloak, the image of the Virgin was found imprinted on the fabric.

The legend of this miraculous apparition, commemorated in hundreds of carved and painted images (Figure 20.2), became the basis for the most important religious cult in Mexican history: the cult of the Virgin of Guadalupe. The colonial cult of Guadalupe worships the Virgin in the traditional medieval guise of mother, intercessor, and protector, but it also exalts her as the symbol of Mexican national consciousness. At her shrine—the goal of thousands of pilgrims each year—and at hundreds of chapels throughout

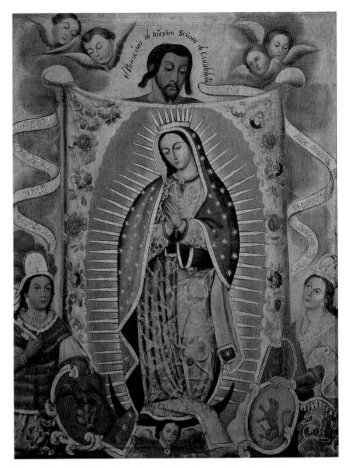

Figure 20.2 *The Virgin of Guadalupe,* 1746. Oil on wood. The cloak of Juan Diego bears the imprint of the Virgin surrounded by an illumined mandorla and the roses that miraculously fell before the bishop. The basilica of Our Lady of Guadalupe in Mexico City remains the second most frequently visited religious shrine in the world.

Mexico, the faithful pay homage to the Madonna, who is shown standing on a crescent moon, surrounded by a corona of sunrays and angels bearing the colors of the Mexican flag. The votive figure of the Virgin of Guadalupe was enthusiastically promoted by the Jesuits beginning in the late sixteenth century, and her widespread popularity as protectress of Mexico has persisted even into modern times: in 1910, she was made an honorary general of the Mexican Revolution.

Literature and the Catholic Reformation

The ideals of the Catholic Reformation infused the arts of the sixteenth and seventeenth centuries. In literature, there appeared a new emphasis on heightened spirituality and on personal visionary experience. Like the Reformation itself, a number of its greatest mystics came from Spain. Juan de Yepes Alvarez, better known as Saint John of the Cross (1542–1591), left some of the finest religious poetry in the corpus of Spanish literature. His *Dark Night of the Soul* (1585) describes the journey of the soul from its bodily prison to spiritual union with God. A Carmelite priest and friar, Saint John worked to eliminate moral laxity and restore absolute poverty in the monasteries. His efforts at establishing new Carmelite houses in Spain were shared by the Carmelite nun, Teresa of Avila.

Teresa of Avila

The early life of Teresa of Avila (1515–1582) was spent founding religious houses and defending the Carmelite practice of going without shoes (as an expression of humility). Traveling all over Spain, she became notorious as "the roving nun." It was not until she was almost forty years old that her life as a visionary began. Teresa's visions describe her firsthand experience of frequent visitations by Jesus Christ over a two-year period. Like the twelfth-century mystic, Hildegard of Bingen (see chapter 12), Teresa embraced the intuitive knowledge of God. But unlike Hildegard, whose writings engage natural and supernatural details, Teresa's experience is physical (and explicitly sensory). Her love is the longing for oneness with God. In the *Visions* physical suffering evokes psychic bliss; and her union with the divine, as illustrated in the following excerpt, is couched in the language of erotic desire and fulfillment. As the Lord's flaming arrow is withdrawn from her body, Teresa is left "completely afire."

READING 20.2 From Saint Teresa's *Visions* (1611)

It pleased the Lord that I should sometimes see the following   1
vision. I would see beside me, on my left hand, an angel in
bodily form—a type of vision which I am not in the habit of
seeing, except very rarely. Though I often see representations
of angels, my visions of them are of the type which I first
mentioned. It pleased the Lord that I should see this angel in
the following way. He was not tall, but short, and very
beautiful, his face so aflame that he appeared to be one of the
highest types of angel who seem to be all afire. They must be
those who are called cherubim: they do not tell me their names   10
but I am well aware that there is a great difference between
certain angels and others, and between these and others still,
of a kind that I could not possibly explain. In his hands I saw a
long golden spear and at the end of the iron tip I seemed to
see a point of fire. With this he seemed to pierce my heart
several times so that it penetrated to my entrails. When he
drew it out, I thought he was drawing them out with it and he
left me completely afire with a great love for God. The pain
was so sharp that it made me utter several moans; and so
excessive was the sweetness caused me by this intense pain   20
that one can never wish to lose it, nor will one's soul be
content with anything less than God. It is not bodily pain, but
spiritual, though the body has a share in it—indeed, a great
share. So sweet are the colloquies of love which pass between
the soul and God that if anyone thinks I am lying I beseech
God, in His goodness, to give him the same experience. …

Q Which strikes you as more effective: the written or the visual version of Saint Teresa's vision? Why so?

Crashaw

The language of religious ecstasy also infused the poetry of the English Catholic Richard Crashaw (1613–1649). Born into a Protestant family, Crashaw converted to Catholicism early in life. His religious poems, written in Latin and English, reflect the dual influence of Loyola's meditations and Teresa's visions. At least two of his most lyrical pieces are dedicated to Saint Teresa: *A Hymn to the Name and Honor of the Admirable Saint Teresa* and *The Flaming Heart, upon the Book and Picture of the Seraphical Saint Teresa, as She Is Usually Expressed with a Seraphim beside Her*. The latter poem suggests that Crashaw was familiar with Bernini's sculpted version of Teresa's vision before it was publicly unveiled in Rome (Figure **20.3**). Representative of this visionary sensibility, the last sixteen lines of *The Flaming Heart*, reproduced in Reading 20.3, are rhapsodic in their intense expression of personal emotion. Erasing boundaries between erotic and spiritual love, Crashaw pleads that Teresa ravish his soul, even as she has been ravished by God.

READING 20.3 From Crashaw's *The Flaming Heart* (1652)

O thou undaunted daughter of desires!
By all thou dower of lights and fires;
By all the eagle in thee, all the dove;
By all thy lives and deaths of love;
By thy large draughts of intellectual day,
And by thy thirsts of love more large than they;
By all thy brim-filled bowls of fierce desire,
By thy last morning's draught of liquid fire;
By the full kingdom of that final kiss
That seized thy parting soul, and sealed thee His;
By all the heavens thou hast in Him,
Fair sister of the seraphim,
By all of Him we have in thee;
Leave nothing of myself in me!
Let me so read thy life that I
Unto all life of mine may die.

Q What is the nature of the love that Crashaw describes?

Q Which images in this poem contribute to its erotic undertone?

The Visual Arts and the Catholic Reformation

Mannerist Painting in Italy

The religious zeal of the Catholic reformers inspired a tremendous surge of artistic activity, especially in Italy and Spain. In Venice and Rome, the centers of Italian cultural life, the clarity and order of High Renaissance art gave way to the visual eccentricities of *Mannerism* (from the Italian *maniera*, meaning "style"). Coined in the twentieth

Figure 20.3 GIANLORENZO BERNINI, *The Ecstasy of Saint Teresa*, 1645–1652. Marble, height of group 11 ft. 6 in.

century, the term "mannerism" describes an art more focused on style than content. Flourishing between ca. 1520 and 1610, and characterized by virtuosity in execution, artificiality, and affectation, the style became a vehicle for the spiritual upheavals of its time. Mannerist artists brought a new level of psychological intensity (bordering on disquiet) to visual expression. Their works mirrored the self-conscious spirituality and deep insecurities generated by Europe's religious wars and political rivalries.

The Mannerist style is already evident in *The Last Judgment* painted by the sixty-year-old Michelangelo on the east wall of the Sistine Chapel (Figure **20.4**). Between 1534 and 1541, only a few years after the armies of the Holy Roman Empire had sacked the city of Rome, Michelangelo

Figure 20.4 MICHELANGELO BUONARROTI, *The Last Judgment* (after restoration), 1536–1540. Fresco, 48 × 44 ft. Below the athletic figure of Christ sits Saint Bartholomew, who suffered martyrdom by being flayed alive. He holds a knife and his own flayed skin, on which some scholars see a self-portrait of Michelangelo.

returned to the chapel whose ceiling he had painted some twenty years earlier with the optimistic vision of salvation. Now, in a mood of brooding pessimism, he filled the altar wall with agonized, writhing figures that press dramatically against one another. Surrounding the wrathful Christ are the Christian saints and martyrs, who carry the instruments of their torture, and throngs of the resurrected—originally depicted nude but in 1564, in the wake of Catholic reform, draped to hide their genitals. Michelangelo has replaced the Classically proportioned figures, calm balance, and spatial clarity of High Renaissance painting with a more troubled and turbulent vision of salvation.

The traits of the Mannerist style can be seen best in the *Madonna of the Long Neck* (Figure **20.5**) by Parmigianino (1503–1540). In this work, the traditional subject of Madonna and Child is given a new mood of theatricality (compare Raphael's *Alba Madonna*; see chapter 17). Perched precariously above a courtyard adorned with a column that supports no superstructure, the unnaturally elongated Mother of God—her spidery fingers affectedly touching her chest—gazes at the oversized Christ Child, who seems to slip lifelessly off her lap. Onlookers crowd into the space from the left, while a small figure (perhaps a prophet) at the bottom right corner of the canvas draws our eye into distant space. Cool coloring and an overall smoky hue make the painting seem even more contrived and artificial, yet, by its very contrivance, unforgettable.

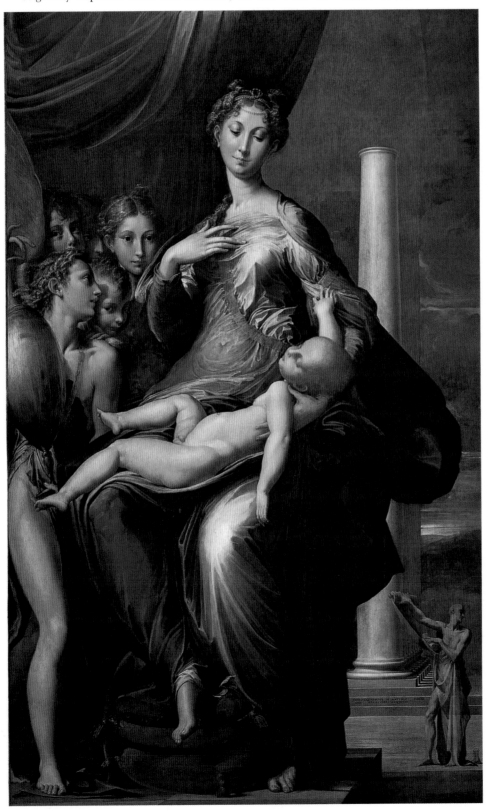

Figure 20.5 PARMIGIANINO,
Madonna of the Long Neck,
1534–1540. Oil on panel,
7 ft. 1 in. × 4 ft. 4 in.

MAKING CONNECTIONS

Figure 20.6 JACOPO TINTORETTO, *The Last Supper*, 1592–1594. Oil on canvas, 12 ft. × 18 ft. 8 in. Pictured against a concentrated burst of light at the upper end of the table, the Savior is pictured distributing the bread and wine to his disciples.

The degree to which the Mannerists rejected the guiding principles of High Renaissance painting is nowhere better illustrated than in a comparison between *The Last Supper* (Figure **20.6**) by the Venetian artist Jacopo Tintoretto (1518–1594) and the fresco of the same subject by Leonardo da Vinci (see chapter 17) executed approximately a century earlier (Figure **20.7**). In his rendering of the sacred event, Tintoretto renounces the symmetry and geometric clarity of Leonardo's composition. The receding lines of the table and the floor in Tintoretto's painting place the viewer above the scene and draw the eye toward a vanishing point that lies in a distant and uncertain space beyond the canvas. The even texture of Leonardo's fresco gives way in Tintoretto's canvas to vaporous contrasts of dark and light, produced by a smoking oil lamp. Clouds of angels flutter spectrally at the ceiling, and phosphorescent halos seem to electrify the agitated figures of the apostles. While Leonardo focuses on the human element of the Last Supper—the moment when Jesus acknowledges his impending betrayal—

Tintoretto illustrates the miraculous moment when Jesus initiates the sacrament by which the bread and wine become his flesh and blood. Yet, in a move toward greater naturalism, he sets the miracle amidst the ordinary activities of household servants, who occupy the entire right-hand portion of the picture

Figure 20.7 LEONARDO DA VINCI, *Last Supper*, ca. 1485–1498. Oil and tempera on plaster, 15 ft. 1⅛ in. × 28 ft. 10½ in.

Figure 20.8 EL GRECO, *The Agony in the Garden*, ca. 1585–1586. Oil on canvas, 6 ft. 1 in. × 9 ft. 1 in.

Mannerist Painting in Spain

The Mannerist passion for pictorial intensity was most vividly realized in the paintings of Domenikos Theotokopoulos, generally known (because of his Greek origins) as El Greco (1541–1614). Born in Crete, his early career was spent in Venice and Rome, but in the 1570s, he settled in Spain, where he remained—serving the Church and the Spanish king Philip II—until his death. El Greco preferred the expressive grace of Tintoretto to the more muscular vitality of Michelangelo. With the inward eye of a mystic, he produced visionary canvases marked by bold distortions of form, dissonant colors, and a daring handling of space. His elongated and flamelike figures, often highlighted by ghostly whites and yellow-grays, seem to radiate halos of light—auras that symbolize the luminous power of divine revelation. *The Agony in the Garden*, the scene of Jesus' final submission to the divine will, takes place in a moonlit landscape in which clouds, rocks, and fabrics billow and swell with mysterious energy (Figure **20.8**). Below the tempestuous sky, Judas (the small figure on the lower right) leads the arresting officers to the Garden of Gethsemane. The sleeping apostles, tucked away in a

cocoonlike shelter, violate rational space: they are too small in relation to the oversized image of Jesus and the angel who hovers above. El Greco's ambiguous spatial fields, which often include multiple vanishing points, his acrid greens and acid yellows, and his "painterly" techniques—his brushstrokes remain engagingly visible on the surface of the canvas—all contribute to the creation of a highly personal style that captured the mystical fervor of the new Catholicism.

The Baroque Style

The Baroque style, which flourished between roughly 1600 and 1750, brought heightened naturalism and a new level of emotionalism to Western art. Derived from the Portuguese word *barocco*, which describes the irregularly shaped pearls often featured in ornamental European decoration, the term *baroque* is associated with such features as ornateness, spatial grandeur, and theatrical flamboyance. In painting, the Baroque is characterized by asymmetric compositions, strong contrasts of light and dark, vigorous brushwork, and bold, illusionistic effects. Baroque sculptors engaged light and space to convey physical energy and dramatic movement. A synthesis of the arts—painting, sculpture, and architecture—promoted the ambitions of rulers and the religious beliefs of Catholics and Protestants.

Baroque Painting in Italy

The Baroque style originated in Italy and came to dominate artistic production throughout Europe and in those parts of the Americas colonized by Spain. Baroque artists worked to increase the dramatic expressiveness of religious subject matter in order to give viewers the sense that they were participating in the action of the scene. They copied nature faithfully and without idealization. Such was the ambition of the north Italian artist Michelangelo Merisi, better known as Caravaggio (1571–1610). The leading Italian painter of the seventeenth century, Caravaggio flouted Renaissance artistic conventions, even as he flouted the law—he was arrested for violent acts that ranged from throwing a plate of artichokes in the face of a tavern keeper to armed assault and murder. Having killed a tennis opponent in 1606, he was forced to flee Rome. In his paintings, Caravaggio renounced the grand style of the High Renaissance, which called for dignity, decorum, and the idealization of figures and setting. He recreated the Christian narrative as though its major events were occurring in the local taverns and streets of sixteenth-century Italy. Caravaggio dramatized these events with strong contrasts of light and

dark that give his figures a sculptural presence. A golden light bathes Christ and his disciples in *The Supper at Emmaus* (see Figure 20.1); Caravaggio "spotlights" Jesus at the moment when, raising his hand to bless the bread, he is recognized as the Christ (Luke 24:30–31). Caravaggio commands our attention by means of explicit theatrical gestures and by the use of a perspective device known as **foreshortening**: Christ's right arm, painted at a right angle to the picture plane, seems to project sharply outward, as if to bless the viewer as well as the bread. At the moment of recognition, the disciple at the right flings his arms outward along a diagonal axis that draws the viewer into the composition, while the figure at the left grips the arm of his chair as though to rise in astonishment. Unlike the visionary El Greco, Caravaggio brings sacred subjects down to earth with an almost cameralike naturalism. Where El Greco's saints and martyrs are ethereal, Caravaggio's are solid, substantive, and often ordinary. Their strong physical presence and frank homeliness transform biblical miracles into human narratives—a bold repudiation of Italian Renaissance conventions of beauty.

Caravaggio composed traditional religious subjects with unprecedented theatrical power and daring. In *The Crucifixion of Saint Peter* (Figure **20.9**), he arranged the figures in a tense, off-centered pinwheel that captures the

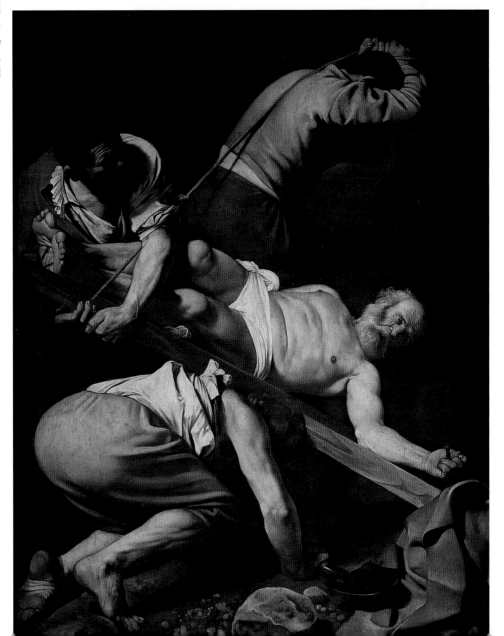

Figure 20.9 CARAVAGGIO,
The Crucifixion of Saint Peter, 1601. Oil on canvas, 7 ft. 6 in. × 5 ft. 9 in. While Caravaggio gives the saint a powerful body, he renders the face with an expression of vulnerability. Note how the highlighted areas of the composition seem to form the spokes of a wheel.

Figure 20.10 ARTEMISIA GENTILESCHI, *Judith Slaying Holofernes*, ca. 1614–1620. Oil on canvas, 6 ft. 6⅓ in. × 5 ft. 4 in.

and impact with Caravaggio's *Crucifixion of Saint Peter* (see Figure 20.9), illustrates the decapitation of an Assyrian general and enemy of Israel at the hands of a clever Hebrew widow. A story found in the Apocrypha (the noncanonical books of the Bible), the slaying of the tyrannical Holofernes was a favorite Renaissance allegory for liberty and religious defiance. Gentileschi brought to this subject the dramatic techniques of Caravaggio: realistically conceived figures, stark contrasts of light and dark, and a composition that brings the viewer painfully close to the event. She invested her subject with fierce intensity—the foreshortened body of the victim and the pinwheel arrangement of human limbs forces the eye to focus on the gruesome action of the swordblade as it severs head from neck in a shower of blood.

Gentileschi's favorite subjects were biblical heroines—she painted the Judith story some seven times. The violence she brought to these depictions may be said to reflect a personal sense of victimization: at the age of eighteen, she was raped by her drawing teacher and (during the sensational trial of her assailant) subjected to torture as a test of the truth of her testimony.

Apocrypha, Book of Judith, 12:16–20; 13:1–10

Holofernes' heart was ravished with [Judith] and his passion was aroused, for he had been waiting for an opportunity to seduce her from the day he first saw her. [17]So Holofernes said to her, "Have a drink and be merry with us!" [18]Judith said, "I will gladly drink, my lord, because today is the greatest day in my whole life." [19]Then she took what her maid had prepared and ate and drank before him. [20]Holofernes was greatly pleased with her, and drank a great quantity of wine, much more than he had ever drunk in any one day since he was born.

[1]When evening came, his slaves quickly withdrew. . . . They went to bed, for they all were weary because the banquet had lasted so long. [2]But Judith was left alone in the tent, with Holofernes stretched out on his bed, for he was dead drunk. . . .

[4]Then Judith, standing beside his bed, said in her heart, "O Lord God of all might, look in this hour on the work of my hands for the exaltation of Jerusalem. [5]Now indeed is the time to help your heritage and to carry out my design to destroy the enemies who have risen up against us."

[6]She went up to the bedpost near Holofernes' head, and took down his sword that hung there. [7]She came close to his bed, took hold of the hair of his head, and said, "Give me strength today, O Lord God of Israel!" [8]Then she struck his neck twice with all her might, and cut off his head. [9]Next she rolled his body off the bed and pulled down the canopy from the posts. Soon afterward she went out and gave Holofernes' head to her maid, [10]who placed it in her food bag.

eccentricity of Saint Peter's torment (he was crucified upside down). By placing these large, vigorously modeled figures up against the picture plane, he reduced the psychological distance between the viewer and the subject. Staged against a darkened background, the action seems to take place within the viewer's space—a space whose cruel light reveals such banal details as the executioner's dirty feet. True to the ideals of the Catholic Reformation, Caravaggio's paintings appealed to the senses rather than to the intellect. They also introduced into European art a new and vigorously lifelike realization of the natural world—one that daringly mingled the sacred and the profane.

Caravaggio's powerful style had considerable impact throughout Europe; however, his most talented follower was also Italian. Born in Rome, Artemisia Gentileschi (1593–1653) was the daughter of a highly esteemed painter, himself a follower of Caravaggio. Artemisia was trained by her father, but soon outstripped him in technical proficiency and imagination. Since women were not permitted to draw from nude male models, they rarely painted large-scale canvases with biblical, historical, or mythological themes that usually required nude figures; instead, their efforts were confined to the genres of portrait painting and still life (see chapter 23). Gentileschi's paintings, however, challenged tradition. Her powerful rendering of Judith slaying Holofernes (Figure **20.10**), which compares in size

Baroque Sculpture in Italy

Gianlorenzo Bernini (1598–1680), Caravaggio's contemporary, brought the theatrical spirit of Baroque painting to Italian architecture and sculpture. A man of remarkable technical virtuosity, Bernini was the chief architect of seventeenth-century Rome, as well as one of its leading sculptors. Under Bernini's direction, Rome became the "city of fountains," a phenomenon facilitated by the early seventeenth-century revival of the old Roman aqueducts. Richly adorned with dolphins, mermaids, and tritons, the fountain—its waters dancing and sparkling in the shifting wind and light—was the favorite ornamental device of the Baroque era (Figure 20.11).

Just as Caravaggio reshaped the tradition of Renaissance painting by way of pictorial illusionism, so Bernini challenged Renaissance sculptural tradition by investing it with a virtuosic naturalism and dramatic movement. He was determined, as he himself confessed, to "render the marble flexible." His life-sized marble sculpture of David (Figure 20.12) portrays this favorite biblical personality in a manner that recreates the very action of his assault on Goliath. In contrast with the languid and effeminate David of Donatello (see Figure 17.2) or the Classically posed hero of Michelangelo (see Figure 17.33), Bernini's David appears in mid-action, stretching the slingshot behind him as he prepares to launch the rock at his adversary: his torso twists

Figure 20.11 GIANLORENZO BERNINI, *Fountain of the Four Rivers*, 1648–1651. Travertine and marble. Piazza Navona, Rome.

Figure 20.12 GIANLORENZO BERNINI, *David*, 1623. Marble, 5 ft. 7 in.

vigorously at the waist, his face contorts with fierce determination, and his muscles strain with tense energy. The viewer, occupying the space "implied" by David's explosive action, is drawn unwittingly into the visual narrative.

Bernini's most important contribution to Baroque religious sculpture was his multimedia masterpiece *The Ecstasy of Saint Teresa* (see Figure 20.3), executed between 1645 and 1652 for the Cornaro Chapel of Santa Maria della Vittoria in Rome (Figure **20.13**). Bringing to life Saint Teresa's autobiographical description of divine seduction (see Reading 20.2). Bernini depicts the swooning saint with head sunk back and eyes half closed. A smiling angel, resembling a teenage cupid, gently lifts her bodice to withdraw the flaming arrow of divine love. Bold illusionism heightens the theatrical effect: the angel's marble draperies flutter and billow with tense energy, while Teresa's slack and heavy gown accents her ecstatic surrender. Teresa reclines on a marble cloud, which floats in heavenly space; the uncertain juxtaposition of the saint and the cloud below her suggests the experience of levitation described in her vision. Sweetness and eroticism dominate this extraordinary image.

But Bernini's conception goes beyond the medium of sculpture to achieve an unparalleled degree of theatrical illusionism. He situates Teresa beneath a colonnaded marble canopy from which gilded wooden rays appear to cast heaven's supernatural light. Real light entering through the glazed yellow panes of a concealed window above the chapel bathes the saint in a golden glow—an effect comparable to the spotlighting in a Caravaggio painting. From the ceiling of the chapel a host of angels both painted and sculpted in **stucco** (a light, pliable plaster) miraculously descends from the heavens. Agate and dark green marble walls provide a somber setting for the gleaming white and gold central image. On either side of the chapel, the members of the Cornaro family (executed in marble) behold Teresa's ecstasy from behind prayer desks that resemble theater boxes. These life-sized figures extend the supernatural space of the chapel and reinforce the viewer's role as witness to an actual event. It is no coincidence that Bernini's illusionistic tour de force appeared contemporaneously with the birth of opera in Italy, for both share the Baroque affection for dramatic expression on a monumental scale.

Baroque Architecture in Italy

The city of Rome carries the stamp of Bernini's flamboyant style. Commissioned to complete the **piazza** (the broad public space in front of Saint Peter's Basilica), Bernini designed a trapezoidal space that opens out to a larger oval—the two shapes form, perhaps symbolically, a keyhole. Bernini's courtyard is bounded by a spectacular colonnade that incorporates 284 Doric columns (each 39 feet high) as well as ninety-six

Figure 20.13 Anonymous, *Cornaro Chapel*, ca. 1644. Oil on canvas, 5 ft. 6¼ in. × 3 ft. 11¼ in.

statues of saints (each 15 feet tall). In a manner consistent with the ecumenical breadth of Jesuit evangelism, the gigantic pincerlike arms of the colonnade reach out to embrace an area that can accommodate more than 250,000 people (Figure **20.14**)—a vast proscenium on which devotional activities of the Church of Rome are staged to this day. The Saint Peter's of Bernini's time was the locus of papal authority; then, as now, popes used the central balcony of the basilica to impart the traditional blessing: "Urbi et Orbi" ("To the city and to the world"). The proportions of Bernini's colonnade are symbolic of the Baroque preference for the grandiose, a preference equally apparent in the artist's spectacular setting for the Throne of Saint Peter and in the immense bronze canopy (*baldacchino*) he raised over the high altar of the basilica (Figure **20.15**).

As with Saint Peter's, Italian Baroque churches were designed to reflect the mystical and evangelical ideals of the Catholic Reformation. Il Gesù (the Church of Jesus) in Rome was the mother church of the Jesuit order and the model for hundreds of Counter-Reformation churches built throughout Europe and Latin America. Designed by Giacomo da Vignola (1507–1573), Il Gesù bears the typical features of the Baroque

Figure 20.14 GIANLORENZO BERNINI, aerial view of colonnade and *piazza* of Saint Peter's, Rome, begun 1656. Travertine, longitudinal axis approx. 800 ft. Copper engraving by Giovanni Piranesi, 1750. The enormous *piazza* in front of the east façade of Saint Peter's can accommodate more than 250,000 people.

church interior: a broad Latin cross nave with domed crossing and deeply recessed chapels (Figure **20.16**). Lacking side aisles, the 60-foot-wide nave allowed a large congregation to assemble close enough to the high altar and the pulpit to see the ceremony and hear the sermon. The wide nave also provided ample space for elaborate religious processions. Il Gesù's interior, with its magnificent altarpiece dedicated to Ignatius Loyola, exemplifies the Baroque inclination to synthesize various media, such as painted stucco, bronze, and precious stones, in the interest of achieving sumptuous and ornate effects.

The most daring of the Italian Baroque architects was Francesco Borromini (1599–1667). Borromini designed

Figure 20.16 GIACOMO DA VIGNOLA, interior of Il Gesù, Rome, 1568–1573. Length approx. 240 ft.

Figure 20.15 (opposite) **GIANLORENZO BERNINI**, *Baldacchino* (canopy) ca. 1624–1633. Bronze with gilding, height 93 ft. 6 in. The four pillars of the *baldacchino* represent the columns of the Temple of Solomon, entwined by the Eucharist vines (symbolizing the New Testament). Decorative and symbolic details—vines, tassels, banners, and angelic figures—are all cast in bronze.

MAKING CONNECTIONS

Figure 20.17 GIACOMO DA VIGNOLA and **GIACOMO DELLA PORTA**, façade of Il Gesù, Rome, ca. 1575–1584. Height 105 ft., width 115 ft.

The exterior façade of Il Gesù, completed by Giacomo della Porta (Figure **20.17**) looks back to Alberti's two-story façade of Santa Maria Novella (Figure **20.18**). A comparison of the two provides insight into the differences between Renaissance and Baroque

Figure 20.18 LEON BATTISTA ALBERTI, façade of Santa Maria Novella, Florence, completed 1470. Width approx. 117 ft.

architectural styles. In contrast with the elegant linearity of the Florentine model, della Porta's façade is deeply carved, almost sculptural in its presence. Like a Caravaggio painting, it exploits dramatic contrasts of light and dark, of shallow and deep space. Pairs of pilasters and engaged Corinthian columns project from the surface, giving it weight and definition. Theatrical effect is heightened by niches bearing life-sized sculptures, by contrasting pediments (round and triangular), and by an ornate **cartouche** (oval tablet) over the central doorway and in the gable. While Alberti's façade was conceived in two dimensions, Il Gesù's was conceived in three. It inspired decades of imitation and architectural embellishment.

Figure 20.19 FRANCESCO BORROMINI, façade of San Carlo alle Quattro Fontane, Rome, 1667. Length 52 ft., width 34 ft., width of façade 38 ft.

the small monastic church of San Carlo alle Quattro Fontane (Saint Charles at the Four Fountains; Figure **20.19**) to fit a narrow site at the intersection of two Roman streets. Rejecting the sobriety of Classical design, he combined convex and concave units to produce a sense of fluid, undulating movement. The façade consists of an assortment of deeply cut decorative elements: monumental Corinthian columns, a scrolled gable over the doorway, and life-sized angels that support a cartouche at the roofline. Borromini's aversion to the circle and the square—the "perfect" shapes of Renaissance architecture—extends to the interior of San Carlo, which is oval in plan. The dome, also oval, is lit by hidden windows that allow light to flood the interior. Carved with geometric motifs that diminish in size toward the apex, the shallow cupola appears to recede deep into space (Figure **20.20**). Such inventive illusionism, accented by dynamic spatial contrasts, characterized Roman Baroque church architecture at its best.

Baroque illusionism went further still, as artists turned houses of God into theaters for sacred drama. Such is the case with the church of Sant'Ignazio in Rome. Its barrel-vaulted ceiling bears a breathtaking *trompe l'oeil* vision of Saint Ignatius' apotheosis—his elevation to divine status (Figure **20.21**). A master of the techniques of linear perspective and dramatic foreshortening, the Jesuit architect and sculptor Andrea Pozzo (1642–1709) made the ceiling above the clerestory appear to open up, so that the viewer gazes "through" the roof into the heavens that receive the levitating body of the saint. Pozzo's cosmic rendering—one of the first of many illusionistic ceilings found in seventeenth- and eighteenth-century European churches and palaces—may be taken to reflect a new perception of the physical world inspired, in part, by European geographic exploration and discovery. Indeed, Pozzo underlines the global ambitions of Roman Catholic evangelism by adding at the four corners of the ceiling the allegorical figures of Asia, Africa, Europe, and America. The vast, illusionistic spatial fields of Italian Baroque frescoes also may be seen as a response to the new astronomy of the Scientific Revolution, which advanced a view of the universe as spatially infinite and dynamic rather than finite and static (see chapter 23). Whatever its inspiration, the spatial illusionism of Baroque painting and architecture gave apocalyptic grandeur to Catholic Reformation ideals.

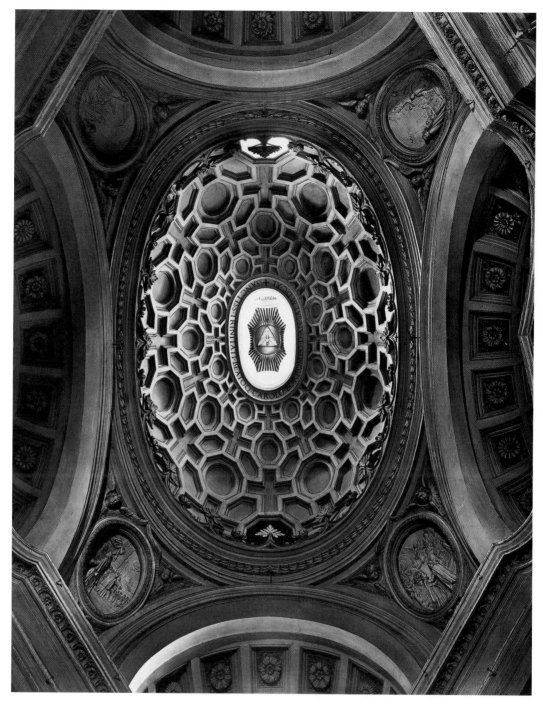

Figure 20.20 FRANCESCO BORROMINI, interior of dome, San Carlo alle Quattro Fontane, Rome, ca. 1638. Width approx. 52 ft. A dove, symbolizing the Holy Spirit, appears in the triangle at the apex of the dome, which is lit by partially hidden windows at its base.

Baroque Music

In an effort to rid sacred music of secular influence, the Council of Trent condemned the practice—common since the Late Middle Ages—of borrowing popular melodies for religious texts. It also banned complex polyphony that tended to obscure the sacred text: the function of music was to serve the text. The most notable representative of the Roman school of musical composition, Giovanni di Palestrina (1525–1594) took these recommendations as strict guidelines: his more than 100 polyphonic Masses and 450 motets feature clarity of text, skillful counterpoint, and regular rhythms. The *a cappella* lines of Palestrina's Pope Marcellus Mass flow with the smooth grace of a Mannerist painting. Often called "the music of mystic serenity," Palestrina's compositions embody the conservative and contemplative side of the Catholic Reformation.

In the religious compositions of Palestrina's Spanish contemporary Tomás Luis de Victoria (1548–1611), there is a brooding but fervent mystical intensity. Like El Greco, his colleague at the court of Philip II, Victoria brought passion and drama to religious themes. Recognizing that the Council of Trent had forbidden Palestrina to compose secular music, Victoria wrote not one note of secular song.

The Genius of Gabrieli

At the turn of the sixteenth century, the opulent city of Venice was the center of European religious musical activity.

Giovanni Gabrieli (1555–1612), principal organist at Saint Mark's Cathedral in Venice and one of the most influential composers of his time, ushered in a dramatic new style of **polychoral** and instrumental religious music. Abandoning the *a cappella* style favored in Rome, he created works that brought together two or more choruses, solo instruments, and instrumental ensembles. The last often included **cornets** (an early type of trumpet) and trombones, commonly used in Venetian ritual street processions (see Figure 17.39).

At Saint Mark's, where two organs were positioned on either side of the **chancel** (the space for clergy and choir surrounding the altar), Gabrieli stationed—on balconies high above the nave—instrumental groups and up to four separate voice choirs. The alternating bodies of sound, gloriously enhanced by the basilica's acoustics, produced a wide range of musical **dynamics** (degrees of loudness and softness), and rich, dramatic effects not unlike those achieved by the contrasts of light and shadow found in Baroque painting. Echo effects created by alternating voices and the use of unseen (offstage) voices achieved a degree of musical illusionism comparable to the pictorial illusionism of Baroque art. The motet *In ecclesiis* illustrates the style of opposing or contrasting sonorities, known as **concertato**, that would become basic to the music of the Baroque era.

Gabrieli was among the first composers to specify an instrument for each part of a musical composition, a talent that earned him the title, "the father of orchestration." He was also one of the first composers to write into his scores the words *piano* (soft) and *forte* (loud) to govern the dynamics of the piece. Gabrieli is also credited with exploring a type of musical organization that would come to dominate Baroque music: *tonality* based on the melodic and harmonic vocabulary of the major–minor key system. **Tonality** refers to the arrangement of a musical composition around a central note, called the "tonic" or "home tone" (usually designated as the "key" of a given composition). A keynote or tonic can be built on any of the twelve tones of the **chromatic scale** (the seven white and five black keys of the piano keyboard). In Baroque music—as in most music written to this day—all of the tones in the composition relate to the home tone. Tonality provided Baroque composers with a way of achieving dramatic focus in a piece of music—much in the way that light served Baroque painters to achieve dramatic focus in their compositions.

Monteverdi and the Birth of Opera

The first master of Baroque music-drama and the greatest Italian composer of the early seventeenth century was Claudio Monteverdi (1567–1643). Monteverdi served the court of Mantua until he became chapel master of Saint Mark's in Venice in 1621, a post he held for the rest of his life. During his long career, he wrote various kinds of religious music, as well as ballets, madrigals, and operas.

Like Gabrieli, Monteverdi discarded the intimate dimensions of Renaissance chamber music and cultivated an expansive, dramatic style, marked by vivid contrasts of texture and color. His compositions reflect a typically Baroque effort to imbue music with a vocal expressiveness that reflected the emotional charge of poetry. "The [written] text," declared Monteverdi, "should be the master of the music, not the servant." Monteverdi linked "affections" or specific emotional states with appropriate sounds: anger, for instance, with the high voice register, moderation with the middle voice register, and humility with the low voice register. While the union of music and speech characterized almost all his religious music and smaller secular pieces, it was essential to the effectiveness of his operas.

Opera—a form of theater that combined music, drama, dance, and the visual arts—was the quintessential musical genre of the Baroque era. Born in Italy, it emerged out of Renaissance efforts to revive the music-drama of ancient Greek theater. While humanist composers had no idea what Greek music sounded like, they sought to imitate the ancient unity of music and poetry. The earliest performances of Western opera resembled the Renaissance masque, a form of musical entertainment that included dance and poetry, along with rich costumes and scenery. Baroque operas were more musically complex, however, and more dramatically cohesive than most Renaissance masques. The first opera house was built in Venice in 1637, and by 1700 Italy was home to seventeen more such houses, a measure of the vast popularity of the new genre. By the end of the seventeenth century, Italian courts and public theaters boasted all of the essential features of the modern theater: the picture-frame stage, the horseshoe-shaped auditorium, and tiers of galleries or boxes (Figure **20.22**). Resplendent with life-sized sculptures and illusionistic frescoes, some of these opera houses are aesthetically indistinguishable from Italian Baroque church interiors (see Figures 20.13 and 20.16).

Orfeo, composed in 1607 for the duke of Mantua, was Monteverdi's first opera and one of the first full-length operas in music history. The **libretto** (literally, "little book") or text of the opera was written by Alessandro Striggio and based on a Classical theme—the descent of Orpheus, the Greek poet-musician, to Hades. *Orfeo* required an orchestra of more than three dozen instruments, including keyboard instruments, ten viols, three trombones, and four trumpets. The instrumentalists opened the performance with the **overture**, an orchestral introduction. They also accompanied the vocal line, which consisted of **arias** (elaborate solo songs or duets) alternating with **recitatives** (passages spoken or recited to sparse chordal accompaniment). The aria tended to develop a character's feelings or state of mind, while the recitative served to narrate the action of the story or to heighten its dramatic effect.

See Music Listening Selections at end of chapter.

Monteverdi believed that opera should convey the full range of human passions. To that end, he exploited the technique of word painting (the manipulation of music to convey the content of the text) popularized by the High Renaissance composer Josquin des Prez (see chapter 17). He engaged this device to reflect the emotional states of his characters, and to convey poetic images: a high tone for words like *stele* (stars) and *sole* (sun), a low tone for *morte* (death). He employed abrupt changes of key to emphasize shifts in mood and action. And he introduced such novel and expressive instrumental effects as **pizzicato**, the technique of plucking rather than bowing a stringed instrument. Integrating music, drama, and visual display, Italian opera became the ideal expression of the Baroque sensibility and the object of imitation throughout Western Europe.

Figure 20.22 PIETRO DOMENICO OLIVIER, *The Teatro Regio, Turin*, painting of the opening night, 26 December 1740. Oil on canvas, 4 ft. 2½ in. × 3 ft. 8⅞ in. Five tiers of boxes are fitted into the sides of the proscenium, one even perched over the semicircular pediment. Note the orchestra, without a conductor; the girls distributing refreshments; and the armed guard protecting against disorder.

LOOKING BACK

The Catholic Reformation

- In the wake of the Protestant Reformation, the Roman Catholic Church launched a reform movement known as the Catholic Reformation.
- Under the leadership of Ignatius Loyola, the Jesuit order became the most influential missionary society of early modern times. Members of the newly formed order worked as missionaries to win back those who had strayed from the "Mother Church."
- Between 1545 and 1563 the Council of Trent undertook papal and monastic reforms that eliminated corruption and restored Catholicism to many parts of Europe.

Catholicism's Global Reach

- Addressing the passions rather than the intellect, the arts broadcast the visionary message of Catholic reform to a vast audience that extended from Europe to Asia and the Americas.
- In China, where European traders were regarded as "ocean devils," Catholic missionaries developed a cordial relationship with the intellectual classes and succeeded in converting a number of Chinese scholars.
- Not all conversion attempts were successful. In 1624, Japan expelled almost all Western foreigners, after a wave of brutal persecutions of both European Christians and Japanese converts to Catholicism.
- Christian evangelism in the Americas proved to be far more successful. In sixteenth-century Latin America, where Spanish

political authority was largely unchallenged, Catholicism went hand in hand with colonization.

Literature and the Catholic Reformation

- The arts of the seventeenth century reflected the religious intensity of the Catholic Reformation. In literature, there appeared a new emphasis on heightened spirituality and on personal visionary experience acquired by way of the senses.
- The writings of Saint John of the Cross and Saint Teresa of Avila set the tone for a new, more mystical Catholicism.
- The English Catholic Richard Crashaw wrote rhapsodic lyrics that fused sensual and spiritual yearnings.

The Visual Arts and the Catholic Reformation

- The Mannerist paintings of Parmigianino, Tintoretto, and El Greco mirrored the climate of insecurity in religiously divided and politically turbulent Europe.
- Mannerism anticipated the Baroque style by its use of figural distortions, irrational space, bizarre colors, and its general disregard for the "rules" of Renaissance painting.

The Baroque Style

- The Baroque style brought new levels of naturalism and emotionalism to Western art. It featured dynamic contrasts of light and dark, an expanded sense of space, and the theatrical staging of the subject matter.
- Caravaggio and Gentileschi explored a variety of illusionistic techniques to draw the spectator into the space and action of the pictorial representation.
- Bernini challenged sculptural tradition by combining illusionism, naturalism, and implied movement. He brought a flamboyant style to the city of Rome, both in his fountain sculptures and in his designs for Italian Baroque churches.
- Italy's Catholic churches became ornate settings for the performance of ritual. Bernini's *The Ecstasy of Saint Teresa* and Pozzo's ceiling for the church of Saint Ignatius achieved new heights of illusionistic theatricality.

Baroque Music

- Rome and Venice were fountainheads for Italian Baroque music. Palestrina's polyphonic Masses and motets emphasized clarity of text and calm sublimity.
- Gabrieli's richly orchestrated polychoral compositions initiated the concertato style that would become a major feature of Baroque music.
- The most important development in seventeenth-century European music was the birth of opera as a genre. Borrowing themes from Classical mythology and history, Monteverdi integrated text and music to create the new art of music-drama.
- In its synthesis of all forms of performance—music, literature, and the visual arts—Italian opera became the supreme expression of the theatrical exuberance and vitality of the Baroque style.

Music Listening Selection

CD Two Selection 1 Gabrieli, Motet, "In Ecclesiis," excerpt, 1615.

CD Two Selection 2 Monteverdi, *Orfeo*, aria: "In questo prato adorno," 1607.

Glossary

aria an elaborate solo song or duet, usually with instrumental accompaniment, performed as part of an opera or other dramatic musical composition

cartouche an oval tablet or medallion, usually containing an inscription or heraldic device

chancel the space for clergy and choir surrounding the altar in a church

chromatic scale a series of twelve tones represented by the seven white and five black keys of the piano keyboard; see also Glossary, chapter 5, "scale"

concertato (Italian, concerto = "opposing" or "competing") an early Baroque style in which voices or instruments of different rather than similar natures are used in an opposing or contrasting manner

cornet (French, *cornett*; German, *Kornett*; Spanish, *cururucho*) an early type of trumpet

dynamics the degree of loudness or softness in music

foreshortening a perspective device by which figures or objects appear to recede or project into space

libretto (Italian, "little book") the words of an opera or other textual musical composition

overture an instrumental introduction to a longer musical piece, such as an opera

piazza (Italian) a broad, open public space

pizzicato (Italian) the technique of plucking (with the fingers) rather than bowing a stringed instrument

polychoral music written for two or more choruses, performed both in turn and together

recitative a textual passage recited to sparse chordal accompaniment; a rhythmically free vocal style popular in seventeenth-century opera

stucco a light, pliable plaster made of gypsum, sand, water, and ground marble

tonality the use of a central note, called the *tonic*, around which all other tonal material of a composition is organized, and to which the music returns for a sense of rest and finality

Chapter

21

Absolute Power and the Aristocratic Style

ca. 1550–1750

"Virtue would not go nearly so far if vanity did not keep her company."
La Rochefoucauld

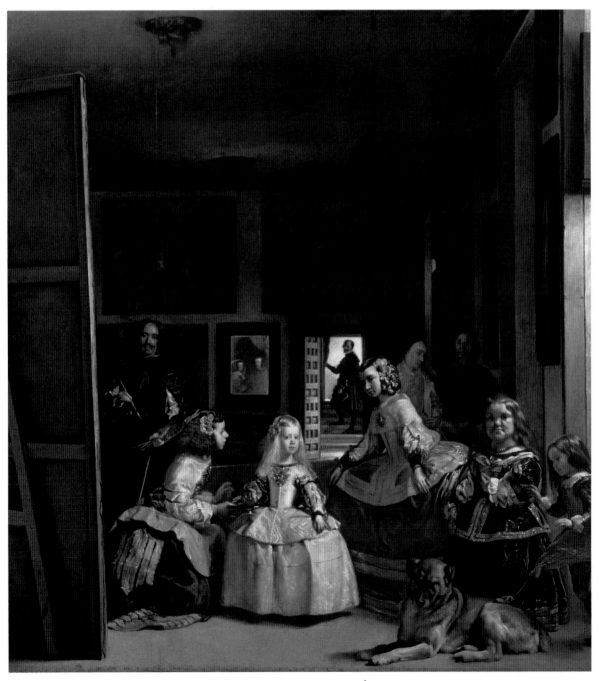

Figure 21.1 DIEGO VELÁZQUEZ, *Las Meninas* (*The Maids of Honor*), 1656. Oil on canvas, 10 ft. 5 in. × 9 ft. This unusual aristocratic group portrait depicts the royal family of Spain: King Philip IV and Queen Mariana are shown reflected in the mirror at the back of the room, while their daughter the Infanta Margarita stands at the center, surrounded by two maids of honor, a dwarf, and other court figures.

The European state system had its beginnings in the early modern era. The first half of the seventeenth century witnessed the Thirty Years' War (1618–1648), a devastating religious conflict involving most of the European powers. In 1648, by the terms of the Treaty of Westphalia, the principle of national sovereignty was firmly established. By that principle, each European state would exercise independent and supreme authority over its own territories and inhabitants. In France a long tradition of absolutism prevailed. Absolutism made the claim that rulers held their power directly from God. During the seventeenth and well into the eighteenth century, divine-right kings exercised unlimited power within the individual nation-states of Europe. But the term "absolutism" is equally appropriate to describe the type of authority exercised in many of the states that prospered outside Europe. The rulers of the three great Muslim empires that flourished between ca. 1550 and 1750—Ottoman, Safavid, and Mogul—held power as divine-right monarchs, exercising unlimited control over vast territories. So too did the Ming and Qing emperors of China, and the Tokugawa rulers in Japan.

Absolute rulers maintained their authority by controlling a centralized bureaucracy and a standing army. They pursued economic policies designed to maximize the wealth of the state. In Western Europe, the mightiest of such potentates was the French king Louis XIV (1638–1715). During the nearly three-quarters of a century that he occupied the throne, he dictated the political, economic, and cultural policies of the country. Under his guidance, France assumed a position of political and military leadership in the West. By his hand, the grandeur of the Baroque style was invested with Classical features. The so-called Classical Baroque style would become the hallmark of French absolutism. It also impressed its stamp on the rest of Europe, and, somewhat later, on an emergent American culture. While absolutist states beyond the West did not share the Classical aspects of the Baroque style, their rulers manifested a typically Baroque taste for ornate theatricality and opulent grandeur. No less than in Louis' France, the aristocratic style that characterized the arts of absolutist regimes outside Europe was an expression of the majesty of the ruler and the wealth and power of the state.

The Aristocratic Style in Europe

Louis XIV and French Absolutism

Like the pharaohs of ancient Egypt and in the tradition of his medieval ancestors, Louis XIV governed France as the direct representative of God on earth (Figure **21.2**). Neither the Church, nor the nobility, nor the will of his subjects limited his power. During his seventy-two years on the throne, the Estates General, France's representative assembly, was never once called into session. As absolute monarch, Louis brought France to a position of political and military preeminence among the European nation-states. He challenged the power of the feudal nobility and placed the Church under the authority of the state, thus centralizing all authority in his own hands. By exempting the nobility and upper middle class from taxation and offering them important positions at court, he turned potential opponents into supporters. Even if Louis never uttered the famous words attributed to him, "I am the state," he surely operated according to that precept. To distinguish his unrivaled authority, he took as his official insignia the image of the Classical sun god Apollo and referred to himself as *le roi soleil* ("the Sun King").

As ruler of France, Louis was one of the world's most influential figures. Under his leadership, the center of artistic patronage and productivity shifted from Italy to France. French culture in all of its forms—from art and architecture to fashions and fine cuisine—came to dominate European tastes, a condition that prevailed until well into the early twentieth century. Although Louis was not an intellectual, he was shrewd and ambitious. He chose first-rate advisers to execute his policies and financed those policies with money from taxes that fell primarily upon the backs of French peasants. Vast amounts of money were spent to make France the undisputed military leader of Western Europe. But Louis, who instinctively recognized the propaganda value of the arts, also used the French treasury to glorify himself and his office. His extravagances left France in a woeful financial condition, one that contributed to the outbreak of the revolution at the end of the eighteenth century. Incapable of foreseeing these circumstances, Louis cultivated the arts as an adjunct to majesty.

Versailles: Symbol of Royal Absolutism

Architecture played a vital role in the vocabulary of absolute power. The French royal family traditionally resided in Paris, at the palace known as the Louvre. But Louis, who detested Paris, moved his capital to a spot from

Science and Technology	
1657	the first fountain pens are manufactured in Paris
1688	the French army introduces bayonets attached to muskets
1698	champagne is invented in France

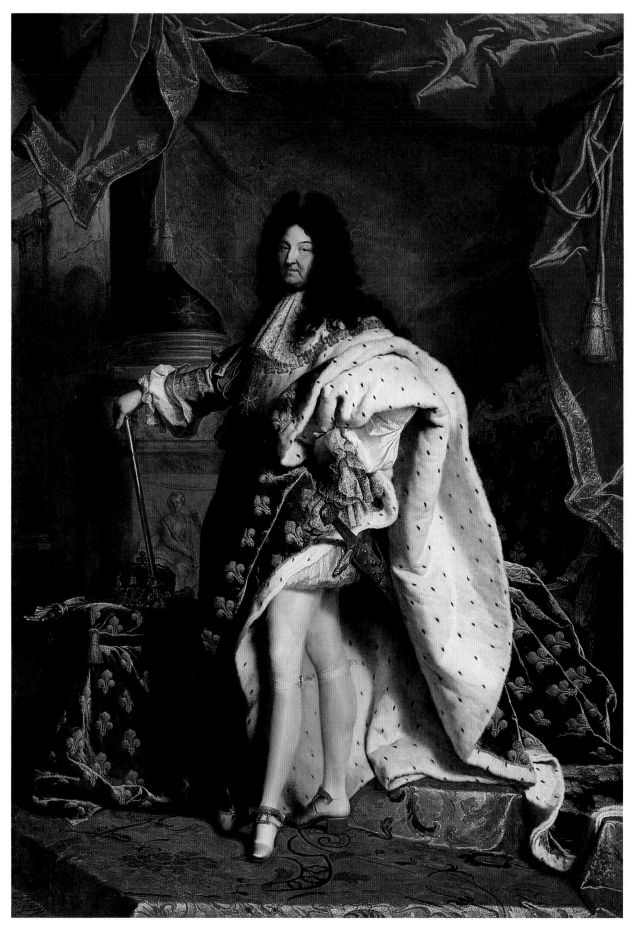

Figure 21.2 **HYACINTHE RIGAUD**, *Portrait of Louis XIV*, 1701. Oil on canvas, 9 ft. 1 in. × 6 ft. 4 in.

crown, and sword of state symbolizing royal authority

lone column signifying fortitude

two royal scepters: staff with fleur-de-lis and "main de justice" (hand of justice), emblems of authority

fleur-de-lis ("lilyflower") heraldic symbol of the French monarchy

brocaded curtains theatrically framing the king and the royal throne

ermine-lined coronation robe

high-heeled shoes designed by Louis XIV to enhance his height

silk stockings, lace cravat, and wig: hallmarks of upperclass wealth

which he might more directly control the nobility and keep them dependent upon him for honors and financial favors. Early in his career he commissioned a massive renovation of his father's hunting lodge at the village of Versailles, some 12 miles from Paris. It took 36,000 workers and nearly twenty years to build Versailles, but, in 1682, the French court finally established itself in the apartments of this magnificent unfortified *château* (castle). More than a royal residence, Versailles was—in its size and splendor—the symbol of Louis' supremacy over the landed aristocracy, the provincial governments, the urban councils, and the Estates General.

The wooded site that constituted the village of Versailles, almost half the size of Paris, was connected to the old capital by a grand boulevard that (following the path of the sun) ran from the king's bedroom—where most state business was transacted—to the Avenue de Paris. Even a cursory examination of the plan of Versailles, laid out by the French architect Louis Le Vau (1612–1670), reveals esteem for the rules of symmetry, clarity, and geometric regularity (Figure **21.3**). These principles, in combination with a taste for spatial grandeur, dramatic contrast, and theatrical display, were the distinguishing features of the Classical Baroque style.

Shaped like a winged horseshoe, the almost 2000-foot-long palace—best viewed in its entirety from the air—was the focus of an immense complex of parks, lakes, and forest (Figure **21.4**). Its central building was designed by Le Vau, while the two additional wings were added by Jules Hardouin-Mansart (1646–1708). Three levels of vertically aligned windows march across the palace façade like soldiers in a formal procession (Figure **21.5**). Porches bearing

Figure 21.3 LOUIS LE VAU, plan of Versailles.

Figure 21.4 **ISIDORE-LAURENT DEROY**, the park and palace of Versailles, France, nineteenth century.

freestanding Corinthian columns accent the second level, and ornamental statues at the roofline help to relieve the monotonous horizontality of the roofline. In its total effect, the palace is dignified and commanding, a synthesis of Classical and Palladian elements. Its calm nobility provides a striking contrast to the robust theatricality of most Italian Baroque structures (see Figures 20.17 and 20.19).

The grandeur and majesty of Versailles made it the model for hundreds of palace-estates and city planning projects in both Europe and America for the following two centuries. Le Vau's façade became the prototype for the remodeled royal palace in Paris, the Louvre. Designed by Claude Perrault (1613–1688), the east façade of the Louvre echoes the basic Classical Baroque features of Louis' residence at Versailles: strong rectilinear organization, paired Corinthian columns, and a gabled entrance that provides dramatic focus (Figure **21.6**).

The palace at Versailles housed Louis' family, his royal mistresses (one of whom bore him nine children), and hundreds of members of the French nobility whose presence

Figure 21.5 **LOUIS LE VAU** and **JULES HARDOUIN-MANSART**, Parterre du Midi, Palace of Versailles, 1669–1685.

Figure 21.6 CLAUDE PERRAULT, LOUIS LE VAU, and **CHARLES LE BRUN**, east façade of the Louvre, Paris, 1667–1670. Louis XIV had originally commissioned Bernini to design the new Louvre. However, upon finding Bernini's design too ornate, he transferred the commission to his own architects, thus establishing the Classical Baroque as a major feature of the aristocratic style.

was politically useful to Louis. Life at the court of the Sun King was both formal and public—a small army of servants, courtiers, ministers, and pet animals constantly surrounded Louis. All behavior was dictated by protocol. Rank at court determined where one sat at the dinner table and whether one or both panels of Versailles' "French doors" were to be opened upon entering.

Flanking the palace were barracks for honor guards, lodgings for more than 1500 servants, kennels, greenhouses, and an orangery with over 2000 orange trees. Over 7 square miles of gardens were designed by André Le Nôtre with the same compelling sense of order that Le Vau brought to the architecture. The great park featured an array of hedges clipped into geometric shapes (see Figure 21.5), sparkling fountains (that favorite of all Baroque mechanical devices), artificial lakes (Figure **21.7**), grottoes, a zoo, theaters, and outdoor "rooms" for private gatherings and clandestine meetings. When in bloom, the gardens—some planted with over four million tulip bulbs, which Louis imported annually from Holland—were a

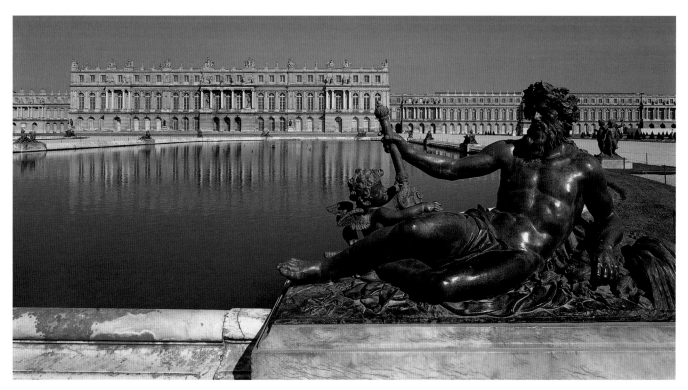

Figure 21.7 Ornamental Lake and Fountain of Latone, Versailles. A bronze sculpture of the Roman river god adorns the lake.

spectacular sight. They embellished the long walkways that radiate from the central building. On the garden side of the palace, artificial pools reflected sculptures whose subject matter glorified the majesty of the king (see Figure 21.7). Itself a kind of outdoor theater, the royal palace provided the ideal backdrop for the ballets, operas, and plays that were regular features of court life (Figure **21.8**).

If the exterior of Versailles symbolized royal grandeur, the interior publicized princely self-indulgence (Figure **21.9**). Though now shorn of many of their original furnishings, Versailles' sumptuous *salons* (drawing rooms) still testify to Louis' success at cultivating French trades in such luxury items as crafted silver, clocks, lace, brocades, porcelain, and fine glass. During the seventeenth century, the silk industry reached its peak, French carpets competed with those of Turkey and Persia, the art of **marquetry** (inlaid wood) rivaled that of Italy, and the tapestries produced at the Gobelins factory in Paris outclassed those woven in Flanders. Versailles' *salons* were adorned with illusionistic frescoes, gilded stucco moldings, crystal chandeliers, and huge, ornate mirrors. The rooms housed some of the most lavish ***objets d'art*** (art objects) in Western history, all of which, it is sobering to recall, were enjoyed at a time when the peasant majority of the French population lived in one-room, thatch-roofed houses filled with coarse wooden furniture. Equally sobering is the fact that despite its splendor the palace lacked any kind of indoor plumbing. Servants carried out the slops, but the unpleasant odor of human waste was difficult to mask, even with the finest French perfumes.

Each of Versailles' rooms illustrates a specific theme: the Salon de Venus was decorated by Charles Le Brun (1619–1690) with ceiling paintings portraying the influence of love on various kings in history. In the Salon de la Guerre (Drawing Room of War) an idealized, equestrian

Figure 21.8 JEAN LE PAUTRE, *Marble Court, Versailles*. Engraving showing a performance of Lully's *Alceste*, 1674.

Figure 21.9 Apartment of the Queen/Salon of the Nobles, Versailles. Length 31 ft.; width 32 ft.; height 24 ft. 8 in.

Louis, carved in low-relief marble, is shown receiving the victor's crown (Figure **21.10**)—though, in fact, Louis himself rarely took part in combat. The most splendid interior space, however, is the 240-foot-long Galerie des Glaces (Hall of Mirrors; Figure **21.11**), which once connected the royal apartments with the chapel. Embellished with glorious frescoes, marble pilasters, and gilded bronze capitals, and furnished with ornate candelabra and bejeweled trees (the latter have since disappeared), the hall features a wall of seventeen mirrored arcades that face an equal number of high-arched windows opening onto the garden. Framing this opulent royal passageway, mirrors and windows set up a brilliant counterpoint of image and reflection. Mirrors were to Versailles what fountains were to Rome: vehicles for the theatrical display of changing light in unbounded space.

Louis as Patron of the Arts

At the center of his court, Louis was the arbiter of fashion and manners. Within his dining *salons*, linen napkins came into use, forks replaced fingers for eating, and elaborate dishes were served to suit the royal palate. Graced with an eye for beauty and a passion for aggrandizement, Louis increased the number of paintings in the French royal collection from the 200 he inherited upon his accession to the throne to the 2000 he left at his death. These paintings formed the basis of the permanent collection at the Louvre, now a world-renowned art museum.

On a grander scale, Louis dictated the standards for all forms of artistic production. Following in the tradition of his father, Louis XIII (1601–1643), who had instituted the French Royal Academy of Language and Literature in 1635, he created and subsidized government-sponsored institutions in the arts, appointing his personal favorites to oversee each. In 1648, at the age of ten, Louis founded the Academy of Painting and Sculpture; in 1661 he established the Academy of Dance; in 1666, the Academy of Sciences; in 1669, the Academy of Music; and in 1671, the Academy of Architecture. The creation of the academies was a symptom of royal efforts to fix standards, but Louis also had something more personal in mind: he is said to have told a group of academicians, "Gentlemen, I entrust to you the most precious thing on earth—my fame." His trust was well placed, for the academies, which brought glory to the king, also set standards that would govern the arts for at least two centuries. These standards were inspired by the legacy of ancient Greece and Rome. Thus *Neoclassicism*—the revival of Classical style and subject matter—became the accepted style of academic art.

A typical example of the Neoclassical style in sculpture is seen in the work of the French academician François Girardon (1628–1715). Girardon drew on Hellenistic models for the ideally proportioned statues that he arranged in graceful tableaux for the gardens of Versailles. In one such tableau, Girardon's Neoclassical nymphs are seen entertaining the sun god Apollo—an obvious reference to Louis as *roi soleil* (Figure **21.12**).

Academic Art: Poussin and Lorrain

Girardon's compositions owed much to the paintings of the leading exponent of French academic art, Nicolas Poussin (1594–1665). Poussin spent most of his life in Rome, absorbing the heritage of the Classical and Renaissance past. He revered the High Renaissance master Raphael as the leading proponent of the Classical style; and, like most Neoclassicists, he shared Raphael's esteem for lofty subjects drawn from Greco-Roman mythology and Christian legend. In an influential treatise on painting, Poussin formalized the rules that would govern academic art for centuries. Enshrined in the works of Raphael and expounded in the aesthetic theories of seventeenth-century Italian painters, these rules would come to characterize the Grand Manner in Western art: artists should choose only serious and elevated subjects (such as battles, heroic actions, and miraculous events) drawn from Classical or Christian history, and reject crude, bizarre, and ordinary subject matter. As to the manner of representation, artists should make the physical action suit the mood of the narrative, avoiding, at all cost, the gross aspects of ordinary existence and any type of exaggeration. They should present their subjects clearly and evenly in harmonious compositions that were free of irrelevant and sordid details. Restraint, moderation, and decorum—that is, propriety and good taste—should govern all aspects of pictorial representation.

Figure 21.10 JULES HARDOUIN-MANSART, Salon de la Guerre (Drawing Room of War), Versailles. Length and width 33 ft. 8 in; height 37 ft. 9 in. The stucco relief by Antoine Coysevox shows a larger-than-life equestrian image of Louis XIV. It is framed by panels of colored marble, mirrors, bronze and gilded sculptures, and ceiling frescoes painted by Le Brun.

Figure 21.11 JULES HARDOUIN-MANSART and **CHARLES LE BRUN**, Galerie des Glaces (Hall of Mirrors), Versailles, ca. 1680. Length 240 ft. The opulence of Louis' court is exemplified in this hall, which functioned as a reception space for official state occasions. Thirty scenes of Louis' achievements were painted by Le Brun's studio on canvas and then attached to the ceiling. A $16 million, three-year renovation of the hall was completed in 2007.

Figure 21.12 FRANÇOIS GIRARDON, *Apollo Attended by the Nymphs*, ca. 1666–1672. Marble, life-sized. Louis XIV entrusted this sculptor with important commissions for the gardens of Versailles. Modeling the central figure on the famous Hellenistic *Apollo Belvedere* (see Figures 5.31 and 26.16), Girardon contributed to the propaganda that linked the Greek sun god with the French king.

Poussin's paintings were faithful to the dictates of the academic style. His *Arcadian Shepherds*, completed in 1639, transports us to the idyllic region in ancient Greece known as Arcadia, a place where men and women were said to live in perfect harmony with nature (Figure **21.13**). Here, three shepherds have come upon an ancient tomb, a symbol of death; on the right, the stately muse of history meditates upon the tomb's inscription, *"Et in Arcadia Ego"* ("I [death] also dwell in Arcadia")—that is, death reigns even in this most perfect of places. Poussin's moral allegory, at once a pastoral elegy and a *memento mori*, instructs us that death is universal. Cool, bright colors and even lighting enhance the elegiac mood, while sharp contours and the sure use of line provide absolute clarity of design. But the real power of the painting lies in its rigorous composition. Poussin arrived at this composition by arranging and rearranging miniature wax models of his figures within a small rectangular box. He then posed these figures—statuesque, heroically proportioned, and idealized—so that their gestures served to narrate the story. All of the elements in the painting, from the muse's feet (which parallel the horizontal picture plane) to the trees in the landscape and at the right edge of the tomb (which

parallel the vertical picture plane) contribute to the geometry of the composition.

Despite the grand theatricality of Poussin's paintings, order dominates spontaneity. Both in form and in content, they are intellectual; they appeal to the mind rather than to the senses. In contrast to such Italian Baroque painters as Caravaggio, whose works he detested, Poussin advanced the aesthetics of Neoclassicism.

Poussin and his contemporary, Claude Gellée (1600–1682), known as Claude Lorrain, were responsible for popularizing the genre known as the "ideal landscape," a landscape painted in the high-minded, idealized style usually found in traditional moral subjects. For such paintings, academic artists made careful renderings of the countryside around Rome. They then returned to the studio to assemble and combine the contents of their sketches according to the Classical ideals of balance and clarity. Lorrain's landscapes, characterized by haunting qualities of light, were tranquil settings for lofty mythological or biblical subjects (Figure **21.14**). Unlike the Dutch landscape painters, who rendered nature with forthright Realism (see Figure 23.10), academic artists imposed a preconceived, rationalized order upon the natural world.

Figure 21.13 NICOLAS POUSSIN, *Arcadian Shepherds*, 1638–1639. Oil on canvas, 33½ × 47⅝ in. Poussin's Classical compositions were an inspiration to the late nineteenth-century artist, Paul Cézanne, who had a copy of this painting in his study.

Figure 21.14 CLAUDE LORRAIN (CLAUDE GELLÉE), *The Marriage of Isaac and Rebekah (The Mill)*, 1642. Oil on canvas, 4 ft. 11 in. × 6 ft. 5 in. The protagonists in the biblical story are barely visible in this idealized landscape. Featuring shepherds and their flocks, such scenes were often called "elevated pastorals."

The Aristocratic Portrait

The Baroque was the great period of aristocratic portraiture. Commissioned by the hundreds by Louis XIV and the members of his court, aristocratic portraits differ dramatically from the portraits of Dürer and Holbein (see chapter 19). Whereas these artists investigated the personalities of their sitters, bringing to their portraits a combination of psychological intimacy and forthrightness, French artists were concerned primarily with outward appearance. The classic example of French aristocratic portraiture is the image of Louis XIV shown at the beginning of this chapter (see Figure 21.2), painted in 1701 by Hyacinthe Rigaud (1659–1743). Rigaud shows the sixty-three-year-old monarch in his coronation garments, with the royal paraphernalia: the scepter, the crown (on the cushion at the left), and the sword of state. He wears ermine-lined coronation robes, silk stockings, a lace cravat, a well-manicured wig, and high-heeled shoes (which he himself designed to compensate for his short stature)—all but the first were fashionable hallmarks of upper-class wealth. Louis' mannered pose, which harks back to Classical models, reflects self-conscious pride in status. Symbolic devices enhance the themes of authority and regality: satin curtains theatrically frame the king, and a lone column compositionally and metaphorically underscores his fortitude. Such devices would become standard conventions in European and American portraits of the eighteenth century (see Figure 26.23).

Velázquez, Rubens, and van Dyck

While the aristocratic phase of the Baroque style was initiated in France, it came to flourish in many other European courts. In Spain, Diego Velázquez (1599–1660), court painter to King Philip IV (1605–1665), became that country's most prestigious artist. Velázquez excelled at modeling forms so that they conveyed the powerful presence of real objects in atmospheric space. For the Spanish court, Velázquez painted a variety of Classical and Christian subjects, but his greatest enterprise was the informal group portrait known as *Las Meninas* (*The Maids of Honor*; see Figure 21.1). In this painting, Velázquez depicted himself at his easel, alongside the members of the royal court: the *infanta* (the five-year-old daughter of the king), her maids of honor, her dwarf, a mastiff hound, and the royal escorts. In the background is a mirror that reflects the images of the king and queen of Spain—presumably the subjects of the large canvas Velázquez shows himself painting in the left foreground. Superficially, this is a group portrait of the kind commissioned by wealthy patrons since the Renaissance. The addition of a mirror that reflects the presence of two figures outside the painting is, indeed, reminiscent of Jan van Eyck's Arnolfini portrait (see Figure 19.5). However, Velázquez's composition is far more complex, for, although the painting is a record of the royal household (its original title was *Family of Philip IV*), it departs from traditional group portraits by minimizing its purported subject: the king and queen. Almost all the subjects in the painting, including the painter himself, are shown gazing at the royal couple, who must be standing outside the picture space in the very spot occupied by the viewer. Velázquez has expanded the spatial field, inviting the beholder into the picture space as if he or she were, in fact, the subject of the painting. His witty invention or "conceit" provokes a visual dialogue between the perceived and the perceiver.

A contemporary of Velázquez, the internationally renowned Flemish painter Peter Paul Rubens (1577–1640) established his reputation in the courts of Europe. Fluent in six languages, he traveled widely as a diplomat and art dealer for royal patrons in Italy, England, and France. He also headed a large studio workshop that trained scores of assistants to help fulfill his many commissions—a total lifetime production of some 1800 paintings. For the Luxembourg Palace of Paris, Rubens and his studio executed twenty-one monumental canvases that glorified Marie de' Medici, Louis XIV's grandmother, and her late husband, King Henry IV of France. Like Poussin, Rubens studied in Italy and was familiar with both Classical and High Renaissance art. Rubens deeply admired the flamboyant colorists Titian and Tintoretto, and he developed a style that, in contrast with Poussin's, was painterly in its brushwork and dynamic in composition.

One of Rubens' most memorable canvases, the *Rape of the Daughters of Leucippus* (Figure **21.15**), depicts the abduction of two mortal women by the mythic heroes

Figure 21.15 PETER PAUL RUBENS, *Rape of the Daughters of Leucippus*, ca. 1618. Oil on canvas, 7 ft. 3 in. × 6 ft. 10 in. The twin sons of Zeus and Leda, Castor and Polydeuces (called the "Dioscuri," or "Sons of Zeus") were popular heroes revered as brave horsemen by both the Greeks and the Romans. Their abduction of two women bethrothed to their cousins provoked a battle in which Castor was killed. When his brother asked Zeus to let him die as well, Zeus granted them immortality.

Castor and Pollux. Rubens' conception of the Classical story explodes with vigor: pressing against the picture plane are the fleshy bodies of the nude maidens, their limbs arranged in the pattern of a slowly revolving pinwheel. The masterful paintstrokes exploit sensuous contrasts of luminous pink flesh, burnished armor, gleaming satins, and dense horsehide. Probably commissioned to commemorate the double marriage of Louis XIII of France to a Spanish princess and Philip IV of Spain to a French princess (and, thus, to celebrate the diplomatic alliance of France and Spain), the painting carries a subtext of (male) power over (female) privilege—and, by extension, of political absolutism. Images of subjugation by force, whether in the form of lion hunts (as in ancient Assyrian reliefs; see chapter 1) or in paintings and sculptures depicting mythological stories of rape, were metaphors for the sovereign authority of the ruler over his subjects, hence a veiled expression of political absolutism.

In England, the most accomplished advocate of the aristocratic style was the Flemish master Anthony van Dyck (1599–1641). Born in Antwerp, van Dyck had been an assistant to Rubens and may have worked with him on the *Rape of the Daughters of Leucippus*. Unwilling to compete with Rubens, he moved to Genoa and then to London, where he became court painter to King Charles I of England (1600–1649). Van Dyck's many commissioned portraits of European aristocrats are striking for their polished elegance and poise, features that are especially evident in his equestrian portrait of Charles I (see Figure 22.2). In this painting, van Dyck shows the king, who was actually short and undistinguished-looking, as handsome and regal. The combination of fluid composition and naturalistic detail, and the shimmering vitality of the brushwork, make this one of the most memorable examples of aristocratic Baroque portraiture.

Music and Dance at the Court of Louis XIV

The court at Versailles was the setting for an extraordinary outpouring of music, theater, and dance. To provide musical entertainments for state dinners, balls, and operatic performances, Louis established a permanent orchestra, the first in European history. Its director, the Italian-born (but French-educated) Jean-Baptiste Lully (1632–1687), also headed the French Academy of Music. Often called the "father of French opera," Lully oversaw all phases of musical performance, from writing scores and conducting the orchestra to training the chorus and staging operatic productions. Many of Lully's operas were based on themes from Classical mythology. Their semidivine heroes, prototypes of the king himself, flattered Louis' image as ruler.

Lully's operas shared the pomp and splendor of Le Brun's frescoes, the strict clarity of Poussin's paintings, and the formal correctness of Classical drama. Though Lully's compositions were generally lacking in spontaneity and warmth of feeling, they were faithful to the Neoclassical unity of words and music. Lully modified the music of the

recitative to follow precisely and with great clarity the inflections of the spoken word. He also introduced to opera the "French overture," an instrumental form that featured contrasts between a slow first part in homophonic texture and a fast, contrapuntal second part. Under Lully's leadership, French opera also developed its most characteristic feature: the inclusion of formal dance.

At the court of Louis XIV, dancing and fencing were the touchstones of aristocratic grace. All members of the upper class were expected to perform the basic court dances, including the very popular *minuet*, and the courtier who could not dance was judged rude and inept. Like his father, Louis XIII, who had commissioned and participated in extravagantly expensive ballets, Louis XIV was a superb dancer. Dressed as the sun, he danced the lead in the 1653 performance of the *Ballet de la Nuit* (Figure **21.16**). Of lasting significance was Louis' contribution to the birth of professional dance and the transformation of court dance into an independent artform. During the late seventeenth century, French ballet masters of the Royal Academy of Dance established rules for the five positions that have

Figure 21.16 King Louis XIV as the sun in the 1653 *Ballet de la Nuit.*

become the basis for classical dance. Clarity, balance, and proportion, along with studied technique—elements characteristic of Classicism in general—became the ideals of the classical ballet.

By 1685 female dancers were permitted to join the previously all-male French dance ensembles in staged performances. And in 1700 Raoul Auget Feuillet published a system of abstract symbols for recording specific dance steps and movements, thus facilitating the art of **choreography**. Ballet, itself a metaphor for the strict etiquette and ceremonial grace of court life, enriched all aspects of the French theater. However, since classical ballet demanded a rigorous attention to proper form, it soon became too specialized for any but professionals to perform, and so there developed the gap between performer and audience that exists to this day in the art of dance.

Seventeenth-Century French Literature

In literature, as with most forms of artistic expression in seventeenth-century France, Neoclassical precepts of form and content held sway. French writers addressed questions of human dignity and morality in a language that was clear, polished, and precise. Their prose is marked by refinement, good taste, and the concentrated presentation of ideas.

One literary genre that typified the Neoclassical spirit was the **maxim**. A maxim is a short, concise, and often witty saying, usually drawn from experience and offering some practical advice. Witty sayings that distilled wisdom into a few words were popular in many cultures, including those of the Hebrews, the Greeks, and the Africans. But in seventeenth-century France, the cautionary or moralizing aphorism was exalted as the ideal means of teaching good sense and decorum. Terse and lean, the maxim exalted precision of language and thought. France's greatest maxim writer was François de La Rochefoucauld (1613–1680), a nobleman who had participated in a revolt against Louis XIV early in his reign. Withdrawing from court society, La Rochefoucauld wrote with a cynicism that reflected his conviction that self-interest, hypocrisy, and greed motivated the behavior of most human beings—including and especially the aristocrats of his day. As the following maxims illustrate, however, La Rochefoucauld's insights into human behavior apply equally well to individuals of all social classes and to any age.

┌─ **READING 21.1** From La Rochefoucauld's
│   *Maxims* (1664)
│
│ Truth does less good in the world than its appearances do harm.
│
│ Love of justice in most men is only a fear of encountering injustice.
│
│ We often do good that we may do harm with impunity.
│
│ As it is the mark of great minds to convey much in few words, so small minds are skilled at talking at length and saying little.

Virtue would not go nearly so far if vanity did not keep her company.

We confess to small faults to create the impression that we have no great ones.

To be rational is not to use reason by chance, but to recognize it, distinguish it, appreciate it.

We all have strength enough to endure the misfortunes of others.

We are never so happy or so unhappy as we imagine we are.

Our minds are lazier than our bodies.

Quarrels would not last long were the wrong all on one side.

─ **Q** What is the effect of brevity in these maxims?

─ **Q** Which of these maxims might apply to the characters in Reading 21.2 (Molière)?

Like La Rochefoucauld's maxims, but on a larger scale, French drama reflected Neoclassical restraint, cool objectivity, and common sense. The leading French tragedian of the seventeenth century, Jean Racine (1639–1699), wrote plays that treated high-minded themes in an elevated language. Racine added to Aristotle's unities of action and time (see chapter 4) a strict unity of place, thus manifesting his abiding commitment to verisimilitude. In the play *Phèdre* (1677), itself based on Greek models, Racine explored the conflict between human passions (Phaedra's "unnatural" infatuation with her stepson) and human reason (Phaedra's sense of duty as the wife of Theseus, king of Athens). As in all of Racine's tragedies, *Phèdre* illustrates the disastrous consequences of emotional indulgence—a weakness especially peculiar to Racine's female characters. Indeed, while Racine created some of the most dramatic female roles in Neoclassical theater, he usually pictured women as weak, irrational, and cruel.

Molière's Human Comedy

Jean-Baptiste Poquelin (1622–1673), whose stage name was Molière, was France's leading comic dramatist. The son of a wealthy upholsterer, he abandoned a career in law in favor of acting and play writing. He learned much from the *commedia dell'arte*, a form of improvised Italian street theater that depended on buffoonery, slapstick humor, and pantomime. Molière's plays involve simple story lines that bring to life the comic foibles of such stock characters as the miser, the hypochondriac, the hypocrite, the misanthrope, and the would-be gentleman. The last of these is the subject of one of Molière's last plays, *Le Bourgeois Gentilhomme* (*The Tradesman Turned Gentleman*). The plot involves a wealthy tradesman (Monsieur Jourdain) who, aspiring to nobility, hires a variety of tutors to school him in the trappings of upper-class respectability. The play's fabric of deceit and self-deception is complicated by Jourdain's refusal to accept his daughter's choice of a partner, the handsome but poor Cléonte. Only after Cléonte appears disguised as the son of the Grand Turk does the unwitting merchant bless the betrothal.

Essentially a farce or comedy of manners, Molière's play (like La Rochefoucauld's maxims) holds up to ridicule the fundamental flaws of human behavior, which might be corrected by applying the Classical norms of reason and moderation. By contrasting incidents of hypocrisy, pomposity, and greed with the solid, good sense demonstrated, for instance, by Mr. Jourdain's wife, Molière probes the excesses of passion and vanity that enfeeble human dignity. *Le Bourgeois Gentilhomme* was designed as a **comédie-ballet**, a dramatic performance that incorporated interludes of song and dance (in a manner similar to modern musical comedy). Lully provided the music, choreographed the ballet, and directed the entire production, which, like many other of Molière's plays, was well received by the king and his court, a court that lavishly and regularly received the ambassadors of "exotic" countries, such as Turkey.

But even beyond Versailles, Molière's hilarious comedy had wide appeal. French aristocrats, convinced that they were above imitation, embraced the play. So did upper-middle-class patrons who, while claiming an increasingly prominent place in the social order, refused to see themselves as merchants longing to be aristocrats. Women found themselves endowed in Molière's play with confidence and guile, while servants discovered themselves invested with admirable common sense. The comedy, for all its farce, reflected the emerging class structure of early modern European society, with its firmly drawn lines between sexes and classes.

In Act II, Scene XIV of *Le Bourgeois Gentilhomme*, Mr. Jourdain—himself descended from shopkeepers—refuses to allow his daughter to marry anyone other than a gentleman. To prevent her from marrying "below" her, he boasts, "I have riches enough for my daughter; all I need is honors, so I shall make her a marquise." To this, his wife exclaims, "'Tis a thing to which I shall never consent. Your marriages with people above you are always subject to wretched vexations. I don't want my daughter to have a husband that can reproach her with her parents, and children that will be ashamed to call me grandma. If she should come to call on me in her fine lady's equipage, and fail by chance to bow to any of the neighbors, they would be sure to say a hundred ill-natured things. . . . I don't want all this cackle, and, in a word, I want a man who shall be beholden to me for my daughter, and to whom I can say: 'Sit down there, son-in-law, and have dinner with me.'" Mr. Jourdain snaps back, "Those are the sentiments of a petty soul, willing to stay forever in a mean station. Don't talk back to me any more. My daughter shall be a marquise, in spite of all the world, and if you provoke me, I'll make her a duchess."

With unparalleled comic wit, *Le Bourgeois Gentilhomme* captured the spirit of the seventeenth century—its class tensions and social contradictions, along with its ambitions and high expectations. Yet, for all its value as a mirror of a particular time and place, *Le Bourgeois Gentilhomme* is universal and timeless. Portions of the first and second acts offer a representative sampling of Molière's rollicking exposition of human nature.

READING 21.2 From Molière's *Le Bourgeois Gentilhomme* (1670)

Characters

Mr. Jourdain	His Scholar
Mrs. Jourdain, *his wife*	A Dancing-Master
Lucile, *his daughter*	A Fencing-Master
Cléonte, *suitor of Lucile*	A Philosophy-Master
Dorimene, *a marquise*	A Master-Tailor
Dorante, *a count, in love with*	A Journeyman-Tailor
Dorimene	Two lackeys
Nicole, *servant to*	Musicians, Dancers, Cooks,
Mr. Jourdain	Journeymen-Tailors, and
Coveille, valet to Cléonte	other characters to dance
A Music-Master	in the interludes

The scene is at Paris

ACT I

Overture, played by a full orchestra; in the middle of the stage the Music-Master's Scholar, seated at a table, is composing the air for a serenade which Mr. Jourdain has ordered.

Scene I

Music-Master, Dancing-Master, Three Singers, Two Violinists, Four Dancers

Music-Master (*To the singers*): Here, step inside, and wait   1
until he comes.

Dancing-Master (*To the dancers*): And you too, this way.

Music-Master (To his scholar): Is it finished?

Scholar: Yes.

Music-Master: Let's see . . . That's good.

Dancing-Master: Is it something new?

Music-Master: Yes, 'tis the air for a serenade which I have
had him compose, while waiting for our gentleman to wake up.

Dancing-Master: May I see it?   10

Music-Master: You shall hear it, with the words, when he
comes. He won't be long.

Dancing-Master: You and I have no lack of occupation now.

Music-Master: That's true. We have found a man here who
is just what we both needed. He's a nice little source of
income for us, this Mr. Jourdain, with his visions of nobility
and gallantry that he has got into his noddle. And 'twould be a
fine thing for your dancing and my music if everybody were
like him.

Dancing-Master: No, no, not quite; I could wish, for his   20
sake, that he had some true understanding of the good things
we bring him.

Music-Master: 'Tis true he understands them ill, but he
pays for them well; and that is what the arts need most
nowadays.

Dancing-Master: For my part, I'll own, I must be fed
somewhat on fame. I am sensitive to applause, and I feel that
in all the fine arts 'tis a grievous torture to show one's talents
before fools, and to endure the barbarous judgments of a dunce
upon our compositions. There's great pleasure, I tell you,   30
in working for people who are capable of feeling the
refinements of art, who know how to give a flattering

reception to the beauties of your work, and recompense your toil by titillating praise. Yes, the most agreeable reward possible for what we do, is to see it understood, to see it caressed by applause that honors us. Nothing else, methinks, can pay us so well for all our labors; and enlightened praise gives exquisite delight.

Music-Master: I grant you that, and I relish it as you do. There is surely nothing more gratifying than such praise as you speak of; but man cannot live on applause. Mere praise won't buy you an estate; it takes something more solid. And the best way to praise, is to praise with open hands. Our fellow, to be sure, is a man of little wit, who discourses at random about anything and everything, and never applauds but at the wrong time. But his money sets right the errors of his mind; there is judgment in his purse; his praises pass current; and this ignorant shopkeeper is worth more to us, as you very well see, than the enlightened lord who introduced us to his house. 40

Dancing-Master: There is some truth in what you say; but methinks you set too much store by money; and self-interest is something so base that no gentleman should ever show a leaning towards it. 50

Music-Master: Yet I haven't seen you refuse the money our fellow offers you.

Dancing-Master: Certainly not; but neither do I find therein all my happiness; and I could still wish that with his wealth he had good taste to boot.

Music-Master: I could wish so too; and 'tis to that end that we are both working, as best we may. But in case, he gives. us the means to make ourselves known in the world; he shall pay for others, and others shall praise for him. 60

Dancing-Master: Here he comes.

[Act I, Scene II: Mr. Jourdain converses with his music- and dancing-masters, who dispute as to which is the more important art: music or dance. A dialogue in music, written by the music-master, follows, then a ballet choreographed by the dancing-master.

Act II, Scene I: Mr. Jourdain dances the minuet for the dancing-master, and then learns how to make a "proper" bow.]

ACT II, Scene II
Mr. Jourdain, Music-Master, Dancing-Master, Lackey

Lackey: Sir, here is your fencing-master. 1

Mr. Jourdain: Tell him to come in and give me my lesson here. (*To the music-master and dancing-master*) I want you to see me perform.

Scene III
Mr. Jourdain, Fencing-Master, Music-Master, Dancing-Master, a Lackey with two foils

Fencing-Master (*Taking the two foils from the lackey and giving one of them to Mr. Jourdain*): Now, sir, your salute. The body erect. The weight slightly on the left thigh. The legs not so far apart. The feet in line. The wrist in line with the thigh. The point of your sword in line with your shoulder. The arm not quite so far extended. The left hand on a level 10 with the eye. The left shoulder farther back. Head up. A bold look. Advance. The body steady. Engage my sword in

quart[1] and finish the thrust. One, two. Recover. Again, your feet firm. One, two. Retreat. When you thrust, sir, your sword must move first, and your body be held well back, and sideways. One, two. Now, engage my sword in tierce,[2] and finish the thrust. Advance. Your body steady. Advance. Now, from that position. One, two. Recover. Again. One, two. Retreat. On guard, sir, on guard (*the fencing-master gives him several thrusts*), on guard. 20

Mr. Jourdain: Well?

Music-Master: You do wonders.

Fencing-Master: I've told you already: the whole secret of arms consists in two things only: hitting and not being hit. And as I proved to you the other day by demonstrative logic, it is impossible that you should be hit if you know how to turn aside your adversary's sword from the line of your body; and that depends merely on a slight movement of the wrist, inwards or outwards.

Mr. Jourdain: So, then, without any courage, one may be 30 sure of killing his man and not being killed?

Fencing-Master: Certainly. Didn't you see the demonstration of it?

Mr. Jourdain: Yes.

Fencing-Master: And by this you may see how highly our profession should be esteemed in the State; and how far the science of arms excels all other sciences that are of no use, like dancing, music . . .

Dancing-Master: Softly, Mr. Swordsman; don't speak disrespectfully of dancing. 40

Music-Master: Learn, pray, to appreciate better the excellences of music.

Fencing-Master: You are absurd fellows, to think of comparing your sciences with mine.

Music-Master: Just see the man of consequence!

Dancing-Master: The ridiculous animal, with his padded stomacher![3]

Fencing-Master: My little dancing-master, I will make you dance to a tune of my own, and you, little songster, I will make you sing out lustily. 50

Dancing-Master: Mr. Ironmonger,[4] I'll teach you your own trade.

Mr. Jourdain (*To the dancing-master*): Are you mad, to pick a quarrel with him, when he knows tierce and quart and can kill a man by demonstrative logic?

Dancing-Master: A fig for his demonstrative logic, and his tierce and his quart.

Mr. Jourdain (*To the dancing-master*): Softly, I tell you.

Fencing-Master (*To the dancing-master*): What, little Master Impudence! 60

Mr. Jourdain: Hey! my dear fencing-master.

Dancing-Master (*To the fencing-master*): What, you great cart-horse!

Mr. Jourdain: Hey, my dear dancing-master.

Fencing-Master: If I once fall upon you . . .

---

[1] A defensive posture in the art of fencing.
[2] Another fencing posture.
[3] Protection used in fencing.
[4] A dealer in hardware.

Mr. Jourdain (*To the fencing-master*): Gently.

Dancing-Master: If I once lay hands on you . . .

Mr. Jourdain (*To the dancing-master*): So, so.

Fencing-Master: I will give you such a dressing . . .

Mr. Jourdain (*To the fencing-master*): I beg you.　70

Dancing-Master: I will give you such a drubbing[5] . . .

Mr. Jourdain (*To the dancing-master*): I beseech you . . .

Music-Master: Let us teach him manners a little.

Mr. Jourdain: Good Heavens! do stop.

Scene IV

Professor of Philosophy, Mr. Jourdain, Music-Master, Dancing-Master, Fencing-Master, Lackey

Mr. Jourdain: Oho! Mr. Philosopher, you've arrived in the nick of time with your philosophy. Do come and set these people here at peace.

The Philosopher: How now? What is the matter, gentlemen?

Mr. Jourdain: They have put themselves in a passion about the precedence of their professions, and even insulted　80 each other and almost come to blows.

The Philosopher: O fie, gentlemen! Should a man so lose his self-control? Have you not read the learned treatise which Seneca composed, *Of Anger*?[6] Is there anything more base or shameful than this passion, which of a man makes a savage beast? Should not reason be mistress of all our emotions?

Dancing-Master: How, how, sir! Here he comes and insults us both, by condemning dancing, which I practice, and music, which is his profession.

The Philosopher: A wise man is above all the insults that　90 can be offered him; and the chief answer which we should make to all offences, is calmness and patience.

Fencing-Master: They both have the insolence to think of comparing their professions with mine!

The Philosopher: Should that move you? 'Tis not for vainglory and precedence that men should contend; what really distinguishes us from each other is wisdom and virtue.

Dancing-Master: I maintain to his face that dancing is a science which cannot be too highly honored.

Music-Master: And I, that music is a science which all　100 ages have reverenced.

Fencing-Master: And I maintain, against both of them, that the science of fencing is the finest and most indispensable of all sciences.

The Philosopher: But what then becomes of philosophy? I think you are all three mighty impertinent to speak with such arrogance before me, and impudently to give the name of science to things which ought not even to be honored with the name of art, and which may best be classed together as pitiful trades, whether of prize-fighters, ballad-mongers, or　110 mountebanks.[7]

Fencing-Master: Go to, dog of a philosopher.

Music-Master: Go to, beggarly pedagogue.

Dancing-Master: Go to, past master pedant.

---

[5] A beating.

[6] A treatise by the first-century Roman Stoic Lucius Annaeus Seneca (see chapter 6).

[7] Charlatans or quacks.

The Philosopher: What, you rascally knaves! . . .

(*He falls upon them, and they all three belabor him with blows.*)

Mr. Jourdain: Mr. Philosopher!

The Philosopher: Villains! varlets! insolent vermin!

Mr. Jourdain: Mr. Philosopher!

Fencing-Master: Plague take the beast!

Mr. Jourdain: Gentlemen!

The Philosopher: Brazen-faced ruffians!　120

Mr. Jourdain: Mr. Philosopher!

Dancing-Master: Deuce take the old pack-mule!

Mr. Jourdain: Gentlemen!

The Philosopher: Scoundrels!

Mr. Jourdain: Mr. Philosopher!

Music-Master: Devil take the impertinent puppy!

Mr. Jourdain: Gentlemen!

The Philosopher: Thieves! vagabonds! rogues! impostors!

Mr. Jourdain: Mr. Philosopher! Gentlemen! Mr. Philosopher! Gentlemen! Mr. Philosopher!　130

(*Exit fighting.*)

Scene V

Mr. Jourdain, Lackey

Mr. Jourdain: Oh! fight as much as you please; I can't help it, and I won't go spoil my gown trying to part you. I should be mad to thrust myself among them and get some blow that might do me a mischief.

Scene VI

The Philosopher, Mr. Jourdain, Lackey

The Philosopher (*Straightening his collar*): Now for our lesson.

Mr. Jourdain: Oh! sir, I am sorry for the blows you got.

The Philosopher: That's nothing. A philosopher knows how to take things aright; and I shall compose a satire against them　140 in Juvenal's manner,[8] which will cut them up properly. But let that pass. What do you want to learn?

Mr. Jourdain: Everything I can; for I have the greatest desire conceivable to be learned; it throws me in a rage to think that my father and mother did not make me study all the sciences when I was young.

The Philosopher: That is a reasonable sentiment; *nam, sine doctrina, vita est quasi mortis imago*. You understand that, for of course you know Latin.

Mr. Jourdain: Yes; but play that I don't know it; and explain　150 what it means.

The Philosopher: It means that, *without learning, life is almost an image of death*.

Mr. Jourdain: That same Latin's in the right.

The Philosopher: Have you not some foundations, some rudiments of knowledge?

Mr. Jourdain: Oh! yes, I can read and write.

The Philosopher: Where will you please to have us begin? Shall I teach you logic?

Mr. Jourdain: What may that same logic be?　160

The Philosopher: 'Tis the science that teaches the three operations of the mind.

---

[8] A Roman satirist of the early second century (see chapter 6).

Mr. Jourdain: And who are they, these three operations of the mind?

The Philosopher: The first, the second, and the third. The first is to conceive aright, by means of the universals; the second, to judge aright, by means of the categories; and the third, to draw deductions aright, by means of the figures: *Barbara, Celarent, Darii, Ferio, Baralipton.*[9]

Mr. Jourdain:There's a pack of crabbed words. This logic 170
doesn't suit me at all. Let's learn something else that's prettier.

The Philosopher: Will you learn ethics?

Mr. Jourdain: Ethics?

The Philosopher: Yes.

Mr. Jourdain: What is your ethics about?

The Philosopher: It treats of happiness, teaches men to moderate their passions, and . . .

Mr. Jourdain: No; no more of that. I am choleric as the whole pack of devils, ethics or no ethics; no, sir, I'll be angry to my heart's content, whenever I have a mind to it. 180

The Philosopher: Is it physics you want to learn?

Mr. Jourdain: And what has this physics to say for itself?

The Philosopher: Physics is the science which explains the principles of natural phenomena, and the properties of bodies; which treats of the nature of the elements, metals, minerals, stones, plants, and animals, and teaches us the causes of all such things as meteors, the rainbow, St. Elmo's fire,[10] comets, lightning, thunder, thunderbolts, rain, snow, hail, winds, and whirlwinds.

Mr. Jourdain: There's too much jingle-jangle in that, too 190
much hurly-burly.

The Philosopher: Then what to do you want me to teach you?

Mr. Jourdain: Teach me spelling.

The Philosopher: With all my heart.

Mr. Jourdain: And afterward, you shall teach me the almanac, so as to know when there's a moon, and when there isn't.

The Philosopher: Very well. To follow up your line of thought logically, and treat this matter in true philosophic 200
fashion, we must begin, according to the proper order of things, by an exact knowledge of the nature of the letters, and the different method of pronouncing each one. And on that head I must tell you that the letters are divided into vowels, so called—*vowels*—because they express the sounds of the voice alone; and consonants, so called—*con-sonants*— because they sound with the vowels, and only mark the different articulations of the voice. There are five vowels, or voices: A, E, I, O, U.

Mr. Jourdain: I understand all that. 210

The Philosopher: The vowel A is formed by opening the mouth wide: A.

Mr. Jourdain: A, A. Yes.

The Philosopher: The vowel E is formed by lifting the lower jaw nearer to the upper: A, E.

Mr. Jourdain: A, E; A, E. On my word, 'tis so. Ah! how fine!

The Philosopher: And the vowel I, by bringing the jaws still nearer together, and stretching the corners of the mouth toward the ears: A, E, I.

Mr. Jourdain: A, E, I, I, I, I. That is true. Science forever! 220

The Philosopher: The vowel O is formed by opening the jaws, and drawing in the lips at the corners: O.

Mr. Jourdain: O, O. Nothing could be more correct: A, E, I, O, I, O. 'Tis admirable! I, O; I, O.

The Philosopher: The opening of the mouth looks exactly like a little circle, representing an O.

Mr. Jourdain: O, O, O. You are right. O. Ah! What a fine thing it is to know something!

The Philosopher: The vowel U is formed by bringing the teeth together without letting them quite touch, and thrusting 230
out the lips, at the same time bringing them together without quite shutting them: U.

Mr. Jourdain: U, U. Nothing could be truer: U.

The Philosopher: Your lips are extended as if you were pouting; therefore if you wish to make a face at anyone, and mock at him, you have only to say U.

Mr. Jourdain: U, U. 'Tis true. Ah! would I had studied sooner, to know all that!

The Philosopher: To-morrow, we will consider the other letters, namely the consonants. 240

Mr. Jourdain: Are there just as curious things about them as about these?

The Philosopher: Certainly. The consonant D, for instance, is pronounced by clapping the tip of the tongue just above the upper teeth: D.

Mr. Jourdain: D, D. Yes! Oh! what fine things! what fine things!

The Philosopher: The F, by resting the upper teeth on the lower lip: F.

Mr. Jourdain: F, F. 'Tis the very truth. Oh! father and mother 250
of me, what a grudge I owe you!

The Philosopher: And the R by lifting the tip of the tongue to the roof of the mouth; so that being grazed by the air, which comes out sharply, it yields to it, yet keeps returning to the same point, and so makes a sort of trilling: R, Ra.

Mr. Jourdain: R, R, Ra, R, R, R, R, R, Ra. That is fine. Oh! what a learned man you are, and how much time I've lost! R, R, R, Ra.

The Philosopher: I will explain all these curious things to you thoroughly. 260

Mr. Jourdain: Do, I beg you. But now, I must tell you a great secret. I am in love with a person of very high rank, and I wish you would help me to write her something in a little love note which I'll drop at her feet.

The Philosopher: Excellent!

Mr. Jourdain: 'Twill be very gallant, will it not?

The Philosopher: Surely. Do you want to write to her in verse?

Mr. Jourdain: No, no; none of your verse.

The Philosopher: You want mere prose? 270

Mr. Jourdain: No, I will have neither prose nor verse.

The Philosopher: It must needs be one or the other.

---

[9] Part of a series of Latin names used by medieval logicians to help remember the valid forms of syllogisms.

[10] Electrical discharges seen by sailors before and after storms at sea and named after the patron saint of sailors.

Mr. Jourdain: Why?

The Philosopher: For this reason, that there is nothing but prose or verse to express oneself by.

Mr. Jourdain: There is nothing but prose or verse?

The Philosopher: No, sir. All that is not prose is verse, and all that is not verse is prose.

Mr. Jourdain: But when we talk, what is that, say?

The Philosopher: Prose. 280

Mr. Jourdain: What! When I say: "Nicole, bring me my slippers and give me my nightcap," that's prose?

The Philosopher: Yes, sir.

Mr. Jourdain: Oh my word, I've been speaking prose these forty years, and never knew it; I am infinitely obliged to you for having informed me of this. Now I want to write to her in a note: *Fair Marquise,*[11] *your fair eyes make me die of love*; but I want it to be put in gallant fashion, and neatly turned.

The Philosopher: Say that the fires of her eyes reduce your heart to ashes; that night and day you suffer for her all the 290 tortures of a. . .

Mr. Jourdain: No, no, no, I want none of all that. I will have nothing but what I told you: *Fair Marquise, your fair eyes make me die of love.*

The Philosopher: You must enlarge upon the matter a little.

Mr. Jourdain: No, I tell you. I'll have none but those very words in the note, but put in a fashionable way, arranged as they should be. Pray tell me over the different ways they can be put, so that I may see.

The Philosopher: You can first of all put them as you said: 300 *Fair Marquise, your fair eyes make me die of love.*
Or else: *Of love to die me make, fair Marquise, your fair eyes.*
Or else: *Your fair eyes of love me make, fair Marquise, to die.*
Or else: *To die your fair eyes, fair Marquise, of love me make.*
Or else: *Me make your fair eyes die, fair Marquise, of love.*

Mr. Jourdain: But which of all these ways is the best?

The Philosopher: The way you said it: *Fair Marquise, your fair eyes make me die of love.*

Mr. Jourdain: And yet I never studied, and I did it at the first try. I thank you with all my heart, and beg you to come 310 again to-morrow early.

The Philosopher: I shall not fail to.

Scene VII

Mr. Jourdain, Lackey

Mr. Jourdain (*To the lackey*): What! Haven't my clothes come yet?

Lackey: No, sir.

Mr. Jourdain: That cursed tailor makes me wait a long while, on a day when I'm so busy. I am furious. May the quartan ague[12] wring this villain of a tailor unmercifully! To the devil with the tailor! Plague choke the tailor! If I had him here now, that wretch of a tailor, that dog of a tailor, that scoundrel 320 of a tailor, I'd. . .

Scene VIII

Mr. Jourdain, A Master-Tailor; A Journeyman-Tailor, *carrying Mr. Jourdain's suit*; Lackey

Mr. Jourdain: Ah! so there you are! I was just going to get angry with you.

Master-Tailor: I could not come sooner. I had twenty men at work on your clothes.

Mr. Jourdain: You sent me some silk stockings so tight that I had dreadful work getting them on, and there are two stitches broke in them already.

Master-Tailor: If anything, they will grow only too loose.

Mr. Jourdain: Yes, if I keep on breaking out stitches. And 330 you made me some shoes that pinch horribly.

Master-Tailor: Not at all, sir.

Mr. Jourdain: What! Not at all?

Master-Tailor: No, they do not pinch you.

Mr. Jourdain: I tell you they do pinch me.

Master-Tailor: You imagine it.

Mr. Jourdain: I imagine it because I feel it. A fine way of talking!

Master-Tailor: There, this is one of the very handsomest and best matched of court costumes. 'Tis a masterpiece to 340 have invented a suit that is dignified, yet not of black; and I'd give the most cultured tailors six trials and defy them to equal it.

Mr. Jourdain: What's this? You have put the flowers upside down.

Master-Tailor: You didn't tell me you wanted them right end up.

Mr. Jourdain: Was there any need to tell you that?

Master-Tailor: Why, of course. All persons of quality wear them this way. 350

Mr. Jourdain: Persons of quality wear the flowers upside down?

Master-Tailor: Yes, sir.

Mr. Jourdain: Oh! that's all right then.

Master-Tailor: If you wish, I will put them right end up.

Mr. Jourdain: No, no.

Master-Tailor: You have only to say the word.

Mr. Jourdain: No, I tell you; you did rightly. Do you think the clothes will fit me?

Master-Tailor: A pretty question! I defy any painter, with 360 his brush, to make you a closer fit. I have in my shop a fellow that is the greatest genius in the world for setting up a pair of German breeches; and another who is the hero of our age for the cut of a doublet.[13]

Mr. Jourdain: Are the wig and the feathers just as they should be?

Master-Tailor: Everything is just right.

Mr. Jourdain (*Looking at the tailor's suit*): Ah! ah! Mr. Tailor here is some of the cloth from my last suit you made me. I know it perfectly. 370

Master-Tailor: The cloth seemed to me so fine that I thought well to cut a suit for myself out of it.

---

[11] The wife of a nobleman ranking below a duke and above an earl or count.

[12] An intermittent fever.

[13] A man's close-fitting jacket.

Mr. Jourdain: Yes; but you ought not to have cabbaged[14] it out of mine.

Master-Tailor: Will you put on your suit?

Mr. Jourdain: Yes; let me have it.

Master-Tailor: Wait. That is not the way to do things. I have brought my men with me to dress you to music; clothes such as these must be put on with ceremony. Ho! enter, you fellows.

Scene IX

Mr. Jourdain, Master-Tailor, Journeyman-Tailor; Dancers, *in the costume of journeymen-tailors*; Lackey

> **Master-Tailor** (*To his journeymen*): Put on the gentleman's **380** suit, in the style you use for persons of quality.

First Ballet

Enter four journeymen-tailors, two of whom pull off Mr. Jourdain's breeches that he has on for his exercise, and the other two his jacket; then they put on his new suit; and Mr. Jourdain walks about among them, showing off his suit, to see if it is all right. All this to the accompaniment of full orchestra.

> **Journeyman-Tailor**: Noble Sir, please give the tailor's men something to drink.
>
> **Mr. Jourdain**: What did you call me?
>
> **Journeyman-Tailor**: Noble Sir. **390**

Mr. Jourdain: Noble Sir! That is what it is to dress as a person of quality! You may go clothed as a tradesman all your days, and nobody will call you Noble Sir. (*Giving him money*) There, that's for Noble Sir.

> **Journeyman-Tailor**: My Lord, we are greatly obliged to you.

Mr. Jourdain: My Lord! Oh! oh! My Lord! Wait, friend; My Lord deserves something, 'tis no mean word, My Lord! There, there's what His Lordship gives you.

> **Journeyman-Tailor**: My Lord, we will all go and drink Your Grace's health. **400**

Mr. Jourdain: Your Grace! Oh! oh! oh! wait; don't go. Your Grace, to me! (*Aside*) Faith, if he goes as far as Your Highness he'll empty my purse. (*Aloud*) There, there's for Your Grace.

> **Journeyman-Tailor**: My Lord, we thank you most humbly for your generosity.

Mr. Jourdain: He did well to stop. I was just going to give it all to him.

Q How does Molière poke fun at aristocratic values?

Q How does he treat middle-class aspirations?

Absolute Power and the Aristocratic Style Beyond Europe

Imperial Islam

Between 1550 and 1700, three major Islamic empires flourished (Map **21.1**): the Ottoman Empire, which stretched from Eastern Europe through Anatolia and Syria, across North Africa and into Arabia; the Safavid Empire in Persia

---

14 Stolen or filched.

(modern-day Iran); and the Mogul Empire, which succeeded in unifying all of India. All three established absolute monarchies that depended on the support of an efficient bureaucracy and a powerful army. As with the kings of France, the rulers of these Muslim empires governed a rigidly stratified society, consisting of a wealthy elite and a large, and often impoverished, agrarian population. And as in early modern Europe, the empires of the Middle East confronted serious religious rifts. The establishment of Islamic authority over non-Muslims, and the militant animosity between Shi'ite and Sunni factions, ignited bitter conflicts not unlike those between Catholics and Protestants in Western Europe.

In the early modern era, both East and West shared a widening global perception that the "Old World" would never again live in isolation. Fueled by curiosity and commercial ambition, cross-cultural contacts between Europe and Asia flourished. In the 1700s, ambassadors of the **shah** (the word means "king") of Persia and of other Asian potentates were splendidly received at Versailles, while, at the same time, Christian missionaries and official representatives of the European monarchs found their way to Hindu, Buddhist, and Muslim lands. France had long maintained diplomatic ties with the Ottoman Turks; in fact, the French king Francis I (1494–1547) had tried to tip the balance of power against the growing power of the Holy Roman Empire by forging an "unholy" alliance with the great Muslim leader, the **sultan** Suleiman (1494–1566).

The Ottoman Empire

The Ottoman Turks were the successors of the Seljuk Turks, who had converted to Islam in the eleventh century (see chapter 10). Having conquered Constantinople in 1453, they went on to establish an empire that, under the leadership of Suleiman, became the most powerful in the world. With a standing army of 70,000 and a navy of some 300 ships, Suleiman governed territories that stretched from Eastern Europe to the Persian Gulf (see Map 21.1). The Turkish infantry consisted of *janissaries*, an elite slave force (originally recruited from conquered lands), who eventually came to receive a regular cash salary for their services to the empire. Suleiman's court, more lavish than that of Louis XIV, supported an army of servants who dressed, bathed, and entertained the ruler, and served his meals on platters of gold and silver. Suleiman's position as caliph gave him religious authority over all Muslims; and while the Ottoman Sunnis militantly opposed the Shi'ites of Persia, Suleiman's regime granted religious toleration to Muslims and non-Muslims alike.

Suleiman's empire was a model of Muslim absolutism. In the sultan's hands lay unlimited political and religious authority. Known as the "Lawgiver," Suleiman oversaw the establishment of a legal code that, while respecting the **sharia** (Muslim sacred law), fixed specific penalties for routine crimes. He also introduced the concept of a balanced financial budget. State revenues some eighty times those of France permitted Suleiman to undertake an extensive program of architectural and urban improvement in the great

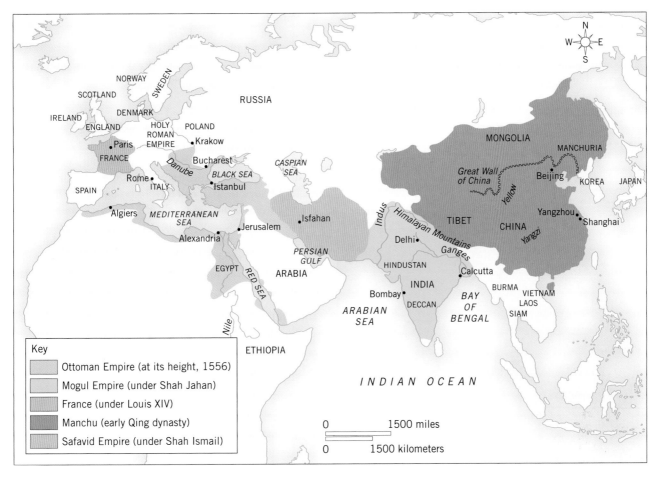

Map 21.1 Empires in the Late Sixteenth and Early Seventeenth Centuries. Note the strategically located capitals: Paris (France), Istanbul (Ottoman), Isfahan (Safavid), Delhi (Mogul), and Beijing (Manchu/Qing).

cities of his empire: Mecca, Constantinople, and Jerusalem. A goldsmith and a poet of some esteem, he initiated a golden age of literature and art. Pomp and luxury characterized Suleiman's court, and the arts that flourished under his patronage shared with those of seventeenth-century France a taste for the ornate and a high degree of technical skill (Figure **21.17**). Suleiman, whom Europeans called "the Magnificent," personally oversaw the activities of official court poets, painters, architects, and musicians. He established a model for imperial patronage that ensured the triumph of the aristocratic style not only in Turkish lands but in all parts of his multi-ethnic empire.

The Safavid Empire

The Ottoman Empire began to decline after Suleiman's death. In Persia, where Shi'ite leaders launched a *jihad* against the reigning Sunnis, the Safavid dynasty rose to power. (By the late seventeenth century, Persia's population was solidly Shi'ite and remains so in modern-day Iran.) Under the leadership of Shah Abbas (1557–1628), the multi-ethnic population of Persia was united. A political pragmatist and a brilliant strategist, Shah Abbas held absolute power over a prosperous empire. Establishing his capital at Isfahan, he commissioned the construction of new mosques, palaces, roads, and bridges. The government

Figure 21.17 Ceremonial canteen, Ottoman Empire, second half of the sixteenth century. Gold decorated with jade plaques and gems.

held monopolies in luxury goods, including silk production, and stimulated trade.

By the year 1600, Persian silk rivaled that of China in European markets. Carpet weaving became a national industry that employed more than 25,000 people in the city of Isfahan alone. Persian tapestries, intricately woven in silk and wool (Figure **21.18**), and finely ornamented

Figure 21.18 Kirman shrub rug, Persia, seventeenth century. Silk and wool, 10 ft. 1 in. × 4 ft. 7 in. Court carpets were among the most magnificent products of sixteenth- and seventeenth-century Persia. This one features flowering trees and bushes that evoke the Qur'anic Garden of Paradise.

ceramics were avidly sought across the world, and Persian manuscripts embellished with brightly printed illustrations came to be imitated throughout Asia.

In the field of architecture, the outstanding monument to Safavid wealth and power was the Imperial Mosque, commissioned by Shah Abbas for the city of Isfahan (Figure **21.19**). Completed in 1637, this magnificent structure, flanked by two minarets, encloses a square main hall covered by a splendid dome that rises to 177 feet. The surfaces of the mosque, both inside and out, are covered with colored glazed tiles (compare to the Ishtar Gate of ancient Babylon, see Figure 1.11) ornamented with calligraphic inscriptions and delicate blue and yellow floral motifs. French aristocrats in the service of Louis XIV brought back to France enthusiastic reports of the Imperial Mosque—a fact that has led scholars to detect the influence of Persian art on some of Louis' more lavish enterprises at Versailles.

The Mogul Empire

Muslims had ruled parts of India for almost a thousand years, but it was not until the sixteenth century that the Muslim dynasty known as the Moguls (the name derives from "Mongol") succeeded in uniting all of India (see Map 21.1). Distant cousins of the Safavid princes, the Moguls ruled India as absolute monarchs from 1526 to 1707. They imported Persian culture and language into India in much the same way that Louis XIV brought Italian culture into France. The creators of a culture that blended Muslim, Hindu, Turkish, Persian, Arabic, and African traditions, the Moguls encouraged the development of an aristocratic style, which—like that of the Sun King—served as an adjunct to majesty.

The founder of the Mogul Empire, Akbar (1542–1605), came to the throne at the age of thirteen. Establishing an integrated state in north India, he laid the foundations for a luxurious court style that his son and grandson would perpetuate. India's most dynamic ruler since Emperor Asoka of the third century B.C.E., Akbar ruled over a court consisting of thousands of courtiers, servants, wives, and concubines. He exercised political control over feudal noblemen and court officials who, unlike their French counterparts, received paid salaries. Amidst the primarily Hindu population, the Muslim ruler pursued a policy of religious toleration. So as not to offend India's Hindus, he became a vegetarian and gave up hunting, his favorite sport. Akbar's religious pluralism reflected his personal quest for a synthesis of faiths. Dedicated to "divine monotheism," he brought learned representatives of Christianity, Judaism, Hinduism, and other religions to his court, to debate with Muslim theologians. He also made every effort to rid India of its outmoded traditions, such as the immolation of wives on their husbands' funeral pyres. Despite Akbar's reforms, however, the lower classes and especially the peasants were taxed heavily (as was also the case in France under Louis XIV) to finance the luxuries of the upper-class elite.

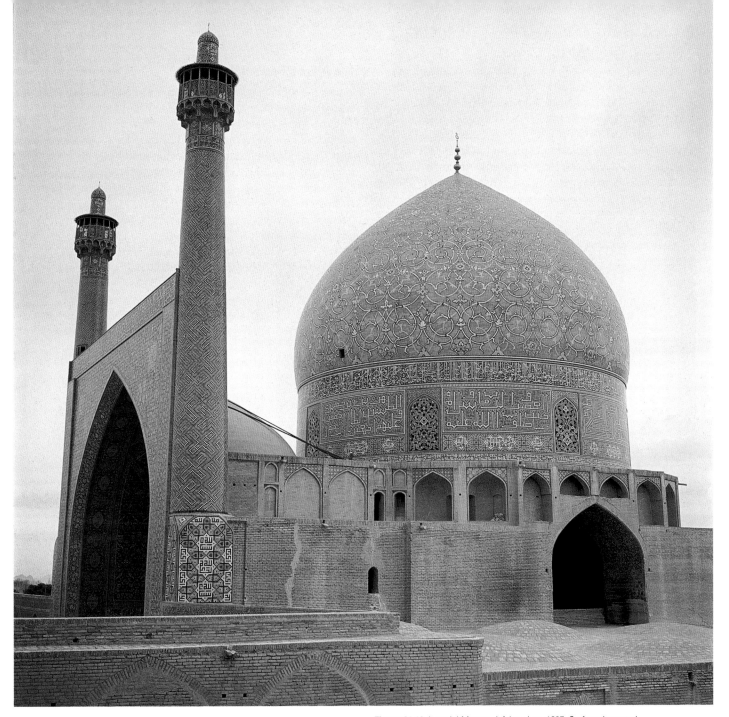

Figure 21.19 Imperial Mosque, Isfahan, Iran, 1637. Surface decorated with colored glazed tiles, height of dome 177 ft. The Imperial Mosque, which dates back to the eighth century, was enlarged and renovated by numerous Muslim rulers. The Safavids were instrumental in making Shia Islam the official religion in Persia.

Science and Technology

1717	inoculation against smallpox is introduced in Europe (from Ottoman Turkey)
1736	expansion of the Indian shipbuilding industry in Bombay
1780	a European version of Chinese silk-reeling machines is introduced in Bengal
1781	Turkish methods for producing high-quality cloth are copied in England
1790	India uses military rockets based on Ottoman technology in warfare

In the seventeenth century, the Moguls governed the wealthiest state in the world, a state whose revenues were ten times greater than those of France. Akbar commissioned magnificent works of music, poetry, painting, and architecture—the tangible expressions of princely affluence and taste. As in Louis' court, most of these exquisite objects were designed for secular, not liturgical, use. A state studio of more than 100 artists working under Persian masters created a library of more than 24,000 illuminated manuscripts, the contents of which ranged from love poetry to Hindu epics and religious tales. One notable Mogul innovation was the practice of recording and illustrating first-hand accounts of specific historical events. A miniature celebrating the birth of Akbar's son, Nurud-din Salim Jahangir, shows courtiers rejoicing: dancers sway to the rhythms of a lively musical ensemble while bread and alms are distributed outside the palace gate (Figure **21.20**). Such miniatures reveal the brilliant union of delicate line, rich color, and strong surface patterns—features that also dominate Asian carpet designs. The absence of Western perspective gives the scene a flat, decorative quality.

Figure 21.20 *Rejoicing at the Birth of Prince Salim in 1569.* Manuscript illustration from the Akbar-Nama.

The Arts of the Mogul Court

Under the rule of Akbar's son Jahangir (ruled 1605–1627), aristocratic court portraiture came into fashion in India. The new genre reflects the influence of European painting, which had been eagerly embraced by the Moguls, and suggests the gradual relaxation of Muslim prohibition against the representation of the human figure. Relatively small in comparison with the aristocratic portraits executed by Rigaud or van Dyck (see Figures 21.2, 22.2), the painted likeness of Jahangir (the name means "world seizer") featured in a small picture album glorifies the monarch in an international context (Figure **21.21**). The artist Bichitr (fl. 1625), whose self-portrait appears in the lower left corner, shows the shah enthroned atop an elaborate hourglass throne, a reference to the brevity of life and to Jahangir's declining health. Jahangir welcomes a Sufi (a Muslim mystic), who stands in the company of a Turkish dignitary and the European King James I of England. While the latter invites the viewer into the scene, the turbaned Turk makes a gesture of submission to Jahangir. Yet Jahangir looks directly at the Sufi, who presents him with a book, perhaps a copy of the Qur'an. Four Western-style angels frame the scene: the upper two seem to lament the impermanence of worldly power, while the bottom two inscribe the base of the hourglass with the prayer, "O Shah, may the span of your life be a thousand years." Just as Louis XIV assumed the guise of the Sun King, so Jahangir— as notorious for his overconsumption of wine and opium as Louis was for fine food and sex—is apotheosized by a huge halo consisting of the sun and the moon. The miniature, an allegorical statement of the superiority of spiritual over secular power, is also an amalgam of Western and Eastern styles and motifs. Western-style illusionistic portraits are framed by an Eastern carpet-like background; the upper two angels are reminiscent of cherubs in Italian Renaissance paintings and the halo is clearly inspired by Hindu and Buddhist art. This little hybrid masterpiece anticipates a global perspective that will overtake the world in the centuries to come.

Well before the seventeenth century, Mogul rulers had initiated the tradition of building huge ceremonial and administrative complexes, veritable cities in themselves. Such complexes symbolized Muslim wealth and authority in India, but, as in France, they were also political manifestations of the cult of royalty. Akbar had personally oversaw the construction of a palace complex near Agra, which, comparable with Versailles, featured an elaborate residence surrounded by courtyards and mosques, as well as by formal gardens and fountains watered by means of artificial conduits. The garden, a this-worldly counterpart of the Qur'anic Garden of Paradise (see chapter 10) and a welcome refuge from India's intense heat, was a characteristic feature of the Mogul palace complex.

Inspired by the elaborate ceremonial centers built by his father and his grandfather, Shah Jahan (1627–1666) commissioned the most sumptuous of all Mogul palaces, the Shahjahanabad (present-day Old Delhi). The red sandstone walls of the Shahjahanabad (nicknamed the "Red Fort") enclosed a palatial residence of white marble, flanked by magnificent gardens, public and private audience halls, courtyards, pavilions, baths, and the largest mosque in India (Figure **21.22**). The Red Fort's 3:4 rectangular plan was bisected by an axis that led through successive courts to the public audience hall, a pattern that anticipated the rigid symmetry of Versailles (compare Figure 21.3).

The hot Indian climate inclined Mogul architects to open up interior space by means of foliated arcades (see chapter 10) and latticed screens through which breezes might blow uninterrupted (Figure **21.23**). These graceful architectural features distinguish the shah's palace at the Red Fort. The most ornate of all Mogul interiors, Shah Jahan's audience hall consists of white marble arcades and ceilings decorated with geometric and floral patterns

Figure 21.21 (above) *Jahangir Preferring a Sufi Shaikh to Kings*, from the *Leningrad Album of Bichitr*, seventeenth century. Color and gold, 10 × 7⅛ in. The inscriptions above the halo hail Jahangir as "Light of the Faith." King James I looks out at us to acknowledge our participation in the scene.

Figure 21.22 Anonymous Delhi artist, *The Red Fort*, ca. 1820. The building dates from the Shah Jahan period, after 1638.

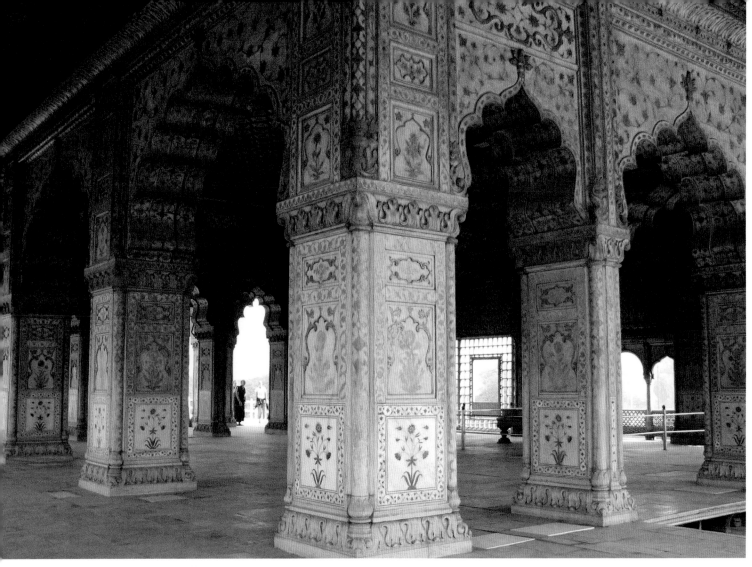

Figure 21.23 Foliated arcades and perforated monolithic screens in the Red Fort (Shahjahanabad), Delhi, Shah Jahan period, after 1638.

popular in Mogul embroidery, a craft traditionally dominated by women. The rich designs consist of inlaid precious and semiprecious stones (***pietra dura***), a type of mosaic work that the Moguls had borrowed from Italy. At the center of the hall, the shah sat on the prized Peacock Throne, fashioned in solid gold and studded with emeralds, rubies, diamonds, and pearls. Above the throne (which served imperial India until it was plundered by Persian warriors in 1732) was a canopy on which stood two gold peacocks, and above the canopy, around the ceiling of the hall, were inscribed the words, "If there is a paradise on the face of the earth, It is this, oh! it is this, oh! it is this."

Surpassing the splendor of the palace at Delhi (badly damaged by the British army during the nineteenth century) is Shah Jahan's most magnificent gift to world architecture: the Taj Mahal (Figure **21.24**). Shah Jahan built the Taj Mahal as a mausoleum to honor the memory of his favorite wife, Mumtaz Mahal (the name means "light of the world"). When Mumtaz died giving birth to their fourteenth child, her husband, legend has it, was inconsolable. He directed his architects to construct alongside the Jumna River a glorious tomb, a twin to one he planned for himself on the adjoining riverbank. Fabricated in cream-colored marble, the Taj rises majestically above a tree-lined pool that mirrors its elegant silhouette so that the

mausoleum seems to be floating in air. Although the individual elements of the structure—slender minarets, bulbous domes, and octagonal base—recall Byzantine and Persian prototypes (see Figure 21.19), its total effect is unique: shadowy voids and bright solids play against one another on the surface of the exterior, while delicate patterns of light and dark animate the latticed marble screens and exquisitely carved walls of the interior. The garden complex, divided into quadrants by waterways and broad footpaths, is an earthly recreation of the Muslim Garden of Paradise. The Taj Mahal is the product of some 20,000 West Asian builders and craftsmen working under the direction of a Persian architect. It is a brilliant fusion of the best aspects of Byzantine, Muslim, and Hindu traditions and, hence, an emblem of Islamic cohesion. But it is also an extravagant expression of conjugal devotion and, to generations of Western visitors, an eloquent tribute to romantic love.

The Decline of the Islamic Empires

As these pages suggest, during the sixteenth and seventeenth centuries the aristocratic courts of Islam ruled vast parts of Asia, including India and the Near East (see Map 21.1). By the mid-eighteenth century, however, the great empires of the Ottomans, the Safavids, and the Moguls were either destroyed or in fatal decline. India came under the rule of Great Britain and parts of the Ottoman Empire were lost to the control of other European powers. While the Islamic empires had depended on the West for modern weapons, they could not compete with the West's rapidly advancing commercialism and military technology. Conservative Muslim elements vigorously resisted all aspects of Western culture, including Western science and Christian learning. Threatened by the culture of the Christian West, some Muslim clerics even opposed the printing of books. Movements of Muslim revivalism would grow more militant in the following centuries, as Islam—once the imperial leader of the Asian world—struggled against European colonialism and the inevitable forces of Modernism.

Absolute Power and the Aristocratic Style in China

The Ming Dynasty

 From the earliest days of Chinese history, Chinese emperors—the "Sons of Heaven"—ruled on earth by divine authority, or, as the Chinese called it, "the Mandate of Heaven" (see chapter 3). In theory, all of China's emperors were absolute rulers. Nevertheless, over the centuries, their power was frequently contested by feudal lords, military generals, and government officials. In 1368, native Chinese rebels drove out the last of the Mongol rulers and

Figure 21.24 Taj Mahal, Agra, India, 1623–1643.

established the Ming dynasty, which ruled China until 1644. The Ming dynasty governed the largest and most sophisticated empire on earth, an empire of some 120 million people. In the highly centralized Chinese state, Ming emperors oversaw a bureaucracy that included offices of finance, laws, military affairs, and public works. They rebuilt the Great Wall (see chapter 7) and revived the ancient Chinese tradition of the examination system, which had been suspended by the Mongols. By the seventeenth century, however, the Ming had become autocrats who, like the foreigners they had displaced, took all power into their own hands. They transformed the civil service into a nonhereditary bureaucracy that did not dare to threaten the emperor's authority. The rigid court protocol that developed around the imperial rulers of the late Ming dynasty symbolized this shift toward autocracy. Officials, for instance, knelt in the presence of the emperor, who, as the Son of Heaven, sat on an elevated throne in the center of the imperial precinct.

The Qing Dynasty

Beset by court corruption and popular revolts, the Ming fell prey to the invading hordes of East Asians (descendants of Mongols, Turks, and other tribes) known as the Manchu. Under the rule of the Manchu, who established the Qing dynasty (1644–1912), the conditions of imperial autocracy intensified. As a symbol of submission, every Chinese male was required to adopt the Manchu hairstyle, by which one shaved the front of the head and wore a plaited pigtail at the back. Qing rulers retained the administrative traditions of their predecessors, but government posts were often sold rather than earned by merit. When

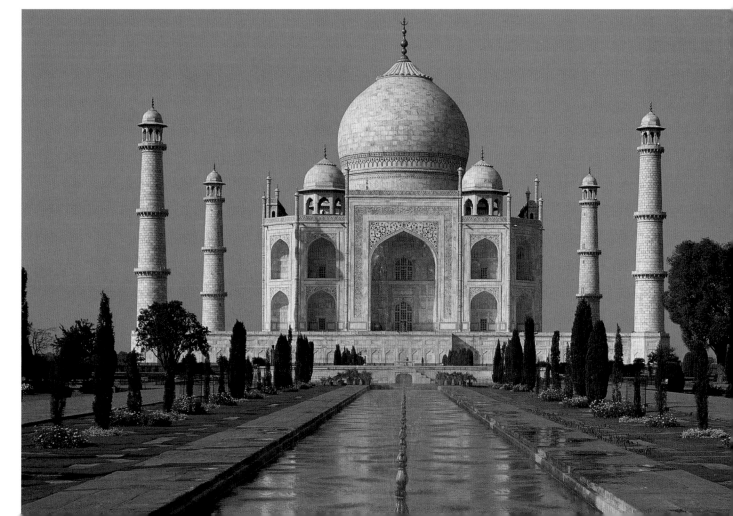

the Qing dynasty reached its zenith—during the very last years that Louis XIV ruled France—it governed the largest, most populous, and one of the most unified states in the world (see Map 21.1). Despite internal peace, uprisings were common. They reflected the discontent of peasant masses beset by high taxes and rents and periodic famines. Like the lower classes of France and India, Chinese villagers and urban workers supported the luxuries of royal princes, government officials, and large landholders, who (as in France and India) were themselves exempt from taxation. The early Manchu rulers imitated their predecessors as royal sponsors of art and architecture. Like Louis XIV and Shah Jahan, the Chinese emperor and his huge retinue resided in an impressive ceremonial complex (Figure 21.25). This metropolis, the symbol of entrenched absolutism and the majesty of the ruler, was known as the Forbidden City—so-called because of its inaccessibility to ordinary Chinese citizens until 1925.

Figure 21.25 XU YANG, *Bird's-Eye View of the Capital*, 1770. Hanging scroll, ink and color on paper, 8 ft. 4¼ in. × 7 ft. 8 in. Commissioned in 1406, the Forbidden City was first occupied by the Ming court in 1421. It is said to have held 9,999 separate rooms; nine, an auspicious number, symbolizes the union of the five elements and the four cosmological directions.

The Forbidden City

Comparable in size and conception to Versailles in the West and to the Mogul palaces of India, the Forbidden City—a walled complex of palaces, tombs, and gardens located in Beijing—was the most elaborate imperial monument of the Ming and Qing eras. Construction on the imperial palace began under fifteenth-century Ming emperors and was continued by the Manchus. For almost 500 years, this vast ceremonial complex—which, like Versailles, is now a park and museum—was the administrative center of China and the home of no fewer than twenty-four Ming and Qing emperors, their families, and the members of their courts. By the eighteenth century, some 9000 people, including guards, concubines, and domestic servants, resided within the complex.

Inside the 10-foot-high walls of the Forbidden City are royal meeting halls, grand avenues, broad courtyards, government offices, mansions of princes and dignitaries, artificial lakes, lush gardens, spacious temples, theaters, a library, and a printing house (Figure **21.26**). Entering from the south, one passes under the majestic, five-towered entranceway through a succession of courtyards and gates reminiscent of the intriguing nests of boxes at which Chinese artisans excel. At the heart of the rectangular complex, one proceeds up the three-tiered stone terrace (Figure **21.27**), into the Hall of Supreme Harmony (approximately 200 by 100 feet), where the Sons of Heaven sat enthroned, and beyond, to the imperial living quarters at the rear of the complex. Fragrant gardens, watered by fountains and artificial pools, once graced the private quarters of the royal officials.

Figure 21.26 Plan of the imperial palace, Forbidden City, Beijing, China.

N

1 Gate of Divine Pride
2 Pavilion of Imperial Peace
3 Imperial Garden
4 Palace of Earthly Tranquility
5 Hall of Union
6 Palace of Heavenly Purity
7 Gate of Heavenly Purity
8 Hall of the Preservation
    of Harmony
9 Hall of Perfect Harmony
10 Hall of Supreme Harmony
11 Gate of Supreme
    Harmony
12 Meridian Gate
13 Kitchens
14 Gardens
15 Former Imperial Printing House
16 Flower Gate
17 Palace of the Culture
    of the Mind
18 Hall of the Worship of
    the Ancestors
19 Pavilion of Arrows
20 Imperial Library
21 Palace of Culture
22 Palace of Peace and Longevity
23 Nine Dragon Screen

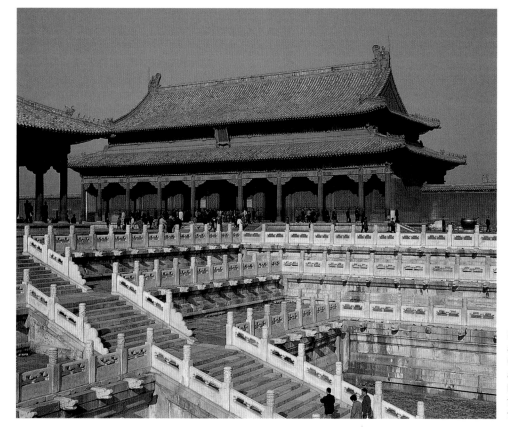

Figure 21.27 Three-tiered stone terrace and Hall of Supreme Harmony, Forbidden City, Beijing, China, Ming dynasty. Hall approx. 200 × 100 ft. Number 10 in Figure 21.26, the largest throne hall in the complex, is positioned centrally on the 2-mile-long ceremonial axis.

Figure 21.28 Flower vase, Qing dynasty. Chinese pottery, "peach-bloom" glaze, height 7¾ in.

During the seventeenth century, courtyard gardening itself developed into a fine art. Often flanked by a covered walkway from which it could be viewed, the Chinese garden was an arrangement of seemingly random (but actually carefully placed) rocks, plants, and trees—a miniature version of the natural world. Like the Chinese landscape scroll, the garden was an object of gentle contemplation, designed to be enjoyed progressively. The garden, with its winding, narrow paths, delicate ferns, and sheltering bamboos, has become a hallmark of East Asian culture.

The Forbidden City was the nucleus of imperial power and the symbol of Chinese absolutism. Laid out with a gridiron regularity that rivaled Mogul and French palatial complexes, the arrangement of buildings, courtyards, gates, and terraces was uniquely Chinese. It adhered to the ancient Chinese practice of *feng shui*, the arrangement of the physical environment in accordance with specific cosmological principles (see chapter 7). Lined up along the cosmic north–south axis, buildings are symmetrical, with square foundations symbolizing Earth, and yellow-tiled roofs symbolizing Heaven. (As the Son of Heaven, the emperor was expected to keep the two in balance.) Palace doors face the "good" southerly direction, while rear walls, facing North, are closed to the cold winds and the attacks of northern barbarians. The Forbidden City, however, also reflects the ceremonial dimension of royal absolutism. The sizes and functions of the buildings were determined by a strict protocol based on rank, age, and gender. During the Ming Era, for instance, imperial legislation prescribed nine rooms for the emperor, seven for a prince, five for a court official, and three for an ordinary citizen.

Most of the buildings of the Forbidden City are no more than a single story high, their walls serving only as screens that divide interior space. What the Chinese sacrificed in monumentality, however, they recovered in ornamental splendor and in the creation of an architecture that achieved harmony with (rather than dominance over) nature. Chinese architects preserved such traditional features as the rectangular hall with fully exposed wooden rafters and the pitched roof with projecting eaves and glazed yellow tiles—the latter symbolic of the mantle of heaven. Bronze lions and gilded dragons (symbols of royal power) guard the great halls and entrances. In the Forbidden City Chinese court culture promoted a lavish aristocratic style that enhanced the majesty of the ruler.

The Arts of the Ming and Qing Courts

The Ming and Qing emperors were great patrons of the arts. They encouraged the traditional schools of landscape painting and oversaw the production of such luxury items as inlaid bronze vessels, carved ivories and jades, lacquerware, embroidered silk, and painted ceramics. Chinese porcelains had been much sought after since the seventh century; by the seventeenth century they were world famous, so much so that in the West the word "Ming" became synonymous with porcelain. (More generally, the word "china" has come to signify fine ceramics and tableware.)

Qing artists used bright colors more freely than in earlier times. Vessels with solid color glazes of ox-blood red and peach-blossom pink (Figure **21.28**) alternated with colorful landscapes filled with songbirds, flowering trees, human figures, and mythical animals. One Qing bowl ornamented with a rich five-color palette shows a group of elegantly attired men, women, and servants in a luxurious interior (Figure **21.29**). As this delightful scene suggests, neither in the porcelains nor in the paintings of this period did the Chinese develop any interest in the kinds of heroic and moralizing themes that dominated Baroque art in the West. This difference notwithstanding, imperial tastes dictated the style of aristocratic art in China every bit as much as the royal academies of France influenced seventeenth-century French style. By 1680, there were over thirty official palace workshops serving the imperial court. Out of these workshops poured precious works of art: gem-encrusted jewelry,

Figure 21.29 *Famille verte*, Qing dynasty, early eighteenth century. Foliated porcelain bowl, diameter 6½ in.

carved wood and lacquerware, painted enamels, *cloisonné* vessels (Figure **21.30**), intricate jade carvings, and heavily embroidered silk and gold textiles (Figure **21.31**). Many of these objects found their way into Europe, where they inspired **chinoiserie**, a style reflecting the influence of Chinese art and a taste for Chinese items that, in the 1700s, developed into something of a mania.

From China, by way of the Dutch, tea ("the Chinese drink") came into use in England, often smuggled into the country to avoid the high import tax. The fashionable tea service became the object of imitation in the West, most notably in the blue and white wares of Delft, Holland. Cultural exchange between East and West, however, was mutual: delegations of Jesuits, who arrived in China in 1601, introduced the rules of linear perspective to Chinese art, even as they transmitted to Europe (often by means of prints and engravings) a knowledge of Chinese techniques and goods. And French prints in turn prompted early Manchu rulers to build a Chinese version of Versailles, complete with fountains, at the imperial summer palace northwest of Beijing.

Figure 21.30 (above) Incense burner in the shape of a *li* (tripod), Ming dynasty, fifteenth or possibly early sixteenth century. *Cloisonné* enamel, diameter 7½ in.

Figure 21.31 (below) Manchu-style man's *jifu* (semiformal court robe), Qing dynasty, second quarter of the eighteenth century. Silk and gold leaf over lacquered paper strips, 4 ft. 4¾ in. × 6 ft. 2⅛ in. The dragon, an age-old symbol of the emperor's supreme power, is the dominant motif on this robe. In the Hall of Supreme Harmony the emperor sat on the Dragon Throne. Some additional 13,000 dragon images adorn the walls, ceilings, and other parts of the building.

Chinese Literature and the Theater Arts

Ming and Qing rulers worked hard to preserve China's rich literary heritage. Under Ming patronage, a group of 2000 scholars began the enormous task of collecting and copying the most famous of China's literary and historical works. The Manchu contemporary of Louis XIV, Emperor Kangxi (1662–1722), hired 15,000 calligraphers and 360 editors to compile a vast assortment of dictionaries, encyclopedias, and a thirty-six-volume anthology of the Chinese classics (Figure **21.32**). Increasing numbers of literate middle-class men and women in China's growing cities demanded printed books for everyday use. These included almanacs, guides to letter writing, short stories, collections of proverbs and maxims, chronicles, ballads, and romances.

Novels, long works of fiction in the colloquial style, had emerged as early as the twelfth century in China and even earlier in Japan (see chapter 14); but in the Ming and Qing eras, this literary genre became ever more popular. The typical Chinese novel recounted historical events and often made fun of religious and secular authorities. In the early eighteenth century, Cao Xueqin produced China's greatest novel, *The Dream of the Red Chamber* (also known as *The Story of the Stone*). This 4000-page work, which was to become the most popular example of Chinese fiction, is a love story involving two aristocratic Beijing families. Filled with realistic detail as well as fantastic dream sequences, the novel provides a fascinating picture of upper-class Qing society.

Plots drawn from popular novels such as *The Dream of the Red Chamber* provided the themes for staged performances, which always included mime, dance, and vocal and instrumental music. This type of theatrical performance—which Westerners might call "opera"—was the only form of drama that existed in China prior to the twentieth century (when, imitating Western drama, Chinese writers began to produce exclusively spoken plays). In the Chinese theater, performers were exclusively male, and male actors played the parts of such stock characters as the coquette or the virtuous maid. Since troupes of players moved from city to city, elaborate costumes and stage scenery were minimal. Chinese theater made use of conventional props to indicate setting or circumstance: a chair might represent a mountain, a whip might signify that the actor was on horseback, and a black cloth might be used to indicate that a character was invisible. Colors symbolized conventional character types: red represented loyalty and dignity, white symbolized villainy or treachery, and so on. During the Ming Era, when sumptuous costumes and masklike makeup became popular, such earlier stage symbols and conventions were still preserved. Indeed, to this day, Chinese theater retains many traditional, highly stylized features.

Despite the differences in their origins, Chinese and European opera developed during the same era—the seventeenth century. By the late eighteenth century the first permanent Chinese opera company emerged in the capital city of Beijing. Chinese opera shunned the dramatic contrasts in texture and timbre that characterize Western opera (and Western music in general). While early

Figure 21.32 UNKNOWN ARTIST, portrait of Emperor Kangxi reading. Kangxi, a Confucian scholar who ruled China for sixty years, is shown seated against a background of string-bound books that made up part of his library. He is said to have introduced Western technology and Western musical instruments into China.

European operas borrowed themes from Greco-Roman mythology and biblical history—themes that might glorify a royal patron or flatter upper-class tastes—Chinese operas mainly drew on a traditional repertory of love stories, social events, and the adventures of folk heroes. Such operas often featured stock characters resembling those of Molière's plays, and, like Molière's plays, they had wide and lasting popularity.

Absolute Power and the Aristocratic Style in Japan

By the seventeenth century, feudal Japan had taken the direction of a unified and centralized state led by members of the Tokugawa dynasty (1600–1868). In contrast to China, whose aristocracy consisted of a scholarly elite recruited through civil service examinations, Japan's aristocracy consisted of a warrior elite (the *samurai*) recruited in battle (see chapter 14). The Tokugawa *shogun* (general-in-chief) demanded that his feudal lords attend his court in Edo (modern-day Tokyo). Here he enforced court etiquette as faithfully as he solidified political and economic control. Unique to Japan was its self-enforced isolation from the West (see chapter 20). In the 1630s, Tokugawa rulers initiated a policy of national seclusion. Determined

See Music Listening Selection 14, CD One, an excerpt from a Chinese opera described in chapter 14.

to maintain internal stability and peace, they expelled foreigners and forbade citizens to travel abroad, thus sealing off Japan from the outside world.

While a large segment of Japan's peasantry led barely subsistent lives, the pleasure-loving court at Edo (a city of one million people by the year 1700) and the rising commercial classes of the towns enjoyed one of the most creative periods in Japanese history. In the Tokugawa court, the traditional Japanese decorative style reached new heights. Luxury items included multipaneled screens (used to divide interior space), hand-painted scrolls, ceramics (including the decorative porcelains known as "Imari ware"), and lacquer boxes used for the tea ceremony. Japan's aristocratic style is best represented in its brightly painted multifold screens, adorned with stylized flowers, birds, or landscape motifs. In the large six-paneled screen by Ogata Korin (ca. 1658–1716), pictured in Figure **21.33**, bold, decorative shapes and the subtle balance of figure and ground (positive and negative space) achieve an astonishing purity of design. Such screens unite simplicity and luxury (the ground of the screen is gold leaf) with an elegance that distinguishes the Japanese court style at its best.

The Floating World

Parallel with the flowering of the aristocratic style in Tokugawa Japan was the rise of popular culture and popular artforms. The new merchant class that occupied Japan's growing commercial cities demanded a variety of lively (and bawdy) entertainments. In the so-called "floating world" (*ukiyo*)—"floating" because Japan's middle class was not bound by aristocratic proprieties—theaters and brothels provided leisure-time pleasures. *Ukiyo* was described by one of Japan's first professional writers, Asai Ryoi (1612–1691), in his *Tales of the Floating World* (ca. 1665):

> Living only for the moment, turning our full
> attention to the pleasures of the moon, the snow,
> the cherry blossoms and the maples, singing songs,
> drinking wine, and diverting ourselves in just
> floating, floating, caring not a whit for the poverty
> staring us in the face, refusing to be disheartened,
> like a gourd floating along with the current:
> this is what we call *ukiyo*.

From the floating world of the Edo district came a new type of staged performance known as **kabuki.** The *kabuki* stage provided an alternative to Japan's oldest form of theater, Nō drama (see chapter 14), whose traditional literary subjects, stylized movements, and use of masks had much in common with ancient Greek theater. In its late-fifteenth-century origins, *kabuki* (literally, "song-dance-art") was a female performance genre. But in 1629, some twenty years after its first appearance, the Japanese government issued an edict that forbade women to appear on stage. Thereafter, male actors wearing elaborate costumes, wigs, and make-up assumed all *kabuki* roles. *Kabuki* plays featured dance, song, and mime. Their plots, drawn from history, myth, puppet plays and daily life, often involved tales of romance marked by violent passions and "love suicides." Action took place on a revolving stage that featured a long ramp leading from the audience to the rear of the stage (Figure **21.34**). Elegant backdrops and scenic effects embellished the action. Three to five plays might be performed in a single day, interrupted by intervals that allowed the audience to visit local teahouses and restaurants.

Woodcut prints celebrating celebrity actors and famous courtesans (some depicted in sexually explicit acts) became one of Japan's most popular genres (Figure **21.35**). Mass-produced and therefore inexpensive, *ukiyo-e* ("pictures of the floating world") were purchased by Edo patrons as souvenirs, much as people today collect posters of famous personalities. Executed in black and white, and (by 1750) colored either by hand or with inked blocks, woodcut prints exemplify Japanese virtuosity in calligraphic

Figure 21.33 OGATA KORIN, *Irises at Yatsuhashi*, from the Tale of Ise (*Ise Monogatari*), Edo period. One of a pair of six-paneled screens, ink and color and gilded paper, with black lacquered frames, each screen 4 ft. 11 in × 11 ft. 3in.

Figure 21.34 MASANOBU (?) (above), *Kabuki* stage, ca. 1740. Colored woodblock print.

Figure 21.35 TOSHUSAI SHARAKU (below), *Bust Portrait of the Actor Segawa Tomisaburo as Yadorigi, the Wife of Ogishi Kurando*, 1794–1795. Woodblock print, 14½ × 9¼ in. Photograph.

design. They share with Korin's screens the typically Japanese mastery of simplicity, elegance, and control.

The Way of Tea and Zen

A classic expression of Japanese culture is the ritual tea ceremony—a unique synthesis of art, theater, and everyday ritual. Introduced into Japan from China during the ninth century, strongly caffeinated tea served as an aid to Buddhist meditation. By the sixteenth century the Way of Tea (as the practice of tea-drinking is called) was closely associated with Zen Buddhism, a strand of Buddhism that seeks spiritual enlightenment through intuitive illumination (see chapter 8). With the cultivation of better types of tea plants, tea-drinking became widely practiced in Japanese society, gradually establishing itself among samurai warriors and wealthy merchants. The four-hour tea ceremony is choreographed according to a strict set of rules and formal etiquette. An intimate ritual, incorporating the arts of ceramics, textiles, and flower-arranging, it remains a paradigm of the cultivated life.

Typical of Zen monastic practice, tea and the etiquette of tea-drinking coincided with a revival of Zen painting among eighteenth-century artist–monks. Zen calligraphers did not consider their paintings as works of art, but, rather, as acts of meditation involving intense concentration and focus. Absence of detail invited the beholder to complete the painting, and thus partake of the meditative process. One of the greatest Zen masters was Hakuin Ekaku (1685–1768), whose magnificent ink scrolls are noted for their vigorous yet subtle brushwork. In *Two Blind Men Crossing a Log Bridge* (Figure **21.36**), Hakuin illustrates his vision of the precarious nature of the human journey to spiritual enlightenment: two monks, one with his sandals hanging on his staff, make their way unsteadily across the narrow bridge. The figures, like the Japanese characters that record the accompanying poem (in the upper left corner), come to life by way of confident, calligraphic brushstrokes. Hakuin's poem reads:

> Both inner life and the floating world outside us
> Are like the blind man's round log bridge—
> An enlightened mind is the best guide.

In their improvisational spirit, the ink scrolls of the Zen master differ from the deliberately stylized Edo screens. Yet, both share the Japanese preference for refinement and utmost simplicity.

Controlled simplicity is a major feature of Tokugawa lyric verse forms, the most notable of which is the *haiku*. The *haiku*—a seventeen-syllable poem arranged in three lines of 5/7/5/ syllables—depends for its effectiveness on the absence of detail and the pairing of contrasting images. The unexpected contrast does not describe a condition or event, but rather evokes a mood or emotion. Much like the art of the Zen calligrapher, the *haiku* creates a provocative void between what is stated and what is left unsaid. In this void there lies an implied "truth," one that aims to close the gap between the world of things and the world of feelings. Witness the following five compositions by Japan's most famous *haiku* poet and Zen monk, Matsuo Bashō (1644–1694):

Figure 21.36 HAKUIN EKAKU, *Two Blind Men Crossing a Log Bridge*, Edo Period (1615–1868). Hanging scroll, ink on paper, 11⅟₁₆ × 33 in.

The beginning of all art
   a song when planting a rice field
      in the country's inmost part.

◆

The first day of the year:
   thoughts come—and there is loneliness;
      the autumn dusk is here.

◆

Oh, these spring days!
   A nameless little mountain,
      wrapped in morning haze!

◆

I'd like enough drinks
   to put me to sleep—on stones
      covered with pinks.

◆

Leaning upon staves
   and white-haired—a whole family
      visiting the graves.

Chronology

1520–1566	Suleiman rules Ottoman Empire
1556–1605	Akbar rules Mogul Empire
1588–1629	Shah Abbas rules Safavid Empire (Persia)
1600–1868	Tokugawa Shogunate in Japan
1607–1627	Jahangir rules Mogul Empire
1627–1666	Shah Jahan rules Mogul Empire
1643–1715	Louis XIV rules France
1661–1722	Kangxi (Qing dynasty) rules China

LOOKING BACK

The Aristocratic Style in Europe

- As absolute monarch, Louis XIV brought France to a position of political and military preeminence among the European nation-states. He challenged the power of the nobility and the Church, centralizing authority in his own hands.
- Under Louis' leadership, the center of artistic patronage and productivity shifted from Italy to France. French culture in all its forms—from art and architecture to fashions and fine cuisine—came to dominate European tastes.

- Louis recognized the propaganda value of the arts. Using the French treasury, he made the arts an adjunct to royalty. His extravagances left France in a woeful financial condition.
- At Versailles, Louis' newly constructed palace emerged as an amalgam of Greco-Roman subject matter, Classical principles of design, and Baroque theatricality. Luxury, grandeur, and technical refinement became the vehicles of French royal authority and the hallmarks of aristocratic elitism.
- Louis was the arbiter of fashion and manners. He dictated the

standards for all forms of artistic production, and created government-sponsored academies in the arts, appointing his personal favorites to each.

- In Spain, Diego Velázquez, court painter to King Philip IV, became the country's most prestigious artist, thanks to aristocratic portraits that conveyed the powerful presence of real objects in atmospheric space.
- The Flemish painter Peter Paul Rubens established his reputation in the courts of Europe. His large studio supported scores of assistants who helped to fulfill his many commissions. As court painter to King Charles I of England, Anthony van Dyck produced elegant, idealized portraits of his patrons.

Music and Dance at the Court of Louis XIV

- The court at Versailles was the setting for music, theater, and dance. To provide musical entertainments for state dinners, balls, and operatic performances, Louis established a permanent orchestra. Its director, the Italian-born Jean-Baptiste Lully, headed the French Academy of Music.
- Lully introduced to opera the "French overture." Under his leadership, French opera also developed its most characteristic feature: the inclusion of formal dance.
- Of lasting significance was Louis' contribution to the birth of professional dance and the transformation of court dance into an independent artform.

Seventeenth-Century French Literature

- François de La Rochefoucauld wrote maxims that reflect the self-interest, hypocrisy, and greed of human beings—including and especially the aristocrats of his day.
- French drama reflected the Neoclassical effort to restrain passionate feeling by means of cool objectivity and common sense. The French tragedian Jean Racine added unity of place to Aristotle's unities of action and time.
- France's leading comic playwright, Molière, brought to life the comic foibles of such stock characters as the miser, the hypochondriac, the hypocrite, the misanthrope, and the would-be gentleman. He learned much from the Italian *commedia dell'arte*, which incorporated buffoonery, slapstick humor, and pantomime.

Absolute Power and the Aristocratic Style beyond Europe

- In Southwest Asia, the Ottoman sultan Suleiman established a pattern of princely patronage that was imitated by Muslim rulers for at least two centuries.
- The Persian Shah Abbas and the Mogul rulers of India were great patrons of the arts and commissioned some of the most magnificent monuments in architectural history.
- Like Versailles in France, the Imperial Mosque in Isfahan, the Red Fort in Old Delhi, and the Taj Mahal in Agra epitomize the wealth, absolute authority, and artistic vision of a privileged minority.

Absolute Power and the Aristocratic Style in China

- The imperial complex at the Forbidden City in Beijing stands as a symbol of the absolutism of China's Ming and Qing emperors.
- Imperial patronage of the arts supported the production of porcelain, *cloisonné*, brocades, and woven textiles, many of which found their way to Europe.
- Under the emperor Kangxi, China's literary and historical writings were compiled and anthologized. Chinese fiction, in the form of the novel, and Chinese opera appealed to growing numbers of the public.

Absolute Power and the Aristocratic Style in Japan

- The Tokugawa dynasty created a unified central state over which the *shogun* assumed political and economic control. After 1630, the Japanese expelled foreigners and sealed themselves off from the world.
- In Japanese multipaneled screens, painted scrolls, lacquerware, and ceramics the decorative tradition in the arts reached new heights of sophistication and refinement.
- Woodcut prints popularized the pleasures of Edo's "floating world" and celebrated the actors of Japan's popular *kabuki* plays.
- Tea and the etiquette of tea-drinking, associated with Zen Buddhist culture, came to define the Japanese way of life.
- The verse form known as *haiku* reflects the controlled simplicity of Zen expression.

Glossary

chinoiserie European imitation of Chinese art, architecture, and decorative motifs; also any objects that reflect such imitation

choreography the art of composing, arranging, and/or notating dance movements

comédie-ballet (French) a dramatic performance that features interludes of song and dance

haiku a light verse form consisting of seventeen syllables (three lines of five, seven, and five)

kabuki (Japanese, "song-dance art") a popular form of Japanese drama

marquetry a decorative technique in which patterns are created on a wooden surface by means of inlaid wood, shell, or ivory

maxim a short, concise, and often witty saying

objet d'art (French) art object

pietra dura (Italian, "hard stone") an ornamental technique involving inlaid precious and semiprecious stones

salon (French, "drawing room") an elegant apartment or drawing room

shah (Persian) king

sharia the body of Muslim law based on the Qur'an and the Hadith

sultan a Muslim ruler

Chapter

22

The Baroque in the Protestant North

ca. 1550–1750

"No man is an island entire of itself; every man is a piece of the continent, a part of the main."
John Donne

Figure 22.1 REMBRANDT VAN RIJN, detail of *Christ Preaching* ("The Hundred-Guilder Print"), ca. 1648–1650. A group of Pharisees stands at the right hand of the preaching Jesus. One turns away from the preacher, a second is lost in thought, while a third, bathed in the light that surrounds the Christ, listens in rapt attention.

LOOKING AHEAD

In Northern Europe, where Protestant loyalties remained strong, there emerged a phase of the Baroque that differed perceptibly from other expressions of that style. The largely middle class populations of England and the Netherlands had little use for the aristocratic Baroque style that glorified absolutist France. The Protestant North also resisted the kinds of florid religious display that characterized the Baroque style of the Catholic Reformation in Italy, Spain, and parts of the Americas.

In contrast with the ornate church interiors of Italy, Northern houses of worship were stripped of ornamentation. In England, the Netherlands, and northern Germany, where Protestants were committed to private devotion rather than public ritual, the Bible exercised an especially significant influence. The Northern Baroque style emphasized personal piety and private devotion. It reflected the spirit of Pietism, a seventeenth-century German religious movement, and the ideals of the Puritans, English Protestants who advocated a "purity" of worship, doctrine, and morality. To both of these movements, as to the arts of the European North, the Bible was prized as the means of cultivating the "inner light."

The Rise of the English Commonwealth

In England, Queen Elizabeth I (1533–1603) was succeeded by the first Stuart monarch, James I (1566–1625). A Scot, and a committed proponent of absolute monarchy, James claimed, "There are no privileges and immunities which can stand against a divinely appointed King." His son, Charles I (1600–1649; Figure 22.2), shared his father's view that kings held a God-given right to rule. Charles alienated Parliament by governing for more than a decade without its approval. He antagonized the growing number of Puritans, who demanded Church reform and greater strictness in religious observance). Allying with antiroyalist factions, mostly of the emergent middle class, the Puritans constituted a powerful political group. With their support, leaders in Parliament raised an army to oppose King Charles, ultimately defeating the royalist forces in a civil war that lasted from 1642 to 1648 and executing the king in 1649 on charges of treason. The government that followed this civil war, led by the Puritan general Oliver Cromwell (1599–1658), was known as the "Commonwealth."

Bearing the hallmarks of a republic, the new government issued a written constitution that proposed the formation of a national legislature elected by universal manhood suffrage. The Commonwealth, however, was unable to survive. A sorely reduced Parliament abolished many offices of state, and a newly formed one, which proved inept, was dissolved

by Cromwell. The "Protector of the Realm" took on the role of a dictator, alienating many segments of English society. When Cromwell died, the monarchy was restored with Charles I's son, Prince Charles (1635–1685), returning from exile to become king. Charles II's successor, James II (1633–1701), came to power in 1685; but when he converted to Catholicism two years later, and attempted to fill a new Parliament with his Catholic supporters, the opposition rebelled.

In 1688, the English expelled the king and offered the crown to William of Orange, ruler of the Netherlands, and his wife Mary, the Protestant daughter of James II. Following the "Glorious Revolution" of 1688, Parliament enacted a Bill of Rights prohibiting the king from suspending parliamentary laws or interfering with the ordinary course of justice. The Bill of Rights was followed by the Toleration Act of 1689, which guaranteed freedom of worship to non-Anglican sects. By 1689, Parliament's authority to limit the power of the English monarch was firmly established. The "bloodless revolution" reestablished constitutional monarchy and won a victory for popular sovereignty.

The King James Bible

These dramatic political developments, so closely tied to religious issues, occurred in the years following one of the most influential cultural events of the seventeenth century: the new English translation of the Bible. Recruited by James I of England, a committee of about fifty scholars had begun the work of translation in 1604. Drawing on a number of earlier English translations of Scripture, they produced an English-language edition of the Old and New Testaments that would have a shaping influence on the English language and on all subsequent English literature. Published in 1611, the "authorized" edition of Scripture came about in part as a response to the problems that Puritan factions of the Anglican Church detected in earlier translations of the Bible. While this version was not actually authorized by any ministerial body, it quickly became the official Bible of the Church of England (and of most English-speaking Protestant sects). As the product of the decades that also witnessed the last works of William Shakespeare, it reflects the moment when the English language reached its peak in eloquence.

The new translation of Scripture preserved the spiritual fervor of the Old Testament Hebrew and the narrative vigor of the New Testament Greek. Some appreciation of these qualities may be gleaned from comparing the two following translations. The first, a sixteenth-century translation based on Saint Jerome's Latin Vulgate edition and published in the city of Douay in France in 1609, lacks the concise language, the poetic imagery, and the lyrical rhythms of the King James version (the second example), which, though deeply indebted to a number of sixteenth-century English translations, drew directly on manuscripts written in the original Hebrew.

Figure 22.2 ANTHONY VAN DYCK, *Charles I on Horseback*, ca. 1638. Oil on canvas, 12 ft. × 9 ft. 7in.

READING 22.1 The Twenty-Third Psalm

From the Douay Bible (1609)

Our Lord ruleth me, and nothing shall be wanting to me; in place of pasture there he hath placed me.

Upon the water of refection he hath brought me up; he hath converted my soul.

He hath conducted me upon the paths of justice, for his name.

For although I shall walk in the midst of the shadow of death, I will not fear evils; because thou art with me.

Thy rod and thy staff, they have comforted me.

Thou hast prepared in my sight a table against them that trouble me.

Thou hast fatted my head with oil, and my chalice inebriating, how goodly is it!

And thy mercy shall follow me all the days of my life.

And that I may dwell in the house of our Lord in longitude of days.

From the King James Bible (1611)

The Lord is my shepherd; I shall not want.

He maketh me to lie down in green pastures: he leadeth me beside the still waters.

He restoreth my soul: he leadeth me in the paths of righteousness for his name's sake.

Yea, though I walk through the valley of the shadow of death, I will fear no evil: for thou art with me; thy rod and thy staff they comfort me.

Thou preparest a table before me in the presence of mine enemies: thou anointest my head with oil; my cup runneth over.

Surely goodness and mercy shall follow me all the days of my life: and I will dwell in the house of the Lord for ever.

Q What aspects of the King James version of the Twenty-Third Psalm make this translation memorable?

English Literature of the Seventeenth Century

John Donne

One of the most eloquent voices of religious devotionalism in the Protestant North was that of the poet John Donne (1571–1631). Born and raised as a Roman Catholic, Donne studied at Oxford and Cambridge, but he renounced Catholicism when he was in his twenties. He traveled widely, entered Parliament in 1601, and converted to Anglicanism fourteen years later, soon becoming a priest of the Church of England.

A formidable preacher as well as a man of great intellectual prowess, Donne wrote eloquent sermons that challenged the parishioners at Saint Paul's Cathedral in London (Figure **22.3**), where he acted as dean. At Saint Paul's, Donne developed the sermon as a vehicle for philosophic meditation. In *Meditation 17* (an excerpt from which follows), Donne pictures humankind—in typically

Baroque terms—as part of a vast, cosmic plan. His image of human beings as "chapters" in the larger "book" of God's design is an example of Donne's affection for unusual, extended metaphors. The tolling bell that figures so powerfully in the last lines makes reference to an age-old tradition (perpetuated at Saint Paul's) of ringing the church bells to announce the death of a parishioner.

READING 22.2 From Donne's *Meditation 17* (1623)

All mankind is of one author, and is one volume; when one man   **1**
dies, one chapter is not torn out of the book, but translated into
a better language; and every chapter must be so translated. God
employs several translators; some pieces are translated by age,
some by sickness, some by war, some by justice; but God's hand   **5**
is in every translation, and his hand shall bind up all our
scattered leaves again for that library where every book shall lie
open to one another. As therefore the bell that rings to a
sermon calls not upon the preacher only but upon the
congregation to come, so this bell calls us all. . . . No man is an   **10**
island entire of itself; every man is a piece of the continent, a
part of the main. If a clod be washed away by the sea, Europe is
the less, as well as if a promontory were, as well as if a manor
of thy friend's or of thine own were. Any man's death diminishes
me, because I am involved in mankind, and therefore never send   **15**
to know for whom the bell tolls; it tolls for thee.

Q What three metaphors are invoked in Meditation 17?

Donne's poetry was as unconventional as his prose: both abound in "conceits," that is, elaborate metaphors that compare two apparently dissimilar objects or emotions, often with the intention of shocking or surprising. In that the conceits of Donne (and other seventeenth-century writers) borrowed words and images from the new science (see chapter 23), critics called these devices and the poetry they embellished "metaphysical." Metaphysical poetry reflects the Baroque affection for dramatic contrast, for frequent and unexpected shifts of viewpoint, and for the dramatic synthesis of discordant images. These features are apparent in some of Donne's finest works, including the group of religious poems known as the Holy Sonnets.

In the first of the following two sonnets, Donne addresses Death as an imaginary person, regarded by some as "mighty and dreadful." Donne mocks Death as being nothing more than a slave who keeps bad company ("poison, war, and sickness"). He teases his adversary for being less potent than pleasurable sleep. And in the final lines of the sonnet, he arrives at the brilliant paradox that Death itself shall die—in the eternal life afforded by Christianity.

In the second sonnet, Donne compares himself to a fortress that has been seized by the enemies of the Lord. Donne describes Reason as the ruler ("Your viceroy in me") who has failed to defend the fortress. He pleads with God to "ravish" and "imprison" him. The poem abounds in intriguing paradoxes that link sinfulness with deliverance, conquest with liberation, and imprisonment with freedom.

Figure 22.3 CHRISTOPHER WREN, west façade of Saint Paul's Cathedral, London, 1675–1710. Width approx. 90 ft.

Donne's unexpected juxtapositions and paradoxical images are typical of English metaphysical poetry, but his rejection of conventional poetic language in favor of a conversational tone (much celebrated by modern poets) represents a revolutionary development in European literature.

─ READING 22.3 From Donne's *Holy Sonnets* (1610)

Death be not proud, though some have called thee   1
Mighty and dreadful, for thou art not so;
For those whom thou think'st thou dost overthrow
Die not, poor Death, nor yet canst thou kill me.
From rest and sleep, which but thy pictures be,   5
Much pleasure, then from thee much more must flow,
And soonest our best men with thee do go,
Rest of their bones and souls' delivery.
Thou art slave to fate, chance, kings, and desperate men,
And dost with poison, war, and sickness dwell,   10
And poppy[1], or charms[2] can make us sleep as well,
And better than thy stroke; why swell'st[3] thou then?
One short sleep past, we wake eternally,
And Death shall be no more; Death, thou shalt die.

─ ◆ ─

─────────────────────────────

[1] Opium.
[2] Sleeping potion.
[3] Puff with pride.

Batter my heart, three-personed God; for You   15
As yet but knock, breath, shine, and seek to mend;
That I may rise, and stand, o'erthrow me, and bend
Your force, to break, blow, burn, and make me new.
I, like an usurped town to another due,
Labour to admit You, but oh! to no end;   20
Reason, Your viceroy in me, me should defend,
But is captived and proves weak or untrue.
Yet dearly I love You, and would be loved fain,[4]
But am betrothed unto Your enemy.
Divorce me, untie, or break that knot again,   25
Take me to You, imprison me, for I
Except You enthrall me, never shall be free;
Nor ever chaste, except You ravish me.

Q Why might these sonnets
be called "metaphysical?"

Q Is faith, in the second sonnet,
a matter of knowledge or belief?

The Genius of John Milton

John Milton (1608–1674) was a devout Puritan and a defender of the Cromwellian Commonwealth that collapsed in 1658. His career as a humanist and poet began at Cambridge University and continued throughout his eleven-year tenure as secretary to the English Council of State. Though shy and retiring, Milton became a political activist and a persistent defender of religious, political, and intellectual freedom. He challenged English society with expository prose essays on a number of controversial subjects. In one pamphlet, he defended divorce between couples who were spiritually and temperamentally incompatible—a subject possibly inspired by his first wife's unexpected decision to abandon him briefly just after their marriage. In other prose works, Milton opposed Parliament's effort to control free speech and freedom of the press. "Who kills a man kills a reasonable creature," wrote Milton, "but he who destroys a good book, kills reason itself."

Milton's verse compositions include lyric poems and elegies, but the greatest of his contributions are his two epic poems: *Paradise Lost* and *Paradise Regained*. Milton wrote both of these monumental poems during the last decades of his life, when he was totally blind—a condition he erroneously attributed to long nights of reading. Legend has it that he dictated the poems to his two young daughters. In *Paradise Lost* Milton created a cosmic (and earth-centered) vision of Heaven, Hell, and Paradise comparable to that drawn by Dante (see chapter 12) but more philosophic in its concern with the issues of knowledge, sin, and free will. Considered the greatest of modern epics, *Paradise Lost* is impressive in its vast intellectual sweep, its wide-ranging allusions to history and literature, and its effort to address matters of time, space, and causality.

Milton was already fifty years old when he resolved to compose a modern epic that rivaled the majesty of the classic works of Homer and Virgil. At the outset, he considered various themes, one of which was the story of King Arthur. But he settled instead on a Christian subject that allowed him to examine an issue particularly dear to his Protestant sensibilities: the meaning of evil in a universe created by a benevolent God. The twelve books of *Paradise Lost* retell the story of the fall of Adam and Eve, beginning with the activities of the rebellious archangel Satan and culminating in the expulsion of the First Parents from Paradise. The poem concludes with the angel Michael's explanation to Adam of how fallen Man, through Christ, will recover immortality. This august theme, rooted in biblical history, permitted Milton to explore questions of human knowledge, freedom, and morality and, ultimately, to "justify the ways of God to Men."

Central in this cosmic drama is the figure of Satan, who is painted larger than life. Milton vividly recounts the demon's passage from Hell to Earth and the fall of the rebel angels—a lengthy account that was probably inspired by the English Civil War. The titanic Satan is a metaphor for the Puritan conception of evil in the world. Less vividly drawn, Adam is an expression of Protestant pessimism—a figure who, for all his majesty, is incapable of holding on to Paradise. *Paradise Lost* may be considered a Christian parable of the human condition. In its cosmic scope and verbal exuberance, it is also a mirror of the Baroque imagination.

The language of *Paradise Lost* is intentionally lofty; it is designed to convey epic breadth and to narrate (as Milton promised) "things unattempted yet in prose or rhyme." Like Shakespeare, Milton chose to write in blank verse: unrhymed lines of ten syllables each with accents on every second syllable. This device allowed Milton to carry the thread of a single thought past the end of the line, thereby grouping ideas in rich verse paragraphs. The following excerpts convey some sense of the power and majesty of Milton's verse. In the first twenty-six lines of Book I, Milton announces the subject of the poem: the loss of humankind's spiritual innocence. The second excerpt, also from Book I, relates the manner in which Satan tears himself from Hell's burning lake and proudly assumes his place as ruler of the fallen legions. In the third excerpt (from Book IX), Adam resolves to stand with his beloved partner, Eve, by eating the Forbidden Fruit. Milton's description of Eve and her "fatal trespass" (l. 71) perpetuated the misogynistic trope of flawed womankind well into the late nineteenth century. Finally, in the passage from Book XII, Adam hears the angel Michael's prophetic description of humankind's destiny and prepares to leave Paradise.

READING 22.4 From Milton's *Paradise Lost* (1667)

Book I

Of man's first disobedience, and the fruit   1
Of that forbidden tree, whose mortal taste
Brought death into the world, and all our woe,
With loss of Eden, till one greater Man[1]

---

[4] Willingly.

Restore us, and regain the blissful seat,
Sing Heav'nly Muse, that on the secret top
Of Oreb, or of Sinai,[2] didst inspire
That shepherd, who first taught the chosen seed,
In the beginning how the heav'ns and earth
Rose out of chaos: or if Sion hill   10
Delight thee more, and Siloa's brook[3] that flowed
Fast by the oracle of God; I thence
Invoke thy aid to my advent'rous song,
That with no middle flight intends to soar
Above th' Aonian mount,[4] while it pursues
Things unattempted yet in prose or rhyme.
And chiefly thou O Spirit, that dost prefer
Before all temples th' upright heart and pure,
Instruct me, for thou know'st; thou from the first
Wast present, and with mighty wings outspread   20
Dove-like sat'st brooding on the vast abyss
And mad'st it pregnant: what in me is dark
Illumine, what is low raise and support;
That to the highth of this great argument
I may assert Eternal Providence,
And justify the ways of God to men.

      · · · · · · ·

Forthwith upright he rears from off the pool
His mighty stature; on each hand the flames
Driv'n backward slope their pointing spires, and rolled
In billows, leave i' th' midst a horrid vale.   30
Then with expanded wings he steers his flight
Aloft, incumbent on the dusty air
That felt unusual weight, till on dry land
He lights, if it were land that ever burned
With solid, as the lake with liquid fire,
And such appeared in hue; as when the force
Of subterranean wind transports a hill
Torn from Pelorus,[5] or the shattered side
Of thund'ring Etna, whose combustible
And fuelled entrails thence conceiving fire,   40
Sublimed with mineral fury, aid the winds,
And leave a singèd bottom all involved
With stench and smoke: such resting found the sole
Of unblest feet. Him followed his next mate,
Both glorying to have escaped the Stygian[6] flood
As gods, and by their own recovered strength,
Not by the sufferance of supernal power.
   "Is this the region, this the soil, the clime,"

Said then the lost Archangel, "this the seat
That we must change for heav'n, this mournful gloom   50
For that celestial light? Be it so, since he
Who now is sovran[7] can dispose and bid
What shall be right: farthest from him is best
Whom reason hath equaled, force hath made supreme
Above his equals. Farewell, happy fields,
Where joy for ever dwells: hail horrors, hail,
Infernal world, and thou, profoundest hell
Receive thy new possessor: one who brings
A mind not to be changed by place or time.
The mind is its own place, and in itself   60
Can make a heav'n of hell, a hell of heav'n.
What matter where, if I be still the same,
And what I should be, all but less than he
Whom thunder hath made greater? Here at least
We shall be free; th' Almighty hath not built
Here for his envy, will not drive us hence:
Here may we reign secure, and in my choice
To reign is worth ambition though in hell:
Better to reign in hell, than serve in heav'n."

      · · · · · · ·

Book IX

On th' other side, Adam, soon as he heard   70
The fatal trespass done by Eve, amazed,[8]
Astonied[9] stood and blank, while horror chill
Ran through his veins, and all his joints relaxed;
From his slack hand the garland wreathed for Eve
Down dropped, and all the faded roses shed:
Speechless he stood and pale, till thus at length
First to himself he inward silence broke.
   "O fairest of creation, last and best
Of all God's works, creature in whom excelled
Whatever can to sight or thought be formed,   80
Holy, divine, good, amiable, or sweet!
How art thou lost, how on a sudden lost,
Defaced, deflow'red, and now to death devote?[10]
Rather how hast thou yielded to transgress
The strict forbiddance, how to violate
The sacred fruit forbidd'n! some cursèd fraud
Of enemy hath beguiled thee, yet unknown,
And me with thee hath ruined, for with thee
Certain my resolution is to die;
How can I live without thee, how forgo   90
Thy sweet converse and love so dearly joined,
To live again in these wild woods forlorn?
Should God create another Eve, and I
Another rib afford, yet loss of thee
Would never from my heart; no no, I feel
The link of nature draw me: flesh of flesh,
Bone of my bone thou art, and from thy state
Mine never shall be parted, bliss or woe."
   So having said, as one from sad dismay

---

[1] Christ.
[2] As was the case with epic poets of old, Milton here invokes a divine source of inspiration. Milton's muse, however, is an abstraction of Judeo-Christian wisdom, identified with the muse that inspired Moses at Mount Horeb (Deut. 4.10) or on Mount Sinai (Exod. 19.20).
[3] A spring near Mount Zion in Jerusalem where, in the Hebrew Bible, God spoke to his people.
[4] In Greece, the muses were thought to live on Mount Helicon, also known as the "Aonian mountain."
[5] A promontory near the volcanic Mount Etna in Sicily.
[6] Referring to the River Styx, in Greek mythology the principal river of the underworld.

[7] Sovereign.
[8] Confused, terror-stricken.
[9] Stunned.
[10] Devoted, doomed.

Recomforted,[11] and after thoughts disturbed   **100**
Submitting to what seemed remédiless,
Thus in calm mood his words to Eve he turned.
  "Bold deed thou hast presumed, advent'rous Eve,
And peril great provoked, who thus hast dared
Had it been only coveting to eye
That sacred fruit, sacred to abstinence,
Much more to taste it under ban to touch.
But past who can recall, or done undo?
Not God omnipotent, nor fate; yet so
Perhaps thou shalt not die, perhaps the fact[12]   **110**
Is not so heinous now, foretasted fruit,
Profaned first by the serpent, by him first
Made common and unhallowed ere our taste;
Nor yet on him found deadly, he yet lives,
Lives, as thou saidst, and gains to live as man
Higher degree of life, inducement strong
To us, as likely tasting to attain
Proportional ascent, which cannot be
But to be gods, or angels demi-gods.
Nor can I think that God, Creator wise,   **120**
Though threat'ning, will in earnest so destroy
Us his prime creatures, dignified so high,
Set over all his works, which in our fall,
For us created, needs with us must fail,
Dependent made; so God shall uncreate,
Be frustrate, do, undo, and labor lose,
Not well conceived of God, who though his power
Creation could repeat, yet would be loath
Us to abolish, lest the Adversary
Triumph and say; 'Fickle their state whom God   **130**
Most favors, who can please him long? Me first
He ruined, now mankind; whom will he next?'
Matter of scorn, not to be given the Foe.
However I with thee have fixed my lot,
Certain to undergo like doom; if death
Consort with thee, death is to me as life;
So forcible within my heart I feel
The bond of nature draw me to my own.
My own in thee, for what thou art is mine;
Our state cannot be severed, we are one,   **140**
One flesh: to lose thee were to lose myself."

    . . . .

Book XII

[. . . to the Angel] Adam last replied.
"How soon hath thy prediction, seer blest,
Measured this transient world, the race of time,
Till time stand fixed: beyond is all abyss,
Eternity, whose end no eye can reach.
Greatly instructed I shall hence depart,
Greatly in peace of thought, and have my fill
Of knowledge, what this vessel can contain;
Beyond which was my folly to aspire.   **150**

Chronology

1625	Charles I becomes king of England
1642–1648	English Civil War
1649	Charles I executed
1649–1660	English Commonwealth
1660	Restoration of monarchy
1685	James II becomes king
1688	Glorious Revolution
1689	English Bill of Rights; Toleration Act

Henceforth I learn, that to obey is best,
And love with fear the only God, to walk
As in his presence, ever to observe
His providence, and on him sole depend,
Merciful over all his works, with good
Still overcoming evil, and by small
Accomplishing great things, by things deemed weak
Subverting worldly strong, and worldly wise
By simply meek; that suffering for truth's sake
Is fortitude to highest victory,   **160**
And to the faithful death the gate of life;
Taught this by his example whom I now
Acknowledge my Redeemer ever blest."
  To whom thus also th' angel last replied:
"This having learnt, thou hast attained the sum
Of wisdom; hope no higher, though all the stars
Thou knew'st by name, and all th' ethereal powers,
All secrets of the deep, all nature's works,
Or works of God in heav'n, air, earth, or sea,
And all the riches of this world enjoy'dst,   **170**
And all the rule, one empire; only add
Deeds to thy knowledge answerable, add faith,
Add virtue, patience, temperance, add love,
By name to come called charity, the soul
Of all the rest: then wilt thou not be loath
To leave this Paradise, but shalt possess
A paradise within thee, happier far.
Let us descend now therefore from this top
Of speculation; for the hour precise
Exacts our parting hence; and see the guards,   **180**
By me encamped on yonder hill, expect
Their motion,[13] at whose front a flaming sword,
In signal of remove,[14] waves fiercely round;
We may no longer stay: go, waken Eve;
Her also I with gentle dreams have calmed
Portending good, and all her spirits composed
To meek submission: thou at season fit
Let her with thee partake what thou hast heard,
Chiefly what may concern her faith to know,

---

[11] Comforted, refreshed.
[12] Crime, deed.

[13] Await their marching orders.
[14] Departure.

The great deliverance by her seed to come   190
(For by the Woman's Seed) on all mankind.
That ye may live, which will be many days,
Both in one faith unanimous though sad,
With cause for evils past, yet much more cheered
With meditation on the happy end."

— **Q** Describe the appearance and the
personality of Satan (Book I).

— **Q** Why does Adam decide to stay
with the fallen Eve (Book IX)?

— **Q** What message does the angel
give to Adam (Book XII)?

The London of Christopher Wren

London at the time of Donne and Milton was a city of vast extremes. England's commercial activities in India and the Americas made its capital a center for stock exchanges, insurance firms, and joint-stock companies. Yet living amongst the wealthy Londoners, a great number of people remained poor. One-fourth of London's 250,000 inhabitants could neither read nor write; meanwhile, English intellectuals advanced scientific learning. For some time Londoners enjoyed some of the finest libraries and theaters in Western Europe, but, under the Puritan-dominated Parliament of the 1640s, stage plays were suppressed, and many old theaters, including Shakespeare's Globe, were torn down. The restoration of the monarchy in 1660 brought with it a revived interest in drama and in the construction of indoor theaters (as opposed to the open-air theaters of Shakespeare's time).

In 1666, a devastating fire tore through London and destroyed three-quarters of the city, including 13,000 homes, eighty-seven parish churches, and the cathedral church of Saint Paul's, where John Donne had served as dean some decades earlier. Following the fire, there was an upsurge of large-scale building activity and a general effort to modernize London. The architect Christopher Wren (1632–1723) played a leading role in this effort. A child prodigy in mathematics, then an experimental scientist and professor of astronomy at London and Oxford, Wren was one of the founding fathers of the Royal Society of London for Improving Natural Knowledge. Following the Great Fire, Wren prepared designs for the reconstruction of London. Although his plans for new city streets (based on Rome) were rejected, he was commissioned to rebuild more than fifty churches, including Saint Paul's—the first church in Christendom to be completed during the lifetime of its architect.

Wren's early designs for Saint Paul's featured the Greek-cross plan that Michelangelo had proposed for Saint Peter's in Rome (see chapter 17). However, the clergy of Saint Paul's preferred a Latin-cross structure. The final design was a compromise that combined Classical, Gothic, Renaissance, and Baroque architectural features. Saint Paul's handsome two-story façade, with its ornate twin clock towers and its strong surface contrasts of light and dark (see Figure 22.3), looks back to Borromini (see Figure 20.19), but its massive scale and overall design—a large dome set upon a Latin-cross basilica—are reminiscent of Saint Peter's (see Figure 20.14). As at Saint Peter's, Wren's dome, which physically resembles that of Bramante's Tempietto (see Figure 17.29), is equal in its diameter (102 feet) to the combined width of the nave and side aisles. The dimensions of the cathedral are colossal: 366 feet from ground level to the top of the lantern cross (Saint Peter's reaches 452 feet).

Wren envisioned a dome that was both impressive from the outside and easily visible from the inside. He came up with an inventive and complex device: two domes, one exterior (made of timber covered with lead) and the other interior (made of light brick), are supported by a third, cone-shaped, middle dome, which is hidden between the other two (Figure **22.4**). The monumental silhouette of Wren's dome, which became the model for the United States capitol, remains an impressive presence on the London skyline. From within the church, there is the equally impressive illusionism of the *trompe l'oeil* heavens painted on the inner surface of the central cupola. Like Milton's *Paradise Lost*, Wren's Saint Paul's is a majestic synthesis of Classical and Christian traditions, while its huge size, dramatic exterior, and light-filled interior are Baroque in conception and effect.

Figure 22.4 Cross section of Saint Paul's showing Wren's three domes.

Protestant Devotionalism in the Netherlands

Since 1560, when Spain had invaded the Dutch Lowlands, the seventeen provinces of the Netherlands had been engaged in a bitter struggle against the Catholic forces of the Spanish king Philip II. In 1579, after years of bloodshed, the Dutch forced Philip's armies to withdraw. Two years later, the seven provinces of the north Netherlands declared their independence. By the end of the century the predominantly Calvinist Dutch Republic (later called "Holland") was a self-governing state and one of the most commercially active territories in Western Europe. Dutch shipbuilders produced some of the finest trading vessels on the high seas, while skilled Dutch seamen brought those vessels to all parts of the world. In Amsterdam, as in hundreds of other Dutch towns, merchants and craftspeople shared the responsibilities of local government, profiting handsomely from the smooth-running, primarily maritime, economy.

The autonomous towns of the north Netherlands, many of which supported fine universities, fostered freedom of thought and a high rate of literacy. Hardworking, thrifty, and independent-minded, the seventeenth-century Dutch enjoyed a degree of independence and material prosperity unmatched elsewhere in the world. Their proletarian tastes, along with a profound appreciation for the physical comforts of home and hearth, inspired their preference for such secular subjects as portraits, still lifes, landscapes, and scenes of domestic life (see chapter 23). Since Calvinism strongly discouraged the use of religious icons, sculpture was uncommon in the Protestant North. But paintings, especially those with scriptural subjects, were favored sources of seventeenth-century moral knowledge and instruction. The Old Testament was particularly popular among the Dutch, who viewed themselves as God's "chosen" people, elected to triumph over the forces of Catholic Spain.

Rembrandt

In this milieu emerged one of the world's great painters, Rembrandt van Rijn (1609–1669). Born in the city of Leiden, Rembrandt moved to Amsterdam, the new business capital of the Netherlands, in 1631, where he rose to fame as a portraitist (see chapter 23). In his religious works, he often chose subjects that were uncommon in Catholic art, focusing on the human, and even intimately personal, aspects of Old and New Testament stories. Rembrandt's Anabaptist upbringing, characterized by a fundamentalist approach to Scripture and a solemn attention to the role of individual conscience, surely contributed to this unique approach. The people who roamed the streets of Amsterdam, and the Spanish and Jewish refugees he regularly sketched in the city's ghettos, provided him with a cast of characters who populated his religious paintings. His sympathetic and largely unidealized treatment of sacred subject matter captured the spirit of Protestant devotionalism.

A case in point is Rembrandt's moving painting, *The Return of the Prodigal Son* (Figure **22.5**). Here, the artist has brought to life the moment when the wayward son of the parable (Luke 15:11–32), having returned home in rags, kneels humbly before his father to beg forgiveness. For theatrical effect, Rembrandt has pulled the figures out of the shadowy depths of the background. The father and son, bathed in golden light, form an off-center triangle balanced

Figure 22.5 REMBRANDT VAN RIJN, *The Return of the Prodigal Son*, ca. 1662–1668. Oil on canvas, 8 ft. 8 in. × 6 ft. 8 in.

by the sharply lit vertical of the figure on the right. Rich areas of bright **impasto** (thick layers of pigment) contrast with dark, brooding passages, created by way of thinly brushed layers of oil paint. Rembrandt learned much about theatrical staging from the Italian Baroque master Caravaggio (see chapter 20), but in this simple and restrained composition, he reaches below surface appearance to explore the psychological subtleties of the drama.

Rembrandt's technical virtuosity as a draftsman made him more famous in his own time as a printmaker than as a painter. His medium of choice was **etching** (Figure **22.6**). Like the woodcuts and engravings of his Northern European predecessors Dürer and Holbein (see chapter 19), Rembrandt's etchings met the demands of middle-class patrons who sought private devotional images that—by comparison with paintings—were inexpensive. A consummate and prolific printmaker, Rembrandt used the **burin** (a steel cutting tool) to develop dramatic contrasts of rich darks and brilliant lights. These talents are evident in one of his most famous prints, *Christ Preaching* (Figure **22.7**)—also known as "The Hundred-Guilder Print," because it sold at a seventeenth-century auction for the then unimaginably high price of 100 Dutch guilders. Illustrating the Gospel of Matthew, it depicts Jesus addressing the members of the Jewish community: the sick and the lame (foreground), "the little children" (middle left), the ill and infirm (right), and an assembly of Pharisees (far left). With an extraordinary economy of line—no more than a few

Figure 22.6 Etching is an intaglio printing process. A metal plate is coated with resin (a) then images are scratched through the coating with a burin, or graver (b). Acid is applied, which "eats" or etches the metal exposed by the scratches (c). The resin is then removed and ink is rubbed into the etched lines on the metal plate (d). After the plate is wiped clean, it is pressed onto the paper and the ink-filled lines are deposited on the paper surface. Other intaglio processes include engraving and aquatint.

deft strokes of the pen—the artist has captured the lot of the poor, the downtrodden, and the aged (see Figure 22.1). So colloquial is Rembrandt's handling of the biblical story that it seems an event that might have taken place in Rembrandt's own time and place.

Figure 22.7 REMBRANDT VAN RIJN, *Christ Preaching* ("The Hundred-Guilder Print"), ca. 1648–1650. Etching, 11 × 15½ in.

The Music of the Protestant North

Handel and the English Oratorio

If the Protestant North produced memorable art, it also generated great music. The careers of two extraordinary German composers, George Frideric Handel (1685–1756) and Johann Sebastian Bach (1685–1750), represent the flowering of the Baroque style in Northern European music.

Born in the Lutheran trading city of Halle, Germany, George Frideric Handel was determined to pursue his childhood musical talents. When his father, who intended for him a career in law, refused to provide him with a musical instrument, he smuggled a small clavichord into the attic. After proving himself at the keyboard and as a successful violinist and composer in the courts of Hamburg, Rome, Paris, Naples, and Venice, he emigrated to London in 1710, becoming a British citizen in 1726. Like many of his contemporaries, Handel began his career as a student of Italian opera. He composed forty-six operas in Italian and four in his native German. He also produced a prodigious number of instrumental works. But it was for his development of the **oratorio** that he earned fame among the English, who called him "England's greatest composer."

An oratorio is the musical setting of a long sacred or epic text; it is performed in concert by a narrator, soloists, chorus, and orchestra (Figure **22.8**). Like operas, oratorios are large in scale and dramatic in intent but, unlike opera, they are produced without scenery, costumes, or dramatic action. Soloists and chorus assume the roles of the main characters in the narrative. The word "oratorio" refers to a church chapel, and most oratorios are religious in content; however, they were never intended for church services. Rather, they were performed in public concert halls. With the oratorio came the shift from music written and performed for church or court to music composed for concert halls (or opera houses) and enjoyed by the general public. Appropriately, in the late seventeenth century, public concerts (and entrance fees) made their first appearance in the social history of music.

In his lifetime, Handel composed more than thirty oratorios. Like the works of Rembrandt and Milton (whose verses he borrowed for the oratorio *Samson*), Handel's music brought Scripture to life. The most famous of Handel's oratorios is *Messiah*, which was written in the English of the King James Bible. Composed, remarkably enough, in twenty-four days, it was performed for the first time in Dublin in 1742. It received instant acclaim. One of the most moving pieces of choral music ever written, *Messiah* celebrates the birth, death, and resurrection of Jesus. Unlike most of Handel's oratorios, it is not a biblical dramatization but rather a collection of verses from the Old and New Testaments. The first part of the piece recounts Old Testament prophecies of a Savior, the second relates the suffering and death of Jesus, and the

Figure 22.8 Performance of an oratorio; Handel (far right) is conducting. Woodcut.

third rejoices in the redemption of humankind through Christ's resurrection.

Messiah is typical of the Baroque sensibility: indeed, the epic proportions of its score and libretto call to mind Milton's *Paradise Lost*. It is also Baroque in its style, which features vigorous contrasts of tempo and dynamics and dramatic interaction between participating ensembles—solo voices, chorus, and instruments. A master of theatrical effects, Handel made use of word painting and other affective devices throughout the piece. For example, the music for the last words of the sentence, "All we, like sheep, have gone astray," consists of deliberately divergent melodic lines.

The best-loved choral work in the English language, *Messiah* has outlasted its age. In many Christian communities, it has become traditional to perform the piece during both the Christmas and Easter seasons. The jubilant "Hallelujah Chorus" (which ends the second of the three parts of the oratorio) still brings audiences to their feet, as it did King George II of England, who introduced this tradition by rising from his seat when he first heard it performed in London in 1743.

Handel's *Messiah* features polyphonic textures at the start of many of the choruses, such as the "For unto us, a Child is born." Nevertheless, like Handel's other oratorios, *Messiah* is essentially **homophonic**; that is, its musical organization depends on the use of a dominant melody supported by chordal accompaniment. Homophony is the musical opposite of polyphony, the many-voiced texture that characterized most music prior to the seventeenth century. The chords in a homophonic composition serve to support—or, in the visual sense, to "spotlight"—a primary melody. In the seventeenth century, there evolved a form of musical shorthand that allowed musicians to fill in the harmony for the principal melody of a homophonic piece. The **figured bass**, as this shorthand was called, consisted of a line of music with numbers written below it to indicate the harmony accompanying the primary melody. The use of the figured bass (also called the "continuo," since it played throughout the piece) was one of the main features of Baroque music.

Bach and Religious Music

Johann Sebastian Bach (Figure **22.9**) was born in the small town of Eisenach, very near the castle in which Martin Luther—hiding from the wrath of the Roman papacy—had first translated the Bible into German. Unlike the cosmopolitan Handel, Bach never strayed more than a couple of hundred miles from his birthplace; the last twenty-seven years of his career were spent in nearby Leipzig. Nor did he depart from his Protestant roots: Luther's teachings and Lutheran hymn tunes were Bach's major sources of religious inspiration, and the organ—the principal instrument of Protestant church music—was one of his favorite instruments. The Germans were the masters of the organ, and Bach was acknowledged to be the finest of organ virtuosi.

Figure 22.9 ELIAS GOTTLOB HAUSSMAN,
Johann Sebastian Bach, 1746. Oil on canvas.

He even served as a consultant for the construction of Baroque organs, whose ornately embellished casings made them the glory of many Protestant churches (Figure **22.10**). As organ master and choir director of the Lutheran church of Saint Thomas in Leipzig, Bach assumed the responsibility of composing music for each of the Sunday services and for holy days. A pious Lutheran, who, in the course of two marriages, fathered twenty children (five of whom became notable musicians), Bach humbly dedicated his compositions "to the glory of God."

Bach's religious vocal music included such forms as the oratorio, the Mass, and the **cantata**. The cantata is a multimovement work with a verse text sung by chorus and soloists and accompanied by a musical instrument or instruments. Like the oratorio, the cantata may be sacred or secular in subject matter and lyric or dramatic in style. Bach's 195 surviving cantatas are musical commentaries on the daily scriptural lessons of the Lutheran church service. Unparalleled in their florid counterpoint, they were inspired by the simple melodies of Lutheran chorales, with their regular rhythms and rugged melodies. Cantata No. 80 is based on Luther's "A Mighty Fortress is Our God," the 𝄞 most important hymn of the Lutheran Church (see chapter 19). Its melody unifies the eight movements of the cantata, which concludes with a four-part setting of the chorale melody, sung in the style of the congregational hymn. Bach drew on Protestant chorales not only for his cantatas but as the basis for many of his instrumental compositions (see chapter 23), including the 170 organ **preludes** that he composed to precede and set the mood for congregational singing.

At the apex of Bach's achievement in vocal music is the *Passion According to Saint Matthew*, an oratorio written in 1727 for the Good Friday service at the church of Saint Thomas in Leipzig. This majestic work consists of the sung texts of chapters 26 and 27 of Matthew's Gospel, which describe Christ's Passion: the events between the Last Supper and the Resurrection. It is written for a double chorus, with soloists who take the parts of Jesus, the disciples, the Pharisees, and other characters in the Gospel account. A solo tenor sings the part of the Evangelist, who narrates the story. A double orchestra and two organs accompany the voices. Alternating with the Gospel verses, passages of commentary (a text written by a local German poet) moralize the narrative and develop the states of minds of the individual "characters."

The three-and-a-half-hour-long piece consists of two parts, the first originally to be sung before the vespers sermon and the second after it. In Bach's time, the church congregation participated in the performance of the choral portions, thus adding to the sheer volume of sound produced by choirs and orchestras. Performed today in the church or in the concert hall, Bach's oratorio still conveys the devotional spirit of the Protestant North. In its imaginative use of Scripture, as well as in its compositional complexity, the *Passion According to Saint Matthew* compares with Rembrandt's religious paintings, Handel's *Messiah*, and Milton's *Paradise Lost*.

Figure 22.10 GOTTFRIED SILBERMANN, organ in Freiburg Cathedral (Saxony), Germany, 1710–1714.

LOOKING BACK

The Rise of the English Commonwealth

- Charles I, like his French counterparts, believed kings held a God-given right to rule. He alienated Parliament and antagonized the growing number of English Puritans until Parliament raised an army and initiated a civil war in 1642.
- After the execution of the king, the English Commonwealth, led

by the Puritan general Oliver Cromwell, bore the hallmarks of a republic.
- Though the monarchy was reestablished after Cromwell's death, a rebellious Protestant opposition brought about the Glorious Revolution of 1688. Parliament's authority to limit the power of

the English monarch was firmly established in 1689 after the passage of the Bill of Rights and the Toleration Act.

The King James Bible

- Drawing on a number of earlier English translations of Scripture made during the sixteenth century, and manuscripts in the original Hebrew, a committee of about fifty scholars produced in 1611 an English-language edition of the Old and New Testaments known as the King James Bible.
- The King James Bible had a shaping influence on the English language and on all subsequent English literature.

English Literature of the Seventeenth Century

- Born and raised as a Roman Catholic, John Donne converted to Anglicanism, becoming a priest of the Church of England. His sermons, developed as philosophical meditations, and his metaphysical sonnets, featured ingenious conceits, extended metaphors, and paradoxical perspectives.
- John Milton, Puritan, humanist, and defender of Cromwell's Commonwealth, was the most notable English-language poet of the seventeenth century. His verse compositions include lyric poems and elegies; his two epic poems, *Paradise Lost* and *Paradise Regained*, are considered his greatest contributions to the humanistic tradition.
- *Paradise Lost* is impressive in its vast intellectual sweep, its wide-ranging allusions to history and literature, and its (typically Baroque) effort to address matters of time, space, and causality.

The London of Christopher Wren

- Following the devastating fire that destroyed three-quarters of London, Christopher Wren, an architect, scientist and professor, and one of the founding fathers of the Royal Society of London, was commissioned to prepare designs for the city's reconstruction.
- Wren's design for Saint Paul's Cathedral was an ingenious combination of Classical, Gothic, Renaissance, and Baroque architectural features. Its huge size, dramatic exterior, and light-filled interior had a lasting impact on the field of architecture.

Protestant Devotionalism in the Netherlands

- The religious paintings of the Dutch master Rembrandt van Rijn represent a visual parallel to the deeply devotional works of Milton and Donne.
- Rembrandt illustrated the contents of Holy Scripture in paintings, drawings, and etchings that were at once realistic, theatrical, and psychologically profound. His bold compositions and inventive use of light recreated sacred events as though they were occurring in his own time and place.

The Music of the Protestant North

- German composer George Frideric Handel dramatized scriptural narrative by means of the oratorio, a new musical form that typified the Baroque taste for rich color and dramatic effect. Handel's *Messiah*, an early landmark in homophonic composition, remains one of the most stirring examples of choral music.
- Handel's Lutheran contemporary, Johann Sebastian Bach, dedicated much of his life to composing music that honored God. His cantatas and preludes employ melodies borrowed largely from Lutheran hymns. His *Passion According to Saint Matthew* brought religious choral music to new heights of dramatic grandeur.

Music Listening Selections

CD Two Selection 3 Handel, *Messiah*, "Hallelujah Chorus," 1742.

CD Two Selection 4 Bach, Cantata No. 80, "Eine feste Burg ist unser Gott" ("A Mighty Fortress is Our God"), Chorale, 1724.

Glossary

burin a steel tool used for engraving and incising

cantata (Italian, *cantare* = "to sing") a multimovement composition for voices and instrumental accompaniment; smaller in scale than the oratorio

etching a kind of engraving in which a metal plate is covered with resin, then incised with a *burin*; acid is applied to "eat" away the exposed lines, which are inked before the plate is wiped clean and printed; see Figure 22.6

figured bass in Baroque music, the line of music with numbers written below (or above) it to indicate the required harmonies, usually improvised in the form of keyboard chords accompanying the melody; also called "continuo"

homophony a musical texture consisting of a dominant melody supported by chordal accompaniment that is far less important than the melody; compare polyphony (see Glossary, chapter 13)

impasto the thick application of pigment to the surface of a painting

oratorio (Latin, *oratorium* = "church chapel") a musical setting of a long text, either religious or secular, for soloists, chorus, narrator, and orchestra; usually performed without scenery, costumes, or dramatic action

prelude a piece of instrumental music that introduces either a church service or another piece of music

Chapter 23

The Scientific
Revolution and
the New Learning
ca. 1550–1750

*"Read not to contradict and confute; nor to believe and take for
granted; nor to find talk and discourse, but to weigh and consider."*
Francis Bacon

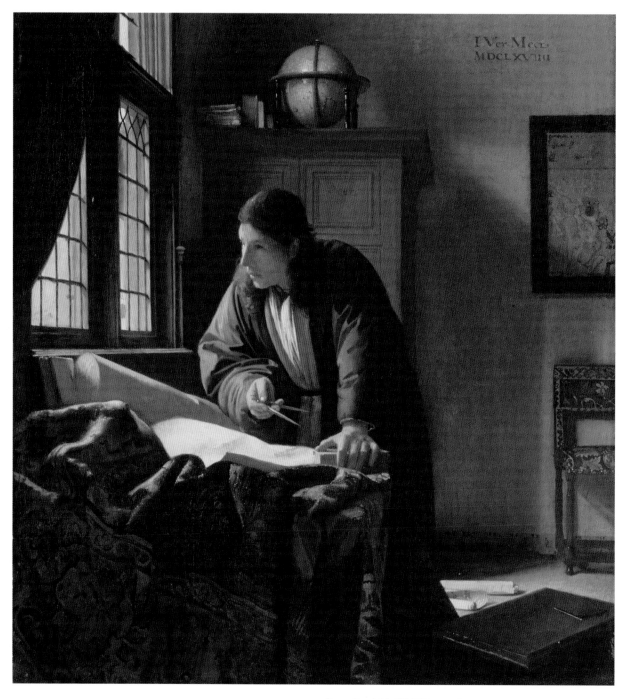

Figure 23.1 JAN VERMEER, *The Geographer*, ca. 1668. Oil on canvas, 20⅞ ×
18¼ in. Vermeer renders the geographer at the moment when he pauses
thoughtfully from his work. The painting, enriched by closely observed details,
captures the spirit of intellectual inquiry that typified the Age of Science.

LOOKING AHEAD

While the early modern era was a time of heightened spirituality, it was also an age of scientific discovery. Between 1550 and 1700, European scientists challenged the model of the universe that had prevailed from the time of Aristotle to the sixteenth century. Advancing the sciences of physics, astronomy, and geology, they demystified nature, taking it out of the hands of priests and poets, and putting it into the laboratory. The Scientific Revolution would have a three-part focus: 1) the exercise of direct observation and experimentation; 2) the reliance on mathematical verification, and 3) the invention of instruments by which to measure natural phenomena, test hypotheses, and predict the operations of nature.

The scientists of the early modern era differed from their predecessors in separating *scientia* (the Latin word for "knowledge") from religious truths. While their forerunners perceived the universe as the creation of an absolute and eternal God, they described it as a mechanism that operated according to the laws of nature. In consort with the new learning, a program of inquiry focused on inductive and deductive reasoning, they laid the groundwork for clear and objective thinking, and, ultimately, for the birth of modern philosophy and modern science.

The alliance of scientific inquiry and critical thinking ushered in a phase of the Baroque marked by an empirical attention to the real world; in art, an emphasis on light and space, and an increased demand for subjects that gave evidence of everyday experience: landscape, portraiture, still life, and the domestic interior. Developments in Baroque instrumental music, unique to this era, met the demands for secular entertainment made by a growing middle class.

The Scientific Revolution

The Background

The Scientific Revolution was not entirely sudden, nor were its foundations exclusively European. It owed much to a long history of empirical and theoretical inquiry that began in ancient Egypt and was furthered in China, in Hellenistic cities, and across the Muslim world. That history ranged from the invention of the magnetic compass to the formulation of Euclidian geometry, the birth of algebra, and the science of optics. Beginning with the Renaissance, however, as artist–scientists probed the workings of the visible world, the ambition to control nature by way of practical knowledge gained greater impetus in the West. In the pioneering efforts of Leonardo da Vinci, the empirical thrust of the Scientific Revolution was already initiated. Inspired by Leonardo's drawings of the human body, particularly those that investigated the internal organs, the Flemish physician Andreas Vesalius (1514–1564) published the first accurate analysis of human anatomy. Vesalius' treatise, *On the Workings of the Human Body*, became the virtual bible for seventeenth-century medical science.

A near contemporary of Vesalius, the Swiss alchemist Philippus Ambrosius Paracelsus (1493–1541) anticipated modern chemistry by compounding medical remedies from minerals rather than from botanical substances. At the same time, the Polish physician and astronomer Nicolas Copernicus (1473–1543) published his landmark treatise, *On the Revolution of the Heavenly Spheres* (1543). Based solely on mathematical calculations, Copernicus formulated a theory according to which the earth and all the planets circle around the sun. The **heliocentric** (sun-centered) model of the cosmos (Figure **23.2A**) stood in contradiction to the **geocentric** (earth-centered) model advanced by the renowned second-century Hellenistic astronomer Claudius Ptolemy. While some earlier astronomers had argued in favor of a sun-centered universe, Ptolemy's detailed studies popularized the ancient Greek conception of the heavens as a series of concentric crystalline spheres (occupied individually by the Moon, Mercury, Venus, the Sun, Mars, Jupiter, and Saturn), with Earth at the center (Figure **23.2B**)—a cosmos enshrined in Dante's *Divine*

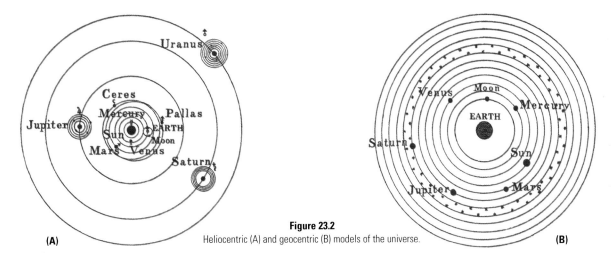

Figure 23.2
Heliocentric (A) and geocentric (B) models of the universe.

(A)

(B)

Comedy (see chapter 12). Planetary motion was circular, directed, according to Aristotle, by a first Cause or Unmoved Mover (in the later, Christian view, God). During the 100 years that followed the publication of Copernicus' treatise, these theories came under close scrutiny.

Kepler

The German mathematician Johannes Kepler (1571–1630) was among the first to make detailed records of planetary movements that substantiated the heliocentric theory. Challenging the conventional assumption that the planetary orbits were perfectly circular, Kepler also showed that the five known planets moved around the sun in elliptical paths. He argued that the magnetic force emitted by the sun determined their movements and their distances from the sun. Kepler's new physics advanced the idea of a universe in motion, contradicting the Aristotelian notion of a fixed and unchanging cosmos. It also generated strong opposition in religious circles. The theory of heliocentricity itself conflicted with the Bible—where, for example, the Hebrew hero Joshua is described as making the sun stand still (Joshua 10: 12–13), a miraculous event that could have occurred only if the sun normally moved around the earth. The earth, according to Genesis (1: 9–13), preceded the sun in the Divine Creation. Ultimately, then, the model of the universe defended by Kepler deprived human beings of their central place in the universe; it made humanity seem incidental to God's plan. Although Catholics and Protestants were at odds on many theological matters, in defending the inviolable truth of Scripture against the claims of the new science, they were united.

Galileo

Kepler's Italian contemporary Galileo Galilei (1574–1642) further advanced Kepler's research—and imperiled his own life by doing so. Galileo's inquiries into motion and gravity resulted in the formulation of the Law of Falling Bodies, which proclaims that the earth's gravity attracts all objects—regardless of shape, size, or density—at the same rate of acceleration. (Legend has it that he tested his theory by dropping different-sized weights from the top of the leaning Tower of Pisa.)

In 1608, a Dutch lensmaker invented an instrument that magnified objects seen at a great distance. Intrigued by the device, Galileo went on to perfect it. His telescope literally revealed new worlds. Through its lens, one could see the craters of the moon, the rings of Saturn, and the moons of Jupiter, which, Galileo observed, operated exactly like earth's moon. The telescope turned the heliocentric theory into fact.

Galileo's discoveries immediately aroused opposition from Catholics and Protestants committed to maintaining orthodox Christian beliefs, especially as set forth in Scripture. The first institutional attack on "the new science" had occurred in 1600, when the Catholic Inquisition tried, condemned, and publicly executed the Italian astronomer Giordano Bruno, who had asserted that the

universe was infinite and without center. Bruno had also suggested that other solar systems might exist in space. Sixteen years after Bruno was burned at the stake, the Church of Rome issued an edict that condemned Copernican astronomy as "false and contrary to Holy Scripture." The writings of Copernicus were put on the Catholic Index of Forbidden Books. Galileo added to the controversy by making his own findings public, and available to a wider audience because he wrote in Italian rather than in Latin, the traditional language of Western authority.

More inflammatory still was the publication of Galileo's *Dialogue Concerning the Two Principal Systems of the World* (1632), a fictional conversation between a Copernican and the defenders of the old order, one of whom resembled the pope. Earlier in his career, when it had become evident that his gravitational theories contradicted Aristotle, Galileo had been forced to give up his position as mathematics professor at the university of Pisa. Now, ill with kidney stones and arthritis, he was dragged to Rome and brought before the Inquisition. After a long and unpleasant trial, Church officials, threatening torture, forced the aging astronomer to "admit his errors."

Legend has it that after publicly denying that the earth moved around the sun, he muttered under his breath, "Eppur si muove" ("But it *does* move!"). Though condemned to indefinite imprisonment, Galileo was permitted to reside—under "house arrest"—in a villa outside of Florence. Imprisonment, however, did not daunt his ingenuity or his sense of awe. On developing the compound microscope, he marveled, "I have observed many tiny animals. . . among which the flea is quite horrible, the gnat and the moth very beautiful; and with great satisfaction I have seen how flies and other little animals can walk attached to mirrors, upside down." His books banned by the Church, Galileo continued to receive personal visits from eminent figures, including the English poet John Milton.

The Instruments of the New Science

The Scientific Revolution produced new instruments for measurement and new procedures for experimentation and analysis. The slide rule, the magnet, the microscope, the mercury barometer, and the air pump (Figure 23.3) were among the many products of the quest to calculate, investigate, and predict the workings of nature. Seventeenth-century scientists investigated the function of the human

---

Science and Technology

1608	Galileo improves the design of Dutch telescopes to obtain three-power magnification
1609	Hans Lippershey and Zacharias Janssen invent the compound microscope
1619	William Harvey accurately traces the circulation of the blood

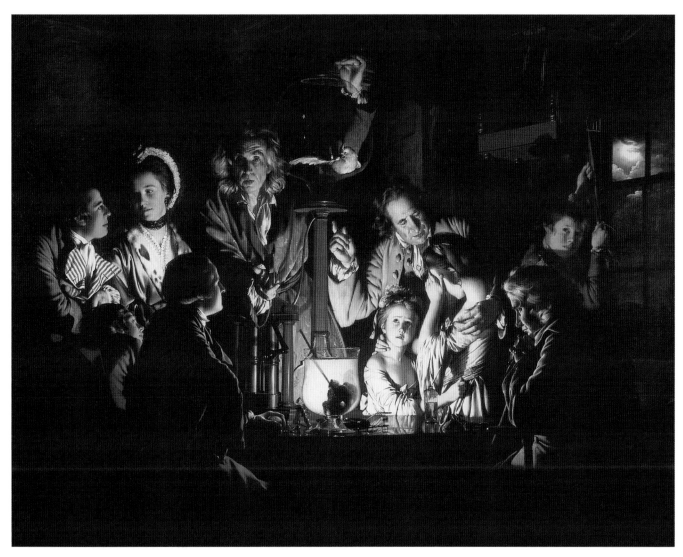

Figure 23.3 JOSEPH WRIGHT, *An Experiment on a Bird in the Air Pump*, 1768. Oil on canvas, 5 ft. 11⅜ in. × 7 ft. 11¾ in. Wright was the first Western artist to use scientific experimentation as dramatic subject matter. A vacuum is created by removing air from a glass bowl, which deprives the bird of oxygen. In a manner borrowed from Baroque religious art, Wright uses light to bring attention to the various expressions on the faces of the middle-class family.

eye and explored the genesis and propagation of light, thus advancing the science of optics beyond the frontiers of Islamic and Renaissance scholarship. They accurately described the action of gases and the circulation of the blood. By 1660, with the aid of a more highly powered microscope, they identified protozoa and human blood cells. The mysterious process known to ancient and medieval societies as "generation" was described with some precision, when, between 1665 and 1680, scientists at the university of Leiden made key discoveries concerning human and animal reproduction. Based on William Harvey's hypothesis that all animals emerge from an egg, and Anton van Leeuwenhoek's microscopic studies of spermatozoa, science advanced an accurate theory of reproduction (see Science and Technology boxes).

Before the end of the century, the great minds of the age formulated the branches of higher mathematics known as analytic geometry, trigonometry, and infinitesimal calculus, by means of which modern scientists might analyze the phenomena of space and motion.

The New Learning

Bacon and the Empirical Method

One of the most characteristic features of the Scientific Revolution was its advancement of the empirical method. This method of inquiry depends on direct observation and scientific experimentation as the bases from which one arrives at general conclusions. The process that draws on the particulars of sensory evidence for the formulation of general principles (or axioms) is known as **inductive reasoning**.

The leading advocate for the empirical method was the English scientist and politician Francis Bacon (1561–1626). In 1620, Bacon published his *Novum Organum* ("New Method"), an impassioned plea for objectivity and clear thinking and the strongest defense of the empirical method ever written. "Man, being the servant and interpreter of Nature," wrote Bacon, "can do and understand so much and so much only as he has observed in fact or in thought of the course of Nature: beyond this he neither knows anything nor can do anything."

Bacon argued that human beings might become "the masters and possessors of Nature" only by means of scientific study guided by precise methods. He promoted an objective system of experimentation, tabulation, and record keeping that became the touchstone of modern scientific inquiry.

Unlike earlier humanists, Bacon turned his back on Aristotle and Classical science. A prophet of the new learning, he sought to eliminate errors in reasoning derived from blind adherence to traditional sources of authority and religious belief. Advancing his own strategy for the acquisition of knowledge, Bacon warned against four "false notions" (or Idols, as he called them) that hinder clear and objective thinking.

READING 23.1 From Bacon's *Novum Organum*
(1620)

39

There are four classes of Idols which beset men's minds. To these for distinction's sake I have assigned names,—calling the first class *Idols of the Tribe*; the second, *Idols of the Cave*; the third, *Idols of the Marketplace*; the fourth, *Idols of the Theatre*.

41

The Idols of the Tribe have their foundation in human nature itself, and in the tribe or race of men. For it is a false assertion that the sense of man is the measure of things. On the contrary, all perceptions as well of the sense as of the mind are according to the measure of the individual and not according to the measure of the universe. And the human understanding is like a false mirror, which, receiving rays irregularly, distorts and discolors the nature of things by mingling its own nature with it.

42

The Idols of the Cave are the idols of the individual man. For every one (besides the errors common to human nature in general) has a cave or den of his own, which refracts and discolors the light of nature; owing either to his own proper and peculiar nature; or to his education and conversation with others; or to the reading of books, and the authority of those whom he esteems and admires; or to the differences of impressions, accordingly as they take place in a mind preoccupied and predisposed or in a mind indifferent and settled; or the like. So that the spirit of man (according as it is meted out to different individuals) is in fact a thing variable and full of perturbation, and governed as it were by chance. Whence it was well observed by Heraclitus[1] that men look for sciences in their own lesser worlds, and not in the greater or common world.

43

There are also Idols formed by the intercourse and association of men with each other, which I call Idols of the Marketplace, on account of the commerce and consort of men there. For it is by discourse that men associate; and words are imposed according to the apprehension of the vulgar. And therefore the ill and unfit choice of words wonderfully obstructs the understanding. Nor do the definitions or explanations wherewith in some things learned men are wont to guard and defend themselves, by any means set the matter right. But words plainly force and overrule the understanding, and throw all into confusion, and lead men away into numberless empty controversies and idle fancies.

44

Lastly, there are Idols which have immigrated into men's minds from the various dogmas of philosophies, and also from wrong laws of demonstration. These I call Idols of the Theatre; because in my judgment all the received systems are but so many stage-plays, representing worlds of their own creation after an unreal and scenic fashion. Nor is it only of the systems now in vogue, or only of the ancient sects and philosophies, that I speak; for many more plays of the same kind may yet be composed and in like artificial manner set forth; seeing that errors the most widely different have nevertheless causes for the most part alike. Neither again do I mean this only of entire systems, but also of many principles and axioms in science, which by tradition, credulity, and negligence have come to be received.

Q **How does the notion of an "idol" serve Bacon's purpose in writing this treatise?**

Bacon observes that every culture and every age has "worshiped" the Idols. *Idols of the Tribe* are deceptive ideas that have their foundations in human nature (such as our natural inclination to accept and believe what we prefer to be true). He points to the fact that human understanding is self-reflective; it functions like a "false mirror," distorting universal truth. Privately held fallacies (*Idols of the Cave*), on the other hand, derive from individual education and background. One may assert, for instance, that one or another religion is the true faith, that certain racial or ethnic groups are superior to others, or that women should be judged by a different set of standards than those applied to men.

The errors resulting from human association and communication, the *Idols of the Marketplace*, arise, according to Bacon, from an "ill or unfit choice of words." For example: the use of the noun "mankind" to designate all human beings. Finally, *Idols of the Theatre* are false dogmas perpetuated by social and political philosophies and institutions. Bacon probably would have regarded "divine-right monarchy" (see chapter 21) and "separate but equal education" as examples of these. To purge the mind of prejudice and false thinking, one must, argued Bacon, destroy the Idols.

Bacon's clarion call for objectivity and experimentation inspired the founding in 1645 of the Royal Society of London for Improving Natural Knowledge. The first of many such European and American societies for scientific advancement, the Royal Society has, over the centuries, attracted thousands of members. Their achievements have confirmed one nineteenth-century historian's assessment of Bacon as "the man that moved the minds that moved the world."

---

[1] A Greek philosopher of ca. 500 B.C.E., who taught that all of nature was in a state of flux.

Science versus Religion

In an era dominated by fervent spirituality, Bacon demanded a separation of religion and science. "In every age," he observed, "Natural Philosophy has had a troublesome adversary . . . namely, superstition, and the blind and immoderate zeal of religion." In Bacon's time, the term "natural philosophy" (*philosophia naturalis*), described the objective study of nature and the physical universe. It is to this precursor of the natural sciences that Bacon refers in the *Novum Organum*:

> . . . the corruption of philosophy by a combination of superstition and theology is . . . widespread, and does the greatest harm both to whole philosophies and to their parts. Yet, some of the moderns have, with the greatest frivolity, indulged so far . . . as to try to found a natural philosophy on the first chapter of Genesis and the Book of Job and other sacred writings. . . . It is all the more important to guard against and check this foolishness, for an unhealthy mixture of the divine and the human leads not only to fanciful philosophy but also to heretical religion. The healthy course therefore is to keep a sober mind and give to faith only that which is faith's.

The question of setting religious faith apart from science troubled early modern intellectuals, even as it does many thinkers in our own time. Some might argue that science and religion remain "locked in a death struggle." Moderates, however, would defend the idea that reason can function alongside faith to reduce suffering, end disease, and—by giving human beings greater power over nature—improve the conditions of everyday life. Nevertheless, where religion and science seem irreconcilable, such as in the case of current stem-cell research that might give humans the power to "compete with God's creation," the issue remains widely debated.

Science and Technology

1626	Francis Bacon uses snow in experiments to refrigerate chickens
1642	Blaise Pascal invents a mechanical calculator capable of addition and subtraction
1645	Otto von Guericke perfects the air pump
1650	Pascal invents the mercury barometer
1656	Christian Huygens develops the first accurate pendulum clock
1660	Anton van Leeuwenhoek discovers microscopic protozoa

While Bacon wrote his scientific treatises in Latin, he used English for essays on law, rhetoric, and intellectual life. In *The Advancement of Learning* (1605), a sketch of his key ideas concerning methods for acquiring and classifying knowledge, and in the essay *Of Studies*, Bacon demonstrated the masterful use of prose as a tool for theorizing. Written in the poetic prose of the early seventeenth century, *Of Studies* describes the ways in which books serve the individual and society at large. In the excerpt that follows, Bacon defends reading as a source of pleasure, but, equally important, as a source of practical knowledge and power.

READING 23.2 From Bacon's *Of Studies* from *Essays* (1625)

Studies serve for delight, for ornament, and for ability. Their [1] chief use for delight is in privateness and retiring; for ornament, is in discourse; and for ability, is in the judgment and disposition of business. For expert men can execute, and perhaps judge of particulars, one by one; but the general counsels and the plots and marshalling of affairs come best f rom those that are learned. To spend too much time in studies is sloth; to use them too much for ornament is affectation; to make judgment wholly by their rules is the humor of a scholar. They perfect nature, and are perfected by experience: for [10] natural abilities are like natural plants, that need pruning by study; . . . Read not to contradict and confute; nor to believe and take for granted; nor to find talk and discourse, but to weigh and consider. Some books are to be tasted, others to be swallowed, and some few to be chewed and digested; that is, some books are to be read only in parts; others to be read, but not curiously; and some few to be read wholly, and with diligence and attention. . . . Reading maketh a full man; conference a ready man; and writing an exact man. And therefore, if a man write little, he had need have a great [20] memory; if he confer little, he had need have a present wit; and if he read little, he had need have much cunning, to seem to know that he does not. Histories make men wise; poets witty; mathematics subtile; natural philosophy deep; moral [philosophy] grave; logic and rhetoric able to contend. . . .

Q In what ways do "studies," according to Bacon, "perfect nature?"

Q What, in his view, are the benefits of reading, verbal discourse, and writing?

Descartes and the Birth of Modern Philosophy

Born in France, René Descartes (1596–1650) is regarded as the founder of modern Western philosophy. His writings revived the ancient Greek quest to discover how one knows what one knows, and his methods made the discipline of philosophy wholly independent of theology.

Whereas Bacon gave priority to knowledge gained through the senses, Descartes, the supreme rationalist, valued abstract reasoning and mathematical speculation. Descartes did not deny the importance of the senses in the

Figure 23.4 PIERRE LOUIS DUMESNIL THE YOUNGER, Detail of *Queen Christina of Sweden and Her Court*, 1649. Oil on canvas. Like many other monarchs of the seventeenth century, Queen Christina of Sweden invited scholars and artists to her court. At the right, Descartes is seen explaining his work to his female benefactor; he points to papers that lie among books and measuring instruments.

search for truth, but he observed that our senses might deceive us. As an alternative to inductive reasoning, he championed the procedure for investigation called **deductive reasoning**. The reverse of the inductive method, the deductive process begins with clearly established general premises and moves toward the establishment of particular truths. In the *Discourse on the Method of Rightly Conducting the Reason and Seeking for Truth in the Sciences*, the most important of all his philosophic works, Descartes set forth his rules for reasoning: never accept anything as true that you do not clearly know to be true; dissect a problem into as many parts as possible; reason from simple to complex knowledge; and finally, draw complete and exhaustive conclusions. Descartes began the *Discourse* by systematically calling everything into doubt. He then proceeded to identify the first thing that he could not doubt—his existence as a thinking individual. This one clear and distinct idea of himself as a "thinking thing," expressed in the proposition "Cogito, ergo sum" ("I think, therefore I am"), became Descartes' "first principle" and the premise for all of his major arguments.

For Descartes, the clear and unbiased mind was the source of all natural understanding. "Except [for] our own thoughts," he insisted, "there is nothing absolutely in our power." Having established rational consciousness as the only sure point of departure for knowledge, Descartes proceeded to examine the world. He made a clear distinction between physical and psychical phenomena, that is, between matter and mind, and between body and soul.

According to this dualistic model, the human body operates much like a computer, with the immaterial mind (the software) "informing" the physical components of the body (the hardware). **Cartesian dualism**, the view that holds the mind (a thinking entity) as distinct from the body, dominated European philosophic thought until the end of the nineteenth century and still has some strong adherents today.

Beyond the domain of philosophy, Descartes earned renown as the father of analytic geometry, the discipline that uses algebra to solve problems of space and motion (Figure **23.4**). His program for defining geometric shapes by way of numerical information, presented in an appendix to the *Discourse*, provided the foundations for the branch of higher mathematics known as calculus.

READING 23.3 From Descartes' *Discourse on Method* (Part IV) (1637)

. . . I do not know that I ought to tell you of the first meditations 1
there made by me, for they are so metaphysical and so unusual
that they may perhaps not be acceptable to everyone. And yet
at the same time, in order that one may judge whether the
foundations which I have laid are sufficiently secure, I find
myself constrained in some measure to refer to them. For a long
time I had remarked that it is sometimes requisite in common
life to follow opinions which one knows to be most uncertain,
exactly as though they were indisputable, as has been said

above. But because in this case I wished to give myself entirely to the search after Truth, I thought that it was necessary for me to take an apparently opposite course, and to reject as absolutely false everything as to which I could imagine the least ground of doubt, in order to see if afterwards there remained anything in my belief that was entirely certain. Thus, because our senses sometimes deceive us, I wished to suppose that nothing is just as they cause us to imagine it to be; and because there are men who deceive themselves in their reasoning and fall into paralogisms,[1] even concerning the simplest matters of geometry, and judging that I was as subject to error as was any other, I rejected as false all the reasons formerly accepted by me as demonstrations. And since all the same thoughts and conceptions which we have while awake may also come to us in sleep, without any of them being at that time true, I resolved to assume that everything that ever entered into my mind was no more true than the illusions of my dreams. But immediately afterwards I noticed that whilst I thus wished to think all things false, it was absolutely essential that the "I" who thought this should be somewhat, and remarking that this truth "*I think, therefore I am*" was so certain and so assured that all the most extravagant suppositions brought forward by the sceptics were incapable of shaking it, I came to the conclusion that I could receive it without scruple as the first principle of the Philosophy for which I was seeking.

And then, examining attentively that which I was, I saw that I could conceive that I had no body, and that there was no world nor place where I might be; but yet that I could not for all that conceive that I was not. On the contrary, I saw from the very fact that I thought of doubting the truth of other things, it very evidently and certainly followed that I was; on the other hand if I had only ceased from thinking, even if all the rest of what I had ever imagined had really existed, I should have no reason for thinking that I had existed. From that I knew that I was a substance the whole essence or nature of which is to think, and that for its existence there is no need of any place, nor does it depend on any material thing; so that this "me," that is to say, the soul by which I am what I am, is entirely distinct from body, and is even more easy to know than is the latter; and even if body were not, the soul would not cease to be what it is.

After this I considered generally what in a proposition is requisite in order to be true and certain; for since I had just discovered one which I knew to be such, I thought that I ought also to know in what this certainly consisted. And having remarked that there was nothing at all in the statement "*I think, therefore I am*" which assures me of having thereby made a true assertion, excepting that I see very clearly that to think it is necessary to be, I came to the conclusion that I might assume, as a general rule, that the things which we conceive very clearly and distinctly are all true—remembering, however, that there is some difficulty in ascertaining which are those that we distinctly conceive.

Following upon this, and reflecting on the fact that I doubted, and that consequently my existence was not quite perfect (for I saw clearly that it was a greater perfection to

know than to doubt), I resolved to inquire whence I had learnt to think of anything more perfect than I myself was; and I recognised very clearly that this conception must proceed from some nature which was really more perfect. As to the thoughts which I had of many other things outside of me, like the heavens, the earth, light, heat, and a thousand others, I had not so much difficulty in knowing whence they came, because, remarking nothing in them which seemed to render them superior to me, I could believe that, if they were true, they were dependencies upon my nature, in so far as it possessed some perfection; and if they were not true, that I held them from nought, that is to say, that they were in me because I had something lacking in my nature. But this could not apply to the idea of a Being more perfect than my own, for to hold it from nought would be manifestly impossible; and because it is no less contradictory to say of the more perfect that it is what results from and depends on the less perfect, than to say that there is something which proceeds from nothing, it was equally impossible that I should hold it from myself. In this way it could but follow that it had been placed in me by a Nature which was really more perfect than mine could be, and which even had within itself all the perfections of which I could form any idea—that is to say, to put it in a word, which was God. . . .

— Q How does Descartes arrive at his distinction between mind and matter?

— Q Why does he conclude that he is "a substance the whole essence or nature of which is to think?"

Religion and the New Learning

The new learning, a composite of scientific method and rational inquiry, presented its own challenge to traditional religion. From "self-evident" propositions, Descartes arrived at conclusions to which empirical confirmation was irrelevant. His rationalism—like Plato's—involved a process of the mind independent of the senses. Reasoning that the concept of perfection ("something more perfect than myself") had to proceed from "some Nature which in reality was more perfect," Descartes "proved" the existence of God as Absolute Substance. Since something cannot proceed from nothing, argued Descartes, the idea of God held by human beings must come from God. Moreover, the idea of Perfection (God) embraces the idea of existence, for, if something is perfect, it must exist.

Raised by Jesuits, Descartes defended the existence of a Supreme Creator, but he shared with many seventeenth-century intellectuals the view that God was neither Caretaker nor personal Redeemer. Instead, Descartes identified God with "the mathematical order of nature." The idea that God did not interfere with the laws of humanity and nature was central to **deism**, a "natural" religion based on human reason rather than revelation. Deists purged religion of superstition, myth, and ritual. They viewed God as a master mechanic who had created the universe, then stepped aside and allowed his World-Machine to run unattended.

---

[1] Fallacious arguments.

Unlike Bacon, Descartes did not envision any conflict between science and religion. He optimistically concluded that "all our ideas or notions contain in them some truth; for otherwise it could not be that God, who is wholly perfect and veracious, should have placed them in us." Like other deists of his time, Descartes held that to follow reason was to follow God.

Spinoza and Pascal

In Amsterdam, a city whose reputation for freedom of thought had attracted Descartes—he lived there between 1628 and 1649—the Jewish philosopher Baruch Spinoza (1632–1677) addressed the question of the new science versus the old faith. Spinoza posited "a universe ruled only by the cause and effect of natural laws, without purpose or design." Stripping God of his traditional role as Creator (and consequently finding himself ousted from the local synagogue), he claimed "God exists only philosophically." God is neither behind, nor beyond, nor separate from nature but, rather, identical with it. Every physical thing, including human beings, is an expression of God in some variation of mind combined with matter. In this pantheistic spirit, Spinoza held that the greatest good was the union of the human mind with the whole of nature.

For the French physicist–mathematician Blaise Pascal (1623–1662), on the other hand, science and religion were irreconcilable. Having undergone a mystical experience that converted him to devout Roman Catholicism, he believed that the path to God was through the heart rather than through the head. Although reason might yield a true understanding of nature, it could in no way prove God's existence. We are capable, wrote Pascal, of "certain knowledge and of absolute ignorance." In his collected meditations on human nature, called simply *Pensées* ("Thoughts"), Pascal proposed a wager that challenged the indifference of skeptics: if God does *not* exist, skeptics lose nothing by believing in him, but if God *does* exist, they reap eternal life. The spiritual quest for purpose and value in a vast, impersonal universe moved the sharp-minded Pascal to confess: "The eternal silence of these infinite spaces frightens me."

Locke and the Culmination of the Empirical Tradition

The writings of the English philosopher and physician John Locke (1632–1704) championed the empirical tradition in seventeenth-century thought. Written seventy years after Bacon's *Novum Organum*, Locke's *Essay Concerning Human Understanding* (1690) confirmed his predecessor's thesis that everything one knows derives from sensory experience. According to Locke, the human mind at birth is a *tabula rasa* ("blank slate") upon which experience—consisting of sensation, followed by reflection—writes the script. There are no innate moral principles or ideas; human knowledge consists only of the progressive accumulation of the evidence of the senses.

The implications of Locke's principles of knowledge moved European and (later) American thought to assume an optimistic view of human destiny. For, if experience influences human knowledge and behavior, then, surely, improving the social environment will work to perfect the human condition. Locke's ideas became basic to eighteenth-century liberalism, as well as to all ideologies that held that human knowledge, if properly applied, would produce happiness for humankind (see chapter 24).

READING 23.4 From Locke's *Essay Concerning Human Understanding* (1690)

Idea is the Object of Thinking.—Every man being conscious   1
to himself that he thinks, and that which his mind is applied
about whilst thinking, being the ideas that are there, it is past
doubt that men have in their minds several ideas, such as are
those expressed by the words whiteness, hardness, sweetness,
thinking, motion, man, elephant, army, drunkenness, and others.
It is in the first place then to be inquired how he comes by
them. I know it is a received doctrine that men have native ideas
and original characters stamped upon their minds in their
very first being. This opinion I have at large examined already;   10
and I suppose what I have [already] said . . . will be much more
easily admitted when I have shown whence the understanding
may get all the ideas it has, and by what ways and degrees they
may come into the mind; for which I shall appeal to every one's
own observation and experience.

All Ideas come from Sensation or Reflection.—Let us then
suppose the mind to be, as we say, white paper, void of all
characters, without any ideas; how comes it to be furnished?
Whence comes it by that vast store which the busy and
boundless fancy of man has painted on it with an almost endless   20
variety? Whence has it all the materials of reason and
knowledge? To this I answer in one word, from experience; in
that all our knowledge is founded, and from that it ultimately
derives itself. Our observation employed either about external
sensible objects, or about the internal operations of our minds,
perceived and reflected on by ourselves, is that which supplies
our understandings with all the materials of thinking. These two
are the fountains of knowledge from whence all the ideas we
have or can naturally have do spring.

The Objects of Sensation, one Source of Ideas.—First, our   30
senses, conversant about particular sensible objects, do convey
into the mind several distinct perceptions of things, according to
those various ways wherein those objects do affect them: and
thus we come by those ideas we have, of yellow, white, heat,
cold, soft, hard, bitter, sweet, and all those which we call
sensible qualities; which when I say the senses convey into the
mind, I mean, they from external objects
convey into the mind what produces there those perceptions.
This great source of most of the ideas we have, depending
wholly upon our senses, and derived by them to the   40
understanding, I call Sensation.

The Operations of our Minds, the other Source of them.—
Secondly, the other fountain, from which experience furnishes
the understanding with ideas, is the perception of the operations
of our own mind within us, as it is employed about the ideas it
has got; which operations, when the soul comes to reflect on
and consider, do furnish the understanding with another set of

ideas, which could not be had from things without; and such are
perception, thinking, doubting, believing,
reasoning, knowing, willing, and all the different actings of our   50
own minds; which we being conscious of, and observing in
ourselves, do from these receive into our understandings as
distinct ideas, as we do from bodies affecting our senses. This
source of ideas every man has wholly in himself; and though it
be not sense, as having nothing to do with external objects, yet
it is very like it, and might properly enough be called internal
sense. But as I call the other Sensation, so I call this
Reflection, the ideas it affords being such only as the mind
gets by reflecting on its own operations within itself. By
reflection then, in the following part of this discourse, I would   60

be understood to mean that notice which the mind takes of its
own operations, and the manner of them; by reason whereof
there come to be ideas of these operations in the understanding.
These two, I say, viz., external material
things, as the objects of sensation; and the operations of our
own minds within, as the objects of reflection; are to me the only
originals from whence all our ideas take their beginnings. . . .

All our Ideas are of the one or the other of these.—The
understanding seems to me not to have the least glimmering of   70
any ideas which it doth not receive from one of these two.
External objects furnish the mind with the ideas of sensible
qualities, which are all those different perceptions they produce
in us; and the mind furnishes the understanding with ideas of its
own operations.

These, when we have taken a full survey of them, and their
several modes, combinations, and relations, we shall find to
contain all our whole stock of ideas; and that we have nothing in
our minds, which did not come in one of these two ways. Let
any one examine his own thoughts, and thoroughly search into   80
his understanding; and then let him tell me, whether all the
original ideas he has there, are any other than of the objects of
his senses, or of the operations of his mind, considered as
objects of his reflection: and how great a mass of knowledge
soever he imagines to be lodged there, he will, upon taking a
strict view, see that he has not any idea in his mind, but what
one of these two have imprinted. . . .

— **Q** **How does Locke's regard for the senses
differ from Descartes'? On what aspects of
the mind's operations might they agree?**

Newton's Scientific Synthesis

The work of the great English astronomer and mathematician Isaac Newton (1642–1727) represents the culminating synthesis of seventeenth-century physics and
mathematics. A tireless student of the sciences (so intent
on his studies that he often forgot to eat), Newton moved
the new learning from its foundations in methodical
speculation (Copernicus) and empirical confirmation
(Galileo) to its apogee in codification.

With the 1687 publication of *Philosophiae Naturalis
Principia Mathematica* (*Mathematical Principles of Natural
Philosophy*),* commonly known as the *Principia*, Newton

Science and Technology

1666 Isaac Newton uses a prism to analyze light

1671 Gottfried Wilhelm Leibniz invents a calculating
machine that multiplies and divides

1684 Leibniz publishes his first paper on differential
calculus

1687 Newton publishes his *Principia Mathematica*

provided an all-embracing theory of universal gravitation
that described every physical movement in the universe—
from the operation of the tides to the effects of a planet on
its moons. In its 550 pages (written in a mere eighteen
months), he proved that nature's laws applied equally to
terrestrial and celestial matter, thus unifying the work of
Galileo and Kepler. He described the workings of the physical world with a single proposition that explained the universal force of gravity: "Every particle of matter attracts
every other particle with a force propositional to the product of the masses and inversely proportional to the square
of the distances between them" (Book III, Number 7).

The *Principia*, the fundamentals of which would go
unchallenged until the late nineteenth century, proved to
be the greatest work of science ever written. It advanced
the concept of an orderly universe, one that operated as
systematically as a well-oiled machine. Equally important,
however, it promoted the optimistic notion that the physical universe was discoverable and knowable by human
beings. Thus, it was an empowering force in the evolution
of self-awareness. Newton's shaping influence is best
described by his admiring British contemporary, Alexander
Pope (see chapter 24): "Nature and Nature's Laws lay hid
in Night./ God said, *Let Newton be*! And All was Light."

The Impact of the Scientific
Revolution on Art

Northern Baroque Painting

If the new science engendered a spirit of objective inquiry
in philosophy, it also inspired new directions in the visual
arts. In the cities of seventeenth-century Holland, where
Dutch lensmakers had produced the first telescopes and
microscopes, artists paid obsessive attention to the appearance of the natural world. In still lifes, portraits, landscape,
and scenes of everyday life—all secular subjects—Dutch
masters practiced the "art of describing."** The almost
photographic realism of the painting that opens this chapter, Jan Vermeer's *The Geographer* (see Figure 23.1), is typical of the new "Baconian" attention to the evidence of the

---

* The term "natural philosophy" meant primarily physics, astronomy,
  and the science of matter.
** See Svetlana Alpers, *The Art of Describing: Dutch Art in the
  Seventeenth Century*. Chicago: University of Chicago Press, 1983.

senses: from the calipers (a device used to measure distances) held in the geographer's right hand and the crisp parchment maprolls that lie on the table and floor, to the brocaded chair that stands against the wall, the objects of the real world are described with loving detail. References to Holland's global outreach, facilitated by its trading companies, appear in the inclusion of the handsome globe, the sea chart (so detailed that one can read the name of the manufacturer), and the richly patterned carpet, an import from the East, commonly used in domestic interiors as a table cover or wall-hanging. Vermeer bathes these tangible objects in atmospheric light that pours in from the window, unifying space.

Similar attention to detail is apparent in *The Drawing Lesson* (Figure **23.5**), a delightful genre painting by Jan Steen (1626–1679). The Dutch studio interior is filled with artist's paraphernalia—canvases, a sketchbook, an easel, pens, paper, and plaster-cast models—as well as by various mundane items: bottles, books, and jugs. Two students are shown receiving instruction from a drawing master. The young female gazes with bewildered wonder at the skills of her mentor. Steen's representation gives evidence of an important phenomenon in seventeenth-century Dutch art: the growing number of women as master painters. Often excluded from membership in the local guilds, they learned their trade by drawing from plaster-cast reproductions (see Figure 23.5). Forbidden to work from nude male models employed in traditional studio training, they inclined to the painting of portraits and still-life subjects. Rachel Ruysch (1664– 1750), the mother of ten children, produced precisely executed flower pieces for an international circle of patrons. Her works, which reflect the influence of the newly available botanical prints, suggest the close relationship between late seventeenth-century science and art.

One of the most talented of Holland's female artists was Maria van Oosterwyck (1630–1693). Drawing on the tradition of exacting realism initiated by Jan van Eyck, van Oosterwyck brought a naturalist's passion for detail to her paintings. Her *Still Life* of 1668 (Figure **23.6**) includes a radiant Dutch tulip, a worn book, a meticulously painted astrological globe, a rotting skull, various insects (including a moth and a microscopically precise fly), a mouse nibbling at some grain, and a wine carafe (left front) that reflects a minute image of the artist. This illusionistic tour de force, while brilliantly decorative, makes symbolic reference to the transience of temporal things. Red wine, exotic flowers, and musical instruments, mark fleeting pleasures and the brevity of life. The books, entitled *Rekeningh* (*Reckoning*) and *Self-Stryt* (*Self-Struggle*), underline the need to take account of one's moral state. Ostensibly a celebration of earthly pleasures, the painting—a type known as **vanitas**—suggests the corruptibility of worldly goods, the futility of riches, and the inevitability of death.

In addition to still-life subjects, genre paintings (scenes of everyday life and especially family life) were in high demand in the Netherlands in the seventeenth century, generating a virtual golden age of Dutch art. The domestic scenes of Pieter de Hooch (1629–1684) show Dutch art to be societal—they are concerned with conviviality and companionship. In one painting, de Hooch uses a spacious courtyard filled with cool, bright light as the setting for such ordinary pleasures as pipe-smoking and beer-drinking (Figure **23.7**). He captures a mood of domestic intimacy in his loving attention to humble fact: the crumbling brick wall, the gleaming

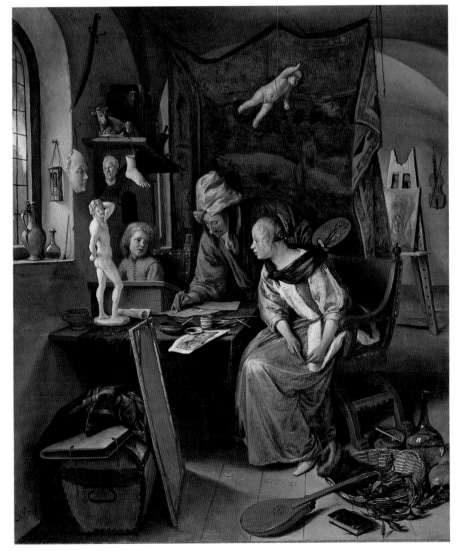

Figure 23.5 JAN STEEN, *The Drawing Lesson*, 1665. Oil on canvas, 19⅜ × 16¼ in. Often humorous and anecdotal, Steen's paintings are usually brilliant in composition. Here, he uses the canvas leaning on the trunk and the lute on the floor to lead our eyes into the scene.

Figure 23.6 MARIA VAN OOSTERWYCK, *Vanitas Still Life*, 1668. Oil on canvas, 29 × 35 in.

flowers, skull, and rotting corn:
symbols of transience and death

moth symbolizing
corruption and decay

astrological globe
implying universality

hourglass symbolizing
the passage of time
and the inevitability
of death

wine carafe signifying
life's pleasures,
with reflection of the
artist in an interior

money bag and
coins alluding to
the futility of riches

recorder signifying
music as a fleeting
pleasure

fly symbolizing
pestilence and
misfortune

mouse symbolizing
pestilence

butterfly: symbol of
the immortal soul

books encouraging the need to
take account of one's moral state

Figure 23.7 (above) **PIETER DE HOOCH**, *A Dutch Courtyard*, 1658–1660. Oil on canvas, 26¾ × 23 in.

Figure 23.8 (below) **PIETER DE HOOCH**, *Portrait of a Family Making Music*, 1663. Oil on canvas, 38⅛ × 45¹⁵⁄₁₆ in.

tankard, the homely matron, and the pudgy child. The strict verticals and horizontals of the composition—established with Cartesian clarity and precision—create a sense of tranquility and order.

Amateur musical performances, one of the major domestic entertainments of the seventeenth century, are the subject of many Northern Baroque paintings, including de Hooch's *Portrait of a Family Making Music* (Figure **23.8**). The growing popularity of musical subjects reflects the emphasis on musical education and the rising number of private musical societies in the towns of the Dutch Republic. In the belief that music-listening and music-making were morally edifying (and thus more desirable than the all too popular pastime of drinking), many churches required musical recitals before and after services and encouraged instrumental and choral expression among members of the congregation. Holland was a center for the manufacture of musical instruments; the Dutch household pictured by de Hooch would have owned the bass viol, recorder, cittern (a type of lute), and violin on which the family performed, their rhythms closely measured by the portly, no-nonsense matron of the house.

Music-making also figures in the delightful painting called *The Suitor's Visit* by Gerard ter Borch (1617–1681). The narrative is staged like a scene from a play: a well-dressed gentleman, who has just entered the parlor of a well-to-do middle-class family, bows before a young woman whose coy apprehension suggests that she is the object of courtship (Figure **23.9**). The father and the family dog take note of the tense moment, while a younger woman, absorbed in playing the lute, ignores the interruption. Ter Borch was famous for his virtuosity in painting silk and satin fabrics that subtly gleam from within the shadowy depths of domestic interiors. Equally impressive, however, was his ability to invest an inconsequential social event with intimacy.

Vermeer and Dutch Painting

Seventeenth-century Dutch artists developed as a major subject the naturalistic landscape (the very word derives from the Dutch *landschap* meaning "landform"). In landscape painting as in genre subjects, they described nature with a close attention to detail and a sensitivity to atmosphere that rivaled the landscapes of their Northern European predecessors, Dürer and Brueghel (see chapter 19). Unlike their seventeenth-century French contemporaries, Poussin and Claude Lorrain (see chapter 21), Dutch landscape painters depicted nature unidealized and free of moralizing narratives; they brought to life a sense of place and the vastness of nature itself.

Such is the case with the *View of Delft* (Figure **23.10**), the only landscape painted by the Delft master

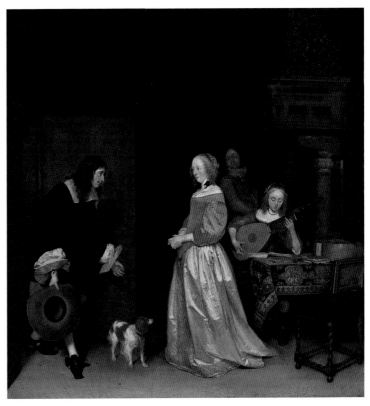

Figure 23.9 GERARD TER BORCH, *The Suitor's Visit*, ca. 1658. Oil on canvas, 31½ × 29⅝ in.

Figure 23.10 JAN VERMEER, *View of Delft*, 1658. Oil on canvas, 3 ft. 2¾ in. × 3 ft. 10 in. This cityscape reflects the pride with which Dutch painters and patrons regarded their home towns. Like other urban centers in the Lowlands, Delft was home to some of Europe's finest mapmakers.

Jan Vermeer (1632–1675). An innkeeper and an art dealer, who produced fewer than forty canvases in his lifetime, Vermeer transformed everyday subjects by way of atmospheric space and evanescent light. His *View of Delft*, a topographical study of his native city, reveals a typically Dutch affection for the visible world. It also reflects the artist's delight in the physical effects of light on matter: the silvery surface of the water interrupted by boats and buildings, the sunlight filtering down to illuminate some segments of the city, while others are clouded into shade. Vermeer lowers the horizon line to give increased attention to the sky—a reflection perhaps of his interest in the new astronomy. While the composition fixes a singular point of view and a precise place, the broad horizon seems to reach beyond the limits of the frame to suggest infinite space. Two groups of tiny figures (in the left foreground) invite us to share the view—as beholders and as minor players on the larger stage of nature.

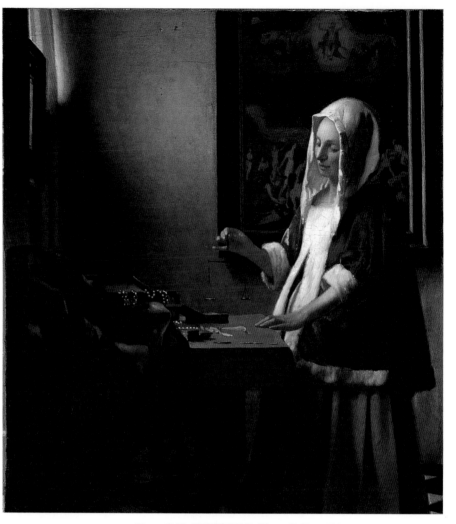

Figure 23.12 JAN VERMEER, *Woman Holding a Balance*, ca. 1664. Oil on canvas, 16¾ × 15 in.

It is likely that Vermeer and other Dutch masters shared an interest in the optical experiments of Galileo and Newton and in the optical devices (such as the *camera lucida*; see chapter 17) that facilitated an accurate and detailed depiction of the physical world. Scholars argue that Vermeer, the exemplar in an age of observation, executed his paintings with the aid of a *camera obscura* (Figure **23.11**), an apparatus that anticipated the modern pinhole camera (while lacking the means of capturing the image on film). The blurred contours and small beads of light that twinkle on the surface of his canvases suggest the use of an optical lens.

Vermeer's favorite subjects—women playing musical instruments, reading letters, or enjoying the company of suitors—are all depicted on small-sized canvases in an intimate interior (possibly that of the artist's studio). Self-contained and self-possessed, and bathed in atmospheric light, they come to life in a strikingly personal manner. In Vermeer's *Woman Holding a Balance* (Figure **23.12**) a woman (perhaps pregnant) stands before a table contemplating a jeweler's balance. On the table, strands of pearls twinkle in the light that filters through the curtained window—a compositional strategy used in *The Geographer* (see Figure 23.1) and in many of Vermeer's domestic interiors. On the wall behind her is a painting of the Last Judgment. Is this a lofty allegory that makes reference to the final weighing of souls, and the balance between worldly and otherworldly rewards? Or is it simply a delicately rendered record of a domestic activity? Either way, its exquisite intimacy and meditative tranquility are unique in Dutch art.

Dutch Portraiture

The vogue for portraiture in Northern Baroque art reflected the self-conscious materialism of a rising middle class. Like the portraits of wealthy Renaissance

Figure 23.11 A *camera obscura*; the image formed by the lens and reflected by the mirror on the ground glass is traced by the artist.

Figure 23.13 **FRANS HALS**, *The Laughing Cavalier*, 1624. Oil on canvas, 33¾ × 27 in.

These qualities also appear in the work of Judith Leyster (1609–1660), a Netherlandish artist from the province of Utrecht, whose canvases until the twentieth century were attributed to her colleague, Frans Hals. Leyster established a workshop in Haarlem and was one of only two females elected to the painters' guild of that city. Almost all her known paintings date from before her marriage at the age of twenty-six. Leyster's *Self-Portrait* achieves a sense of informality through the casual manner in which the artist turns away from her canvas as if to greet the viewer (Figure **23.14**). The laughing violinist that is the subject of the painting-within-the-painting provides an exuberant counterpoint to Leyster's robust visage. Leyster's portrait is a personal comment on the role of the artist as muse and artisan. It conveys the self-confidence of a middle-class woman who competed with the best of Holland's masters.

Figure 23.14 **JUDITH LEYSTER**, *Self-Portrait*, ca. 1630. Oil on canvas, 29⅜ × 25⅞ in. Shortly after her marriage Leyster moved with her husband to Amsterdam, where she bore and reared at least five children. Though she may have helped her husband, Jan Molenaer, execute his paintings, her own artistic output decreased dramatically.

aristocrats (see chapter 17), the painted likenesses of seventeenth-century Dutch burghers fulfilled the ambition to immortalize one's worldly self. But in contrast to Italian portraits, the painted images of middle-class Dutch men and women are usually unidealized and often even unflattering. They capture a truth to nature reminiscent of late Roman portraiture (see chapter 6) but surpass even these in their self-scrutiny and probing, self-reflective character.

Two contemporaries, Frans Hals (1581–1666) and Rembrandt van Rijn (the latter introduced in chapter 22), dominated the genre of portraiture in seventeenth-century Dutch painting. Hals was the leading painter of Haarlem and one of the great realists of the Western portrait tradition. His talent lay in capturing the personality and physical presence of his sitters: the jaunty self-confidence of a courtly Dutch soldier, for instance, whose fleeting sideways glance flirts with the viewer (Figure **23.13**). A master of the brush, Hals brought his forms to life by means of quick, loose, staccato brushstrokes and impasto highlights. Immediacy, spontaneity, and impulsive movement—features typical of Baroque art—enliven Hals' portraits.

Rembrandt's Portraits

Hals' and Leyster's portraits are astute records of surface appearance. By comparison, Rembrandt's portraits are studies of the inner life of his sitters, uncompromising explorations of flesh and blood. A keen observer of human character, Rembrandt became the leading portrait painter in the city of Amsterdam. The commissions he received at the beginning of his career exceeded his ability to fill them. But after a meteoric rise to fame, he saw his fortunes decline. Accumulated debts led to poverty, bankruptcy, and psychological depression—the last compounded by the loss of his beloved wife in 1642.

The history of Rembrandt's career is mirrored in his self-portraits, some forty of which survive. They are a kind of visual diary, a lifetime record of the artist's passionate enterprise in self-scrutiny. The *Self-Portrait* of 1661, with its slackened facial muscles and furrowed brow, engages the viewer with the image of a noble and yet utterly vulnerable personality (Figure **23.15**). Portraiture of this kind,

which has no equivalent in any non-Western culture, may be considered among the outstanding examples of Northern Baroque art.

Among the most lucrative of Rembrandt's commissions was the group portrait, a genre that commemorated the achievements of wealthy Dutch families, guild members, and militia officers. Some of these paintings, which measure more than 12 by 14 feet, reflect the Baroque fondness for colossal proportion and theatrical setting. Even in his smaller-sized group portraits, Rembrandt achieved a unity of dramatic effect typical of the Baroque style. The painting that established Rembrandt's reputation as a master portraitist, *The Anatomy Lesson of Dr. Nicolaes Tulp* (1632), is a case in point (Figure **23.16**). Here the artist has eliminated the posed look of the conventional group portrait by staging the scene as a dissection in progress. As in his religious compositions (compare Figure 22.5), he manipulates light for dramatic purposes: he spotlights the dissected corpse in the foreground and balances the darker area formed by the figure of the doctor with a triangle created by the brightly lit faces of the students (whose names appear on the piece of paper held by the central figure). These faces bear the force of individual personalities and the spirit of inquisitiveness peculiar to the Age of Science.

Figure 23.15 REMBRANDT VAN RIJN, *Self-Portrait as Saint Paul*, 1661. Oil on canvas, 35⅛ × 30¾ in. As part of their training, Rembrandt's students copied the master's self-portraits. Recent scholarship has reduced the number of authentic Rembrandt self-portraits from sixty to around forty.

Figure 23.16 REMBRANDT VAN RIJN, *The Anatomy Lesson of Dr. Nicolaes Tulp*, 1632. Oil on canvas, 5 ft. 3⅜ in. × 7 ft. 1¼ in. Engaged in a public dissection witnessed by his students, the doctor is shown examining the muscles of the arm and hand of an executed prisoner. The large book in the lower right corner is doubtlessly a copy of Vesalius' monumental study, *On the Workings of the Human Body.*

Baroque Instrumental Music

Until the sixteenth century, almost all music was written for the voice rather than for musical instruments. Even during the Renaissance, instrumental music was, for the most part, the result of substituting an instrument for a voice in music written for singing or dancing. The seventeenth century marked the rise of music that lacked an extramusical text. Like a mathematical equation or a geometric formula, the instrumental music of the early modern era carried no explicit narrative content—it was neither a vehicle of religious expression nor a means of supporting a secular vocalized text. Such music was written without consideration for the content traditionally provided by a set of sung lyrics. The idea of music as an aesthetic exercise, composed for its own sake rather than to serve a religious or communal purpose, was a notable feature of seventeenth-century European culture.

Not surprisingly, the rise of instrumental music was accompanied by improvements in instruments and refinements in tuning. Indeed, instrumental music came to dominate musical composition at the very moment that Western musicians were perfecting such stringed instruments as the violin, viola, and cello (see Figure 23.8) and such keyboard instruments as the organ and harpsichord (Figure 23.17). By the early eighteenth century, musicians were adopting the system of tuning known as **equal temperament**, whereby the octave was divided into twelve half-steps of equal size. The collection of preludes and fugues known as the *Well-Tempered* [tuned] *Clavier* (1722–1742) shows how Bach made use of this uniform system of tuning to create sublime music—he wrote two pieces in every possible key. The new attention to improving instruments and systematizing keys mirrored the efforts of scientists and philosophers to bring precision and uniformity to the tools and methods of scientific inquiry.

In the seventeenth century, northern Italy was the world center for the manufacture of violins. The Amati, Guarneri, and Stradivari families of Cremona, Italy, established the techniques of making quality violins that were sought in all of the great courts of Europe. Transmitted from father to son, the construction techniques used to produce these instruments were guarded so secretly that modern violinmakers have never successfully imitated them. Elsewhere, around 1650, earlier instruments were standardized and refined. The ancient double-reed wind instrument known as the shawm, for instance, developed into the modern oboe. While amateur music-making was widespread, professional performance also took a great leap forward, as a new breed of virtuosi inspired the writing of treatises on performance techniques.

Figure 23.17 JOHANNES COUCHET (maker), Flemish Harpsichord-double-banked; compass, four octaves, and a fifth F to C (each keyboard), ca. 1650. Case decorated with carving and gilt gesso work.

Three main types of composition—the sonata, the suite, and the concerto—dominated seventeenth-century instrumental music. All three reflect the Baroque taste for dramatic contrasts in tempo and texture. The **sonata** (from the Italian word for "sounded," that is, music played and not sung) is a piece written for a few instruments—often no more than one or two. It usually consisted of three **movements** of contrasting tempo—fast/slow/fast—each based on a song or dance form of the time.

The **suite**, written for any combination of instruments, is a sequence or series of movements derived from various European court or folk dances—for example, the sarabande, the pavane, the minuet, and the gigue, or jig. Henry Purcell (1659–1695) in England, François Couperin (1668–1733) in France (see chapter 26), and Johann Sebastian Bach (1685–1750) in Germany all contributed to the development of the suite as a musical genre.

Finally, the **concerto** (from the same root as *concertato*, which describes opposing or contrasting bodies of sound; see chapter 20) is a composition consisting of two groups of instruments, one small and the other large, playing in "dialogue." The typical Baroque concerto, the **concerto grosso** ("large concerto") featured several movements, whose number and kind varied considerably.

Vivaldi

The leading Italian instrumental composer of the Baroque era was Antonio Vivaldi (1678–1741), a Roman Catholic priest and the son of a prominent violinist at Saint Mark's Cathedral in Venice. A composer of both sacred music and opera, he earned lasting fame as one of the most influential figures in the history of the concerto grosso. He wrote some

450 concertos, including concerti grossi and solo concertos, the latter mostly for violin. Vivaldi systematized the concerto grosso into a three-movement form (fast/slow/fast) and increased the distinctions between solo and ensemble groups in each movement. He also perfected the form known as ***ritornello*** (literally, "return"), which makes use of a returning or recurring musical passage that (alternating with other musical episodes) brings dramatic unity to the composition.

Of the many compositions Vivaldi wrote for solo violin and orchestra, the most glorious is *The Four Seasons*, a group of four violin concertos, each of which musically describes a single season. Vivaldi intended that this piece be "programmatic," that is, carry meaning outside of the music itself. As if to ensure that the music duplicate the descriptive power of traditional vocal lines, he added poems at appropriate passages in the score for the instruction of the performers. At the section called "Spring," for instance, Vivaldi's verses describe "flowing streams" and "singing birds." While the music offers listeners the challenge of detecting such extramusical references, its brilliance lies not in its programmatic innovations but in its vibrant rhythms, its lyrical solos, and its exuberant "dialogues" between violin and orchestra.

Bach and Instrumental Music

Johann Sebastian Bach, whom we met in chapter 22, served as a brilliant church musician for much of his life. However, he was also one of history's greatest composers of secular music, that is, music with no obvious religious function. Influenced by both Vivaldi's concertos and the Italian music style that inspired the expressive conjunction of solo and orchestral forms, Bach developed the musical potential of the concerto form more completely than any previous composer. He claimed that his study of Vivaldi had taught him to "think musically," and endow the creative process with "order, coherence, and proportion." To the hundreds of concertos produced throughout his lifetime, Bach brought a high degree of rational control, expanding the *ritornello* sections and bringing solo episodes to new levels of complexity.

The six concertos known as the Brandenburg Concertos were composed over a period of several years. In 1721, Bach sent them to Ludwig Christian, the margrave of Brandenburg, in the hope of securing a position at his court. Though there is no record that these concertos were ever performed during Bach's lifetime, they were intended for performance by the Brandenburg court orchestra.

The Brandenburg Concertos employ as soloists most of the principal instruments of the Baroque orchestra: violin, oboe, recorder, trumpet, and harpsichord. Bach applied himself to developing rich contrasts of tone and texture between the two "contending" groups of instruments—note especially the massive sound of the orchestra versus the lighter sounds of the small group (consisting of a violin and

♪ See Music Listening Selections at end of chapter.

two recorders) in the first movement of the fourth concerto. Here, tightly drawn webs of counterpoint are spun between upper and lower instrumental parts, while musical lines, driven by an unflagging rhythm and energy, unfold majestically.

In the ten years before his death in 1750, Bach undertook one of the most monumental works of his career—a compelling example of Baroque musical composition that came to be called *The Art of Fugue*. A **fugue** (literally "flight") is a polyphonic composition in which a single musical theme (or subject) is restated in sequential phrases. As in the more familiar canon known as a "round"—for instance, "Three Blind Mice"—a melody in one voice part is imitated in a succession of other voices, so that melody and repetitions overlap. The musical subject can be arranged to appear backward or inverted (or both), augmented (the time value of the notes doubled, so that the melody moves twice as slowly), or diminished (note values halved, so that the melody moves twice as fast). In the hands of a great composer, this form of imitative counterpoint weaves a majestic tapestry of sound.

Such is the case with *The Art of Fugue*, which explores the contrapuntal possibilities of a single musical subject in

See Music Listening Selections at end of chapter.

eighteen separate compositions. Bach produced this *summa* of seventeenth-century musical science as a tool for instruction in the writing of fugues, which explores the contrapuntal possibilities of a single musical subject in eighteen separate compositions. In the last portion of the work he signed his name with a musical motif made up of the letters of his name—B flat, A, C, and B natural (pronounced as an H in German). Even the listener who cannot read music or understand the complexities of Bach's inventions is struck by their concentrated brilliance. No less than Newton's codification of the laws of nature, *The Art of Fugue* is a triumphant expression of the Age of Science.

Chronology

1543	Copernicus publishes *De revolutionibus orbium*
1619	Kepler formulates three laws of planetary motion
1620	Bacon publishes *Novum Organum*
1633	Trial of Galileo
1637	Descartes publishes *Discourse on Method*
1662	Royal Society of London founded

LOOKING BACK

The Scientific Revolution

- Following Copernicus, European scientists confirmed the reality of a heliocentric cosmos that operated according to fixed and understandable laws.
- Johannes Kepler's inquiries on planetary movements confirmed Copernicus' theories, and showed that the planets moved around the sun in elliptical paths.
- Galileo formulated the Law of Falling Bodies and used the telescope to confirm empirically the previously theoretical heliocentric universe.
- Between 1600 and 1700, new tools were invented for accurately measuring the physical world; the sciences of physics and astronomy, and the language of higher mathematics, were firmly established.
- The tenets of the new science contradicted scriptural teachings and met with opposition from both Catholics and Protestants.

The New Learning

- While scientists demystified nature, the new learning provided a methodology for more accurately describing and predicting its operations.
- English scientist Francis Bacon, author of the *Novum Organum*, championed induction and the empirical method, which gave priority to knowledge gained through the senses.
- English philosopher and physician John Locke defended the empirical tradition with the theory that all experience is imprinted on the human mind, a *tabula rasa* ("blank slate") at birth.
- Questioning the authority of the inductive method, René Descartes, the father of modern Western philosophy, gave priority to deductive reasoning and mathematical analysis in his *Discourse on Method*.
- Descartes, along with many other intellectuals of new learning, embraced deism, which identified God as a master mechanic who did not interfere with the laws of nature.

Newton's Scientific Synthesis

- Bridging physics and mathematics, Isaac Newton moved the new learning from its theoretical and empirical phases to the stage of codification.
- Newton's *Principia* promoted the idea of a uniform and intelligible universe that operated as systematically as a well-oiled machine; his monumental work became the basis of modern physics.

The Impact of the Scientific Revolution on Art

- The Scientific Revolution and the new learning ushered in a phase of the Baroque style marked by an empirical attention to physical detail and a fascination with light and space.
- An increased demand for such secular subjects as still life, landscape, portraiture, and genre painting reflects the secular preoccupations and growing wealth of middle-class patrons, particularly in Northern Europe.
- The definitive artworks of seventeenth-century Northern Baroque include Vermeer's *View of Delft*, the portraits of Rembrandt, Hals, and Leyster, and the genre paintings of de Hooch and ter Borch, which explore the intimate pleasures of house and home.
- Rembrandt's psychologically penetrating self-portraits are the intimate equivalents of his masterful group portraits.

Baroque Instrumental Music

- During the seventeenth century, instrumental music came to dominate musical composition. String instruments, especially the violin, reached a new level of refinement.
- Keyboard instruments, and musical performance in general, benefited from the development of a uniform system of tuning; treatises on the art of instrumental performance became increasingly popular.
- The seventeenth century saw the rise of wholly instrumental music and of such instrumental forms as the sonata, the suite, and the concerto.
- Vivaldi was the most influential figure in the development of the Baroque concerto, especially the concerto grosso. Bach brought to perfection the art of the fugue in compositions whose complexity and brilliance remain unrivaled. These instrumental forms captured the exuberance of the Baroque spirit and the dynamic intellectualism of the age.

Music Listening Selections

CD Two Selection 5 Vivaldi, *The Four Seasons*, "Spring," Concerto in E Major, Op. 8, No. 1, first movement, 1725.

CD Two Selection 6 Bach, Brandenburg Concerto No. 4 in G Major, first movement, excerpt, 1721.

CD Two Selection 7 Bach, *The Art of Fugue*, Canon in the 12th, harpsichord, 1749–1750.

Glossary

Cartesian of or relating to René Descartes or his philosophy

concerto (Italian, "opposing" or "competing") an instrumental composition consisting of one or more solo instruments and a larger group of instruments playing in "dialogue"

concerto grosso a "large concerto," the typical kind of Baroque concerto, consisting of several movements

deductive reasoning a method of inquiry that begins with clearly established general premises and moves toward the establishment of particular truths

deism a movement or system of thought advocating natural religion based on human reason rather than revelation; deists describe God as Creator, but deny that God interferes with the laws of the universe

dualism the view that holds the mind (a thinking entity) as distinct from the body

equal temperament a system of tuning that originated in the seventeenth century, whereby the octave is divided into twelve half-steps of equal size; since intervals have the same value in all keys, music may be played in any key, and a musician may change from one key to another with complete freedom.

fugue ("flight") a polyphonic composition in which a theme (or subject) is imitated, restated, and developed by successively entering voice parts

geocentric earth-centered

heliocentric sun-centered

inductive reasoning a method of inquiry that begins with direct observation and experimentation and moves toward the establishment of general conclusions or axioms

movement a major section in a long instrumental composition

ritornello (Italian, "a little return") in Baroque music, an instrumental section that recurs throughout the movement

sonata an instrumental composition consisting of three movements of contrasting tempo, usually fast/slow/fast; see also Glossary, chapter 26

suite an instrumental composition consisting of a sequence or series of movements derived from court or folk dances

vanitas (Latin, "vanity") a type of still life consisting of objects that symbolize the brevity of life and the transience of earthly pleasures and achievements

Chapter

24

The Enlightenment:
The Promise of Reason
ca. 1650–1800

"The time will ... come when the sun will shine only on free men who know no other master but their reason."
Antoine Nicolas de Condorcet

Figure 24.1 N. LAVRÉINCE, *Assembly in a Salon*, 1745–1807. Oil on canvas, 1¾ × 2⅓ ft. The painting shows the elegantly dressed men and women of eighteenth-century society enjoying leisure activities in the *salon* of a Parisian townhouse. Such works were reproduced in popular and affordable engravings.

LOOKING AHEAD

In the year 1680 a comet blazed across the skies over Western Europe. The English astronomer Edmund Halley (1656–1742) observed the celestial body, calculated its orbit, and predicted its future appearances. Stripped of its former role as a portent of catastrophe or a harbinger of natural calamity, Halley's comet now became merely another natural phenomenon, the behavior of which invited scientific investigation. This new, objective attitude toward nature and the accompanying confidence in the liberating role of reason were hallmarks of the Enlightenment—the intellectual movement that occurred between 1687 (the date of Newton's *Principia*) and 1789 (the beginning of the French Revolution).

Also known as the Age of Reason, this era marks the divide between the medieval view of the world as governed by God and the principles of faith, and the modern, secular view of the world as dominated by humankind and the principles of reason. The light of reason, argued enlightened intellectuals, would dispel the mists of human ignorance, superstition, and prejudice. This spirit of buoyant optimism infused Enlightenment efforts to create a kind of happiness on earth that in former ages had been thought to exist only in heaven.

During the Age of Enlightenment learning freed itself from the Church, and literacy became widespread. Among middle-class Europeans, 90 to 100 percent of men and almost 75 percent of women could read and write. This new, more literate middle class competed with a waning aristocracy for social and political prestige. The public interest in literature and the arts spurred the rise of the newspaper, the encyclopedia, the novel, and the symphony. While the major intellectual and cultural ideals of the Enlightenment did not directly touch the lives of millions of peasants and villagers, they influenced the course of modern history, not only in the West, but, gradually, throughout the world.

Liberty and Political Theory

Natural Law

Eighteenth-century intellectuals were heirs to Newtonian science. As Newton had established the natural laws of the physical universe, so these rationalists sought to establish general laws of human behavior. As Newton had defined the operations of celestial bodies in the context of unchanging nature, so Enlightenment thinkers perceived human behavior in terms of *natural law*. Natural law, the unwritten and divinely sanctioned law of nature, held that

there are certain principles of right and wrong that all human beings, by way of reason, can discover and apply in the course of creating a just society. "Natural rights" included the right to life, liberty, property, and just treatment by the ruling order.

Enlightenment thinkers argued that a true understanding of the human condition was the first step toward progress, that is, toward the gradual betterment of human life. It is no wonder, then, that the eighteenth century saw the birth of the social sciences: anthropology, sociology, economics, and political science. Devoted to the study of humankind, these new disciplines were put at the service of an enlightened social order.

Hobbes and Locke

An enlightened social order required a redefinition of the role of government and the rights of citizens. In the early modern era, when European nation-states were on the rise, this subject dominated intellectual circles. Not since the Golden Age of Athens was so much attention given to the relationship between the ruler and the ruled.

During the sixteenth century, the pioneer political theorist Machiavelli had argued that the survival of the state was more important than the well-being of its citizens. Later in that century, the French lawyer Jean Bodin (1530–1596) employed biblical precepts and long-standing tradition to defend theories of divine-right monarchy. In the seventeenth century, the Dutch statesman Hugo Grotius (1583–1645) proposed an all-embracing system of international law based on reason, which he identified with nature. Grotius' idea of a political contract based in natural law profoundly influenced the thinking of two of England's finest philosophers, Thomas Hobbes (1588–1679) and John Locke, the latter of whom we met in chapter 23.

Though a generation apart, Hobbes and Locke took up the urgent question of human rights versus the sovereignty of the ruler. Shaken by the conflict between royalist and antiroyalist factions that had fueled the English Civil War (see chapter 22), both thinkers rejected the principle of divine-right monarchy. Instead, they advanced the idea that government must be based in a **social contract**. For Hobbes, the social contract was a covenant among individuals who willingly surrendered a portion of their freedom to a governing authority or ruler, in whose hands should rest ultimate authority. Locke agreed that government must be formed by a contract that laid the basis for social order and individual happiness. But he believed that power must remain with the ruled.

The divergent positions of Hobbes and Locke proceeded from their contrasting perceptions of human nature. Whereas Locke described human beings as naturally equal, free, and capable (through reason) of defining the common good, Hobbes viewed human beings as selfish, greedy, and warlike. Without the state, he argued, human life was "solitary, poor, nasty, brutish, and short." Bound by an irrevocable and irreversible social contract, government under one individual or a ruling assembly was, according to

Hobbes, society's only hope for peace and security. The collective safety of society lay in its willingness to submit to a higher authority, which Hobbes called the "Leviathan," after the mythological marine monster described in the Bible. Hobbes aired these views in a treatise called the *Leviathan*, which he published in 1651—only two years after England's antiroyalist forces had beheaded the English monarch, Charles I.

─ READING 24.1 From Hobbes' *Leviathan* (1651)

Part I   Chapter 13: Of the Natural Condition of Mankind as Concerning their Felicity and Misery

Nature has made men so equal in the faculties of the body and mind as that, though there be found one man sometimes manifestly stronger in body or of quicker mind than another, yet, when all is reckoned together, the difference between man and man is not so considerable as that one man can thereupon claim to himself any benefit to which another may not pretend as well as he. For as to the strength of body, the weakest has strength to kill the strongest, either by secret machination or by confederacy with others that are in the same danger with himself. . . .   10

From this equality of ability arises equality of hope in the attaining of our ends. And therefore if any two men desire the same thing, which nevertheless they cannot both enjoy, they become enemies; and in the way to their end, which is principally their own conservation, and sometimes their delectation[1] only, endeavor to destroy or subdue one another. And from hence it comes to pass that where an invader has no more to fear than another man's single power, if one plant, sow, build, or possess a convenient seat, others may probably be expected to come prepared with forces united to dispossess   20 and deprive him, not only of the fruit of his labor, but also of his life or liberty. And the invader again is in the like danger of another. . . .

So that in the nature of man we find three principal causes of quarrel: first, competition; secondly, diffidence;[2] thirdly, glory.

The first makes men invade for gain, the second for safety, and the third for reputation. The first use violence to make themselves masters of other men's persons, wives, children, and cattle; the second, to defend them; the third, for trifles, as a   30 word, a smile, a different opinion, and any other sign of undervalue, either direct in their persons or by reflection in their kindred, their friends, their nation, their profession, or their name.

Hereby it is manifest that, during the time men live without a common power to keep them all in awe, they are in that condition which is called war, and such a war as is of every man against every man. For war consists not in battle only, or the act of fighting, but in a tract of time wherein the will to contend by battle is sufficiently known; and therefore the notion of time is   40 to be considered in the nature of war as it is in the nature of

weather. For as the nature of foul weather lies not in a shower or two of rain but in an inclination thereto of many days together, so the nature of war consists not in actual fighting but in the known disposition thereto, during all the time there is no assurance to the contrary. All other time is PEACE.

Whatsoever, therefore, is consequent to a time of war where every man is enemy to every man, the same is consequent to the time wherein men live without other security than what their own strength and their own invention shall furnish them   50 withal. In such condition there is no place for industry, because the fruit thereof is uncertain; and consequently no culture of the earth; no navigation nor use of the commodities that may be imported by sea; no commodious building; no instruments of moving and removing such things as require much force; no knowledge of the face of the earth; no account of time; no arts; no letters; no society; and, which is worst of all, continual fear and danger of violent death; and the life of man solitary, poor, nasty, brutish, and short. . . .

Part II   Chapter 17: Of the Causes, Generation, and Definition of a Commonwealth

The final cause, end, or design of men, who naturally love   60 liberty and dominion over others, in the introduction of that restraint upon themselves in which we see them live in commonwealths, is the foresight of their own preservation, and of a more contented life thereby—that is to say, of getting themselves out from that miserable condition of war which is necessarily consequent . . . to the natural passions of man when there is no visible power to keep them in awe and tie them by fear of punishment to the performance of their covenants and observations of [the] laws of nature. . . .

For the laws of nature—as *justice, equity, modesty, mercy*,   70 and, in sum, *doing to others as we would be done to*—of themselves, without the terror of some power to cause them to be observed, are contrary to our natural passions, that carry us to partiality, pride, revenge, and the like. And covenants without the sword are but words, and of no strength to secure a man at all. Therefore, notwithstanding the laws of nature . . ., if there be no power erected, or not great enough for our security, every man will—and may lawfully—rely on his own strength and art for caution against all other men. . . .

The only way to erect such a common power as may be able   80 to defend them from the invasion of foreigners and the injuries of one another, and thereby to secure them in such sort as that by their own industry and by the fruits of the earth they may nourish themselves and live contentedly, is to confer all their power and strength upon one man, or upon one assembly of men that may reduce all their wills, by plurality of voices, unto one will; which is as much as to say, to appoint one man or assembly of men to bear their person, and everyone to own and acknowledge to himself to be author of whatsoever he that so bears their person shall act or cause to be acted in those things   90 which concern the common peace and safety, and therein to submit their wills every one to his will, and their judgments to his judgment. This is more than consent or concord; it is a real unity of them all in one and the same person, made by covenant of every man with every man, in which manner as if every man should say

---

[1] Enjoyment; delight.
[2] Lack of confidence.

to every man, *I authorize and give up my right of governing myself to this man, or to this assembly of men, on this condition, that you give up your right to him and authorize all his actions in like manner.* This done, the multitude so united in one person is called a COMMONWEALTH, in Latin CIVITAS. This is the generation of that great LEVIATHAN (or rather, to speak more reverently, of that *mortal god*) to which we owe, under the *immortal God*, our peace and defense. For by this authority, given him by every particular man in the commonwealth, he has the use of so much power and strength conferred on him that, by terror thereof, he is enabled to form the wills of them all to peace at home and mutual aid against their enemies abroad. And in him consists the essence of the commonwealth, which, to define it, is *one person, of whose acts a great multitude, by mutual covenants one with another, have made themselves every one the author, to the end he may use the strength and means of them all as he shall think expedient for their peace and common defense.* And he that carries this person is called SOVEREIGN and said to have sovereign power: and everyone besides, his SUBJECT. 100 110

The attaining to this sovereign power is by two ways. One, by natural force. . . . The other is when men agree among themselves to submit to some man or assembly of men voluntarily, on confidence to be protected by him against all others. This latter may be called a political commonwealth, or commonwealth by *institution*, and the former a commonwealth by *acquisition*. . . . 120

Part II   Chapter 30: Of the Office of the Sovereign Representative

The office of the sovereign, be it a monarch or an assembly, consists in the end for which he was trusted with the sovereign power, namely, the procuration of the *safety of the people*; to which he is obliged by the law of nature, and to render an account thereof to God, the author of that law, and to none but him. But by safety here is not meant a bare preservation but also all other contentments of life which every man by lawful industry, without danger or hurt to the commonwealth, shall acquire to himself. 130

And this is intended should be done, not by care applied to individuals further than their protection from injuries when they shall complain, but by a general providence contained in public instruction, both of doctrine and example, and in the making and executing of good laws, to which individual persons may apply their own cases.

And because, if the essential rights of sovereignty . . . be taken away, the commonwealth is thereby dissolved and every man returns into the condition and calamity of a war with every other man, which is the greatest evil that can happen in this life, it is the office of the sovereign to maintain those rights entire, and consequently against his duty, first, to transfer to another or to lay from himself any of them. For he that deserts the means deserts the ends. . . . 140

Q   What is Hobbes' view of human nature?

Q   What is the function of a "Leviathan?"

Locke's Government of the People

John Locke (Figure **24.2**) rejected Hobbes' view of humankind as self-serving and aggressive. If, as he argued, human beings were born without any preexisting qualities, their natural state must be one of perfect freedom. Whether people became brutish or otherwise depended solely upon their experiences and their environment. People have, by their very nature as human beings, reasoned Locke, the right to life, liberty, and estate (or "property"). Government must arbitrate between the exercise of one person's liberty and that of the next. The social contract thus preserves the natural rights of the governed. While individuals may willingly consent to give up some of their liberty in return for the ruler's protection, they may never relinquish their ultimate authority. If a ruler is tyrannical or oppressive, the people have not only the right but the obligation to rebel and seek a new ruler. Locke's defense of political rebellion in the face of tyranny served as justification for the "Glorious Revolution" of 1688. It also inspired the revolutions that took place in America and in France toward the end of the eighteenth century.

If for Hobbes the state was supreme, for Locke sovereignty rested with the people, and government existed only to protect the natural rights of its citizens. In his first treatise, *On Government* (1689), Locke argued that individuals might attain their maximum development only in a society free from the unnatural restrictions imposed by absolute rulers. In his second treatise, *Of Civil Government* (an excerpt from which follows), Locke expounded the idea that government must rest upon the consent of the governed. While Locke's views were basic to the development

Figure 24.2 JOHN GREENHILL, *Portrait of John Locke*, ca. 1672–1676. Oil on canvas, 22⅛ × 18½ in.

of modern liberal thought, Hobbes' views provided the justification for all forms of tyranny, including the enlightened despotism of such eighteenth-century rulers as Frederick of Prussia and Catherine II of Russia, who claimed that their authority was founded in the general consent of the people. Nevertheless, the notion of government as the product of a social contract between the ruler and the ruled has become one of the dominating ideas of modern Western—and more recently of Eastern European and Asian—political life.

READING 24.2 From Locke's *Of Civil Government*
(1690)

Book II   Chapter II: Of the State of Nature

To understand political power right and derive it from its **1** original, we must consider what state all men are naturally in, and that is a state of perfect freedom to order their actions and dispose of their possessions and persons as they think fit, within the bounds of the law of nature without asking leave or depending upon the will of any other man.

A state also of equality, wherein all the power and jurisdiction is reciprocal, no one having more than another; there being nothing more evident than that creatures of the same species and rank, promiscuously born to all the same **10** advantages of nature and the use of the same faculties, should also be equal one amongst another without subordination or subjection; unless the Lord and Master of them all should, by any manifest declaration of his will, set one above another and confer on him, by an evident and clear appointment, an undoubted right to dominion and sovereignty. . . .

Chapter V: Of Property

God, who hath given the world to men in common, hath also given them reason to make use of it to the best advantage of life and convenience. The earth and all that is therein is given to men for the support and comfort of their being. And though **20** all the fruits it naturally produces and beasts it feeds belong to mankind in common . . ., there must of necessity be a means to appropriate them some way or other before they can be of any use, or at all beneficial to any particular man. . . .

Though the earth and all inferior creatures be common to all men, yet every man has a property in his own person: this nobody has any right to but himself. The labor of his body, and the work of his hands we may say, are properly his. Whatsoever then he removes out of the state that nature has provided and left it in, he has mixed his labor with and joined **30** to it something that is his own, and thereby makes it his property. . . .

Chapter VIII: The Beginning of Political Societies

Men being, as has been said, by nature all free, equal, and independent, no one can be put out of this estate and subjected to the political power of another without his own consent. The only way whereby any one divests himself of his natural liberty and puts on the bonds of civil society is by agreeing with other men to join and unite into a community for their comfortable, safe, and peaceable living one amongst another, in a secure enjoyment of their properties, and a **40** greater security against any that are not of it. This any number of men may do, because it injures not the freedom of the rest; they are left as they were in the liberty of the state of nature. When any number of men have so consented to make one community or government, they are thereby presently incorporated and make one body politic, wherein the majority have a right to act and conclude the rest.

For when any number of men have, by the consent of every individual, made a community, they have thereby made that community one body, with a power to act as one body, which is **50** only by the will and determination of the majority: . . . And therefore we see that in assemblies empowered to act by positive laws, where no number is set by that positive law which empowers them, the act of the majority passes for the act of the whole and of course determines; as having, by the law of nature and reason, the power of the whole.

And thus every man, by consenting with others to make one body politic under one government, puts himself under an obligation to every one of that society to submit to the determination of the majority and to be concluded by it; or else **60** this original compact whereby he with others incorporate into one society, would signify nothing and be no compact if he be left free and under no other ties than he was in before in the state of nature. . . .

Chapter IX: Of the Ends of Political Society and Government

If man in the state of nature be so free as has been said; if he be absolute lord of his own person and possessions, equal to the greatest, and subject to nobody, why will he part with his freedom, why will he give up this empire and subject himself to the dominion and control of any other power? To which it is obvious to answer that though in the state of nature he has **70** such a right, yet the enjoyment of it is very uncertain and constantly exposed to the invasion of others; for all being kings as much as he, every man his equal and the greater part no strict observers of equity and justice, the enjoyment of the property he has in this state is very unsafe, very unsecure. This makes him willing to quit a condition, which, however free, is full of fears and continual dangers: and it is not without reason that he seeks out and is willing to join in society with others who are already united or have a mind to unite for the mutual preservation of their lives, liberties, and estates, which I call by the general **80** name property.

The great and chief end, therefore, of men's uniting into commonwealths, and putting themselves under government, is the preservation of their property. . . .

Chapter XVIII: Of Tyranny

As usurpation is the exercise of power, which another hath a right to, so tyranny is the exercise of power beyond right, which nobody can have a right to. And this is making use of the power any one has in his hands, not for the good of those who are under it, but for his own private, separate advantage—

when the governor, however entitled, makes not the law, but **90** his will, the rule; and his commands and actions are not directed to the preservation of the properties of his people, but [to] the satisfaction of his own ambition, revenge, covetousness, or any other irregular passion. . . .

Wherever law ends, tyranny begins, if the law be transgressed to another's harm; and whosoever in authority exceeds the power given him by the law, and makes use of the force he has under his command, . . . ceases in that to be a [magistrate]; and, acting without authority, may be opposed as any other man who by force invades the right of another. . . . **100**

"May the commands then of a prince be opposed? may he be resisted as often as any one shall find himself aggrieved, and but imagine he has not right done him? This will unhinge and overturn all politics, and, instead of government and order, leave nothing but anarchy and confusion."

To this I answer that force is to be opposed to nothing but to unjust and unlawful force; whoever makes any opposition in any other case, draws on himself a just condemnation both from God and man. . . .

Q Why, according to Locke, are people willing to give up their freedom?

Q What, in Locke's view, is the function of law?

The Influence of Locke on Montesquieu and Jefferson

Locke's political treatises were read widely. So too, his defense of religious toleration (issued even as Louis XIV forced all Calvinists to leave France), his plea for equality of education among men and women, and his arguments for the use of modern languages in place of Latin won the attention of many intellectuals. Published during the last decade of the seventeenth century, these writings became the wellspring of the Enlightenment in both Europe and America.

In France, the keen-minded aristocrat Charles Louis de Secondat Montesquieu (1689–1755) championed Locke's views on political freedom and expanded on his theories. Intrigued by the ways in which nature appeared to govern social behavior, the Baron de Montesquieu investigated the effects of climate and custom on human conduct, thus pioneering the field of sociology. In an elegantly written thousand-page treatise, *The Spirit of the Laws* (1748), Montesquieu defended liberty as the free exercise of the will. He was among the first to condemn slavery as fundamentally "unnatural and evil."

Montesquieu, a proponent of constitutional monarchy, advanced the idea of a separation of powers among the executive, legislative, and judicial agencies of government, advising that each monitor the activities of the others in order to ensure a balanced system of government. He warned that when legislative and executive powers were united in the same person (or body of magistrates), or when judicial power was inseparable from legislative and executive powers, human liberty might be gravely threatened. Montesquieu's system of checks and balances was

later enshrined in the Constitution of the United States of America (1787).

Across the Atlantic, many of Locke's ideas appeared in the preamble to the statement declaring the independence of the North American colonies from the rule of the British king George III. Written by the leading American apostle of the Enlightenment, Thomas Jefferson (1743–1826; Figure **24.3**), and adopted by the Continental Congress on July 4, 1776, the American Declaration of Independence echoes Locke's ideology of revolt as well as his view that governments derive their just powers from the consent of the governed. Following Locke and Montesquieu, Jefferson advocated the establishment of a social contract between ruler and ruled as the principal means of fulfilling natural law—the "unalienable right" to life, liberty, and the pursuit of happiness. While Jefferson did not include "property" among the unalienable rights, he was, as well, fully committed to the individual's right to own land and goods, including slaves.

Figure 24.3 JEAN-ANTOINE HOUDON, *Thomas Jefferson*, 1789. Marble, height 21½ in.

The Right of Revolution

John Locke was among the many intellectuals—ancient and modern—who explored the relationship between individual rights and the well-being of the community. Like most seventeenth-century thinkers, Locke argued for the need for a social contract that protected both the citizen and the commonwealth. Following the Glorious Revolution of 1688, in his treatise, *Of Civil Government*, he tried to provide justification for popular revolt against a tyrannical ruler. Proclaiming that the function of government is the good of mankind, he asks:

> . . . which is best for mankind, that the people should always be exposed to the boundless will of tyranny, or that rulers should be sometimes liable to be opposed when they grow exorbitant in the abuse of their power, and employ it for the destruction and not the preservation of the properties of their people?

Locke's answer defended the use of force to unseat a ruler who, by his violation of the social contract, forfeited the right to rule. The question remains, however, whether, as Hobbes pointed out, the great masses of human beings (if indeed as selfish and competitive as Hobbes described them) should hold the privilege or the authority to forcefully unseat the sovereign. Might the community, as regulated by the decisions of the sovereign, ultimately be better served if the citizens' right to revolt were limited?

READING 24.3 From Jefferson's Declaration of Independence (1776)

When, in the course of human events, it becomes necessary   1
for one people to dissolve the political bands which have
connected them with another, and to assume among the
powers of the earth, the separate and equal station to which
the laws of nature and of nature's God entitle them, a decent
respect to the opinions of mankind requires that they should
declare the causes which impel them to separation.

  We hold these truths to be self-evident: That all men are
created equal; that they are endowed by their Creator with
certain unalienable rights; that among these are life, liberty   10
and the pursuit of happiness; that to secure these rights
governments are instituted among men, deriving their just
powers from the consent of the governed; that whenever any
form of government becomes destructive of these ends, it is
the right of the people to alter or to abolish it, and to institute
new government, laying its foundation on such principles and
organizing its powers in such form, as to them shall seem most
likely to effect their safety and happiness. . . .

   Q **What is meant by "unalienable rights?"**

   Q **How does Jefferson justify revolution?**

The Declaration of Independence made clear the founding fathers' belief in equality among men. Equality between the sexes was, however, another matter: although both Locke and Jefferson acknowledged that women held the same natural rights as men, they did not consider women—or slaves, or children, for that matter—capable of exercising such rights. Recognizing this bias, Abigail Adams (d. 1818) wrote to her husband, John, who was serving as a delegate to the Second Continental Congress (1777), as follows:

> I . . . hear that you have declared an independency, and, by the way, in the new code of laws which I suppose it will be necessary for you to make, I desire you would remember the ladies and be more generous and favorable to them than were your ancestors. Do not put such unlimited power into the hands of husbands. Remember all men would be tyrants if they could. If particular care and attention are not paid to the ladies we are determined to foment a rebellion, and will not hold ourselves bound to obey any laws in which we have no voice or representation.

Despite the future First Lady's spirited admonitions, however, American women did not secure the legal right to vote or to hold political office until well into the twentieth century.

  If the Declaration of Independence constituted a clear expression of Enlightenment theory in justifying revolution against tyrannical rule, the Constitution of the new United States of America represented the practical outcome of the revolution: the creation of a viable new nation with its government based ultimately on Enlightenment principles. The U.S. Constitution, framed in 1787 and ratified by popular vote in 1788–1789, articulated the mechanics of self-rule. First, it created a form of government new to the modern world: a system of representative government embodying the principle of "Republicanism," that is, government run by the elected representatives of the people. Second, following the precepts of Montesquieu, the framers of the Constitution divided the new government into three branches—legislative, executive, and judicial—each to be "checked and balanced" by the others to prevent the possible tyranny of any one branch. Third, the new republic was granted sufficient power to govern primarily through the authority granted the president to execute national laws and constitutional provisions. Withal, the U.S. Constitution would prove effective for over two centuries, and would serve as the model for the constitutions of almost all the newborn republics created throughout the world.

The Birth of Economic Theory

While Enlightenment thinkers were primarily concerned with matters of political equality, they also addressed questions related to the economy of the modern state. The Scottish philosopher Adam Smith (1723–1790) applied the idea of natural law to the domains of human labor, productivity, and the exchange of goods. His epoch-making synthesis of ethics and economics, *An Inquiry into the Nature and Causes of the Wealth of Nations*, set forth the "laws" of labor, production, and trade with an exhaustiveness reminiscent of Newton's *Principia Mathematica* (see chapter 23).

Smith contended that labor, a condition natural to humankind (as Locke had observed), was the foundation for prosperity. A nation's wealth is not its land or its money, said Smith, but its labor force. In the "natural" economic order, individual self-interest guides the progress of economic life, and certain natural forces, such as the "law of supply and demand," motivate a market economy. Since government interference would infringe on the natural order, reasoned Smith, such interference is undesirable. He thus opposed all artificial restraints on economic progress and all forms of government regulation and control.

The modern concepts of free enterprise and *laissez-faire* (literally, "allow to act") economics spring from Smith's incisive formulations. In the following excerpt, Smith examines the origin of the division of labor among human beings and defends the natural and unimpeded operation of trade and competition among nations.

READING 24.4 From Smith's *An Inquiry into the Nature and Causes of the Wealth of Nations* (1776)

Book I   Chapter II: The Principle which Occasions the Division of Labor

[The] division of labor, from which so many advantages are   1
derived, is not originally the effect of any human wisdom, which
foresees and intends that general opulence to which it gives
occasion. It is the necessary, though very slow and gradual,
consequence of a certain propensity in human nature which has
in view no such extensive utility; the propensity to truck, barter, and
exchange one thing for another.

. . . . [This propensity] is common to all men, and to be found
in no other race of animals, which seem to know neither this
nor any other species of contracts. Two greyhounds, in running   10
down the same hare, have sometimes the appearance of acting
in some sort of concert. Each turns her towards his companion,
or endeavors to intercept her when his companion turns her
towards himself. This, however, is not the effect of any
contract, but of the accidental concurrence of their passions in
the same object at that particular time. Nobody ever saw a dog
make a fair and deliberate exchange of one bone for another
with another dog. . . . In almost every other race of animals
each individual, when it is grown up to maturity, is entirely
independent, and in its natural state has occasion for the   20
assistance of no other living creature. But man has almost
constant occasion for the help of his brethren, and it is in vain
for him to expect it from their benevolence only. He will be more
likely to prevail if he can interest their self-love in his favor, and
show them that it is for their own advantage to do for him what
he requires of them. Whoever offers to another a bargain of any

kind, proposes to do this. Give me that which I want, and you
shall have this which you want, is the meaning of every such
offer; and it is in this manner that we obtain from one another
the far greater part of those good offices which we stand in   30
need of. It is not from the benevolence of the butcher, the
brewer, or the baker, that we expect our dinner, but from their
regard to their own interest. We address ourselves, not to their
humanity, but to their self-love; and never talk to them of our
own necessities, but of their advantages. . . .

As it is by treaty, by barter, and by purchase, that we obtain
from one another the greater part of those mutual good offices
which we stand in need of, so it is this same trucking
disposition which originally gives occasion to the division of
labor. In a tribe of hunters or shepherds a particular person   40
makes bows and arrows, for example, with more readiness and
dexterity than any other. He frequently exchanges them for
cattle or for venison with his companions; and he finds at last
that he can in this manner get more cattle and venison, than if
he himself went to the field to catch them. From a regard to his
own interest, therefore, the making of bows and arrows grows
to be his chief business. . . .

Book IV   Chapter III, Part II: Of the Unreasonableness of Restraints [on Trade]

Nations have been taught that their interest consisted in
beggaring all their neighbors. Each nation has been made to
look with an invidious eye upon the prosperity of all the   50
nations with which it trades, and to consider their gain as its
own loss. Commerce, which ought naturally to be, among
nations as among individuals, a bond of union and friendship,
has become the most fertile source of discord and animosity.
The capricious ambition of kings and ministers has not, during
the present and the preceding century, been more fatal to the
repose of Europe, than the impertinent jealousy of merchants
and manufacturers. The violence and injustice of the rulers of
mankind is an ancient evil, for which, I am afraid, the nature of
human affairs can scarce admit of a remedy. But the mean   60
rapacity, the monopolizing spirit of merchants and
manufacturers, who neither are, nor ought to be, the rulers of
mankind, though it cannot perhaps be corrected, may very
easily be prevented from disturbing the tranquility of anybody
but themselves.

That it was the spirit of monopoly which originally both
invented and propagated this doctrine, cannot be doubted; and
they who first taught it were by no means such fools as they
who believed it. In every country it always is and must be the
interest of the great body of the people to buy whatever they   70
want of those who sell it cheapest. The proposition is so very
manifest, that it seems ridiculous to take any pains to prove it;
nor could it ever have been called in question had not the
interested sophistry of merchants and manufacturers
confounded the common sense of mankind. Their interest is, in
this respect, directly opposed to that of the great body of the
people. . . .

The wealth of a neighboring nation, though dangerous in
war and politics, is certainly advantageous in trade. In a state
of hostility it may enable our enemies to maintain fleets and   80
armies superior to our own; but in a state of peace and

commerce it must likewise enable them to exchange with us to a greater value and to afford a better market, either for the immediate produce of our own industry or for whatever is purchased with that produce. As a rich man is likely to be a better customer to the industrious people in his neighborhood, than a poor, so is likewise a rich nation. . . .

Q **What natural forces dominate the economic life of the nation, according to Smith?**

Q **Would you consider Smith a Realist or an Idealist?**

The *Philosophes*

When Louis XIV died in 1715, the French nobility fled the palace of Versailles and settled in fashionable Paris townhouses. Socially ambitious noblewomen, many of whom championed a freer and more public role for their gender, organized gatherings in the *salons* of these town homes. Here, nobility and middle-class thinkers met to exchange views on morality, politics, science, and religion and to voice opinions on everything ranging from diet to the latest fashions in theater and dress. Inevitably, as new ideas began to circulate in these meetings, Paris became the center of intellectual life (see Figure 24.1). The well-educated individuals who graced the *salons* came to be known as *philosophes* (the French word for "philosophers"). Intellectuals rather than philosophers in the strictest sense of the term, the *philosophes* dominated the literary activity of the Enlightenment. Like the humanists of fifteenth-century Florence, their interests were mainly secular and social. Unlike their Renaissance counterparts, however, the *philosophes* scorned all forms of authority—they believed that they had surpassed the ancients, and they looked beyond the present state of knowledge to the establishment of a superior moral and social order.

Most *philosophes* held to the deist view of God as Creator and providential force behind nature and natural law, rather than as personal Redeemer. They believed in the immortality of the soul, not out of commitment to any religious doctrine, but because they regarded human beings as fundamentally different from other living creatures. They viewed the Bible as mythology rather than as revealed truth, and scorned church hierarchy and ritual. Their antipathy to irrationality, superstition, and religious dogma (as reflected, for instance, in the Catholic doctrine of Original Sin) alienated them from the Church and set them at odds with the established authorities—a position memorably expressed in Voltaire's acerbic pronouncement: "men will not be free until the last king is strangled with the entrails of the last priest." The quest for a nonauthoritarian, secular morality led the *philosophes* to challenge all existing forms of intolerance, inequality, and injustice. The banner cry of the *philosophes*, "Ecrasez l'infame" ("Wipe out all evils"), sparked a commitment to social reforms that provoked the French Revolution (see chapter 25).

Science and Technology

1702	the world's first daily newspaper is published in England
1704	the first alphabetical encyclopedia in English is printed
1714	a London engineer patents the first known typewriter
1765	Diderot's *Encyclopédie* is issued in seventeen volumes

Diderot and the *Encyclopédie*

The reforming ideals of the Enlightenment were summed up in a monumental literary endeavor to which many of the *philosophes* contributed: the thirty-five-volume *Encyclopédie* (including eleven volumes of engraved plates), edited by Denis Diderot (1713–1784; Figure **24.4**), and published between 1751 and 1772. Modeled on the two-volume Chambers' Encyclopedia printed in England in 1751, Diderot's *Encyclopédie*—also known as *The Analytical Dictionary of the Sciences, Arts, and Crafts*—was

Figure 24.4 JEAN-ANTOINE HOUDON, *Diderot*, 1773. Marble, height 20⅞ in.

the largest compendium of contemporary social, philosophic, artistic, scientific, and technological knowledge ever produced in the West. A collection of "all the knowledge scattered over the face of the earth," as Diderot explained, it manifested the zealous desire of the *philosophes* to dispel human ignorance and transform society. It was also, in part, a response to rising literacy and to the widespread public interest in the facts of everyday life. Not all members of society welcomed the enterprise, however: King Louis XV claimed that the *Encyclopédie* was doing "irreparable damage to morality and religion." Although the crown twice banned its printing, some volumes were published and distributed secretly.

Diderot's *Encyclopédie* was the most ambitious and influential literary undertaking of the eighteenth century. Almost 200 individuals contributed 72,000 entries on subjects ranging from political theory, cultural history, and art criticism to the technology of theater machinery, the making of silk stockings, and the varieties of wigs (Figure 24.5). Articles on Islam, India, and China indicate a more than idle curiosity about civilizations that remained to most Westerners remote and exotic. Diderot enlisted as contributors to the *Encyclopédie* the most progressive minds of the Enlightenment: François Marie Arouet (1694–1778), known as Voltaire, wrote on "matters of nature and art"; the French philosopher and educator Jean-Jacques Rousseau (1712–1778; see chapter 25) provided articles on music; François Quesnay wrote on political economy; Montesquieu (whose articles were published posthumously) examined the different types of government; Jean Le Rond d'Alembert (1717–1783) treated the subject of higher education; and Diderot himself prepared numerous entries on art and politics.

The *Encyclopédie* remains a monument to secular knowledge and to the Enlightenment faith in the promise of reason—a spirit summed up in Voltaire's proclamation, "Let the facts prevail." The following excerpts come from the entry on natural law written by the French lawyer Antoine-Gaspart Boucher d'Argis and from the long article on black Africans written by Le Romain (first name and dates unknown).

Figure 24.5 *Wigs*, a plate from the *Encyclopédie* illustrating the varieties of men's wigs that were fashionable in Europe in the 1750s.

READING 24.5 From the *Encyclopédie* (1751–1772)

Law of Nature or Natural Law

In its broadest sense the term is taken to designate certain 1
principles which nature alone inspires and which all animals as well as all men have in common. On this law are based the union of male and female, the begetting of children as well as their education, love of liberty, self-preservation, concern for self-defense.

It is improper to call the behavior of animals natural law, for, not being endowed with reason, they can know neither law nor justice.

More commonly we understand by natural law certain laws 10
of justice and equity which only natural reason has established among men, or better, which God has engraved in our hearts.

The fundamental principles of law and all justice are: to live honestly, not to give offense to anyone, and to render unto each whatever is his. From these general principles derive a great many particular rules which nature alone, that is, reason and equity, suggest to mankind.

Since this natural law is based on such fundamental principles, it is perpetual and unchangeable: no agreement can debase it, no law can alter it or exempt anyone from the 20
obligation it imposes. . . .

The principles of natural law, therefore, form part of the law of nations, particularly the primitive law of nations; they also form part of public and of private law: for the principles of natural law, which we have stated, are the purest source of the foundation of most of private and public law. . . .

The authority of natural laws stems from the fact that they owe their existence to God. Men submit to them because to observe them leads to the happiness of men and society. This is a truth demonstrated by reason. It is equally true that virtue 30
by itself is a principle of inner satisfaction whereas vice is a principle of unrest and trouble. It is equally certain that virtue produces great external advantage, while vice produces great ills. . . .

Negroes[1]

For the last few centuries the Europeans have carried on a trade in Negroes whom they obtain from Guinea and other coasts of Africa and whom they use to maintain the colonies established in various parts of America and in the West Indies. To justify this loathsome commerce, which is contrary to

---

[1] A term originally used by the Spanish and Portuguese to identify black Africans.

natural law, it is argued that ordinarily these slaves find the salvation of their souls in the loss of their liberty, and that the Christian teaching they receive, together with their indispensable role in the cultivation of sugar cane, tobacco, indigo, etc., softens the apparent inhumanity of a commerce where men buy and sell their fellow men as they would animals used in the cultivation of the land.

Trade in Negroes is carried on by all the nations which have settlements in the West Indies, and especially by the French, the English, the Portuguese, the Dutch, the Swedes, and the Danes. The Spaniards, in spite of the fact that they possess the greatest part of the Americas, have no direct way of acquiring slaves but have concluded treaties with other nations to furnish them with Negroes. . . .

As soon as the trade is completed no time must be lost in setting sail. Experience has shown that as long as these unfortunates are still within sight of their homeland, they are overcome by sorrow and gripped by despair. The former is the cause of many illnesses from which a large number perish during the crossing; the latter inclines them to suicide, which they effect either by refusing nourishment or by shutting off their breathing. This they do in a way they know of turning and twisting their tongues which unfailingly suffocates them. Others again shatter their head against the sides of the ship or throw themselves into the sea if the occasion presents itself. . . .

Punishment of the Negroes, policing, and regulations concerning these matters:

If the Negro commits a slight offense the overseer may on his own responsibility punish him with a few strokes of the whip. If, however, it is a serious matter, the master has the culprit clapped in irons and then decides the number of strokes with which he will be punished. If all men were equally just, these necessary punishments would be kept within limits, but it often happens that certain masters abuse the authority which they claim over their slaves and chastise these unfortunates too harshly. Yet the masters themselves may be responsible for the situation which led to the offense. To put an end to the cruelties of these barbarous men who would be capable of leaving their slaves without the basic necessities of life while driving them to forced labor, the officers of His Majesty, who are resident in the colonies, have the responsibility of enforcing the edict of the king, which is called the Black Code. In the French islands of America this code regulates the governing and the administration of justice and of the police, as well as the discipline of the slaves and the slave-trade. . . .

Q What is the relationship between natural law and reason?

Q How is slavery assessed in this reading?

Madame du Châtelet

Although women contributed moral and financial support to the *Encyclopédie*, none was invited to participate in its production. Moreover, not one of the thirty-one entries on women makes reference to the contributions of exceptional eighteenth-century women such as Gabrielle-Emilie Le Tonnelier de Breteuil, the Marquise du Châtelet (1706–1749). An impeccable scholar and a brilliant mathematician, Madame du Châtelet produced an annotated French translation of Newton's *Principia*—a monumental achievement that was near completion when she died, a few days after giving birth to her fourth child.

Proficient in Latin, Italian, and English, the marquise translated the works of Virgil, Horace, and Ovid into eloquent French; she wrote original poetry and conducted experiments in physics and chemistry. She was a reckless gambler, a feminist, a champion of the fashionably low-cut neckline (Figure **24.6**), and the mistress of Voltaire, who lived at her *château* until her death in 1749. As a woman, du Châtelet was deprived of education by the formal secondary schools that welcomed men. Nonetheless, she received independent instruction from some of Paris' most notable scholars, beginning lessons in advanced geometry and algebra at the age of twenty-six, and eventually becoming a respected authority in both of these fields, as well as in physics and calculus. Voltaire confessed that he could hardly live without the marquise, whose intellectual achievements, he insisted, qualified her as "a great man."

The Encyclopedic Cast of Mind

The *Encyclopédie* had an enormous impact on eighteenth-century culture. Although it was read and understood by few, it fostered an encyclopedic cast of mind. Its emphasis on the accumulation, codification, and systematic preservation of knowledge was, in part, a response to the

Figure 24.6 NICOLAS DE LARGILLIÈRE, *Gabrielle-Emilie Le Tonnelier de Breteuil, Marquise du Châtelet*, ca. 1740. Oil on canvas, 4 ft. 3½ in. × 3 ft. 4¼ in. Du Châtelet was the first woman whose writings were published by the French Royal Academy of Sciences. Managing a household, a husband, her children, and a series of lovers, she was forced to pursue her own work between midnight and five a.m.

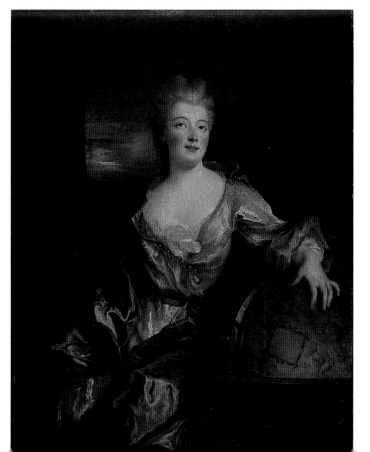

Scientific Revolution and to that other Enlightenment "bible," Newton's *Principia*.

Eighteenth-century scientists made notable advances in the fields of chemistry, electricity, biology, and the medical sciences. They produced the mercury thermometer and the stethoscope and introduced the science of immunology to the West—some seven centuries after the Chinese had invented the first inoculations against smallpox. Antoine Lavoisier (1743–1794) published the *Elementary Treatise of Chemistry* (1789) and launched chemistry as an exact science. The Swede Carolus Linnaeus (1707–1778) produced a systematic method for classifying plants, and the French naturalist Georges Louis Leclerc, Comte de Buffon (1707–1788), made landmark advances in zoology.

Valuable efforts to accumulate and classify knowledge took place in the arts as well. The English critic and poet Samuel Johnson (1709–1784) published the first dictionary of the English language and Rousseau produced the first Western dictionary of music. In the social sciences, Voltaire's seven-volume general history (published in 1756), which included a monumental account of the age of Louis XIV, provided a model for a new universal and rationalist kind of history-writing. Voltaire was among the first to recognize Europe's debt to Arab science and Asian thought. He rejected faith-based explanations of the past and was generally critical of the role played by the Catholic Church in Western history. But it fell to the English historian Edward Gibbon (1737–1794) to provide the rationale that blamed Christianity for contributing to the collapse of Rome. *The Decline and Fall of the Roman Empire* (1776) was the product of Gibbon's unique interpretation of the sociological forces that shaped ancient cultures.

Eighteenth-century China lay beyond the immediate influence of the European Enlightenment; nevertheless, in the East an encyclopedic impulse similar to that prevailing in the West came to a climax at this time. Qing rulers followed their Ming predecessors in directing groups of scholars to assemble exhaustive collections of information, some filling as many as 36,000 manuscript volumes. These "encyclopedias" were actually anthologies of the writings of former Chinese artists and scholars, rather than comprehensive collections of contemporary knowledge. Nevertheless, as in France, some of China's rulers deemed the indiscriminate accumulation of information itself dangerous, and at least one eighteenth-century Qing emperor authorized the official burning of thousands of books.

The Crusade for Progress

Leibniz and Beccaria

Among European intellectuals, the belief in the reforming powers of reason became the basis for a progressive view of human history. The German mathematician and philosopher Gottfried Wilhelm Leibniz (1646–1716) systematically defended the view that human beings live in perfect harmony with God and nature. Leibniz linked optimism to the logic of probability: his *principle of sufficient reason* held, simply, that there must be a reason or purpose for

everything in nature. In response to the question, Why does evil exist in a world created by a good God? Leibniz answered that all events conformed to the preestablished harmony of the universe. Even evil, according to Leibniz, was necessary in a world that was "better than any other possible world"—a position that came to be called "philosophic optimism."

For the *philosophes*, the key to social reform lay in a true understanding of human nature which, they argued, might best be acquired by examining human history. They viewed, for instance, the transition from Paleolithic hunting and gathering to the rise of urban civilization as clear evidence of the steady march toward social improvement. Faith in the reality of that march motivated the Enlightenment crusade for progress. The Italian lawyer and social reformer Cesare de Beccaria (1738–1794) enlisted in this crusade when he wrote his treatise *On Crimes and Punishments*. Here, for instance, he suggested that torturing criminals did not work to deter crime. Rather, argued Beccaria, society should seek methods by which to rehabilitate those who commit crimes. Although Beccaria's publication generated no immediate changes, it went through six editions in eighteen months and ultimately contributed to movements for prison reform in Europe and the United States. The questions that Beccaria raised concerning the value of punishment are still being debated today.

Condorcet

The most passionate warrior in the Enlightenment crusade for progress was the French aristocrat Antoine Nicolas de Condorcet (1743–1794). Condorcet was a mathematician, a social theorist, and a political moderate amidst revolutionary extremists. His *Sketch for a Historical Picture of the Progress of the Human Mind*, written during the early days of the French Revolution, was the preface to a longer work he never completed—he committed suicide shortly after being imprisoned as an "enemy" of the revolution.

Condorcet believed that human nature could be perfected through the application of reason. All errors in politics and morals, he argued, were based in philosophic and scientific errors. "There is not a religious system nor a supernatural extravagance," he wrote, "that is not founded on ignorance of the laws of nature." Fiercely optimistic about the future of humankind, Condorcet was one of the first male champions of sexual equality. He called for the "complete annihilation of the prejudices that have brought about an inequality of rights between the sexes, an inequality fatal even to the party in whose favor it works." Such inequality, he protested, "has its origin solely in an abuse of strength, and all the later sophistical attempts that have been made to excuse it are vain."

In his *Sketch*, the visionary Condorcet traced the "progress" of humankind through ten stages, from ignorance and tyranny to the threshold of enlightenment and equality. The utopian tenth stage, subtitled "The Future Progress of the Human Mind" (an excerpt from which follows), sets forth ideas that were well ahead of their time,

Map 24.1 The Intellectual Revolution of the Seventeenth and Eighteenth Centuries in Western Europe.

such as a guaranteed livelihood for the aged, a universal system of education, fewer work hours, and the refinement of a technology for the accumulation of knowledge. (How digital computers would have delighted this prophet of the Information Age!) The educational goals that Condorcet outlines toward the end of the excerpt still carry the force of sound judgment.

READING 24.6 From Condorcet's *Sketch for a Historical Picture of the Progress of the Human Mind*
(1793)

If man can, with almost complete assurance, predict 1
phenomena when he knows their laws, and if, even when
he does not, he can still, with great expectation of success,
forecast the future on the basis of his experience of the

past, why, then, should it be regarded as a fantastic
undertaking to sketch, with some pretense to truth, the
future destiny of man on the basis of his history? The sole
foundation for belief in the natural sciences is this idea
that the general laws directing the phenomena of the universe,
known or unknown, are necessary
and constant. Why should this principle be any less true for the 10
development of the intellectual and moral faculties of man
than for the other operations of nature? Since beliefs founded
on past experience of like conditions provide the only rule of
conduct for the wisest of men, why should the philosopher be
forbidden to base his conjectures on these same foundations,
so long as he does not attribute to them a certainty superior to
that warranted by the number, the constancy, and the accuracy
of his observations? . . .

The time will therefore come when the sun will shine only
on free men who know no other master but their reason; when 20

tyrants and slaves, priests and their stupid or hypocritical instruments will exist only in works of history and on the stage; and when we shall think of them only to pity their victims and their dupes; to maintain ourselves in a state of vigilance by thinking on their excesses; and to learn how to recognize and so to destroy, by force of reason, the first seeds of tyranny and superstition, should they ever dare to reappear among us.

In looking at the history of societies we shall have had occasion to observe that there is often a great difference between the rights that the law allows its citizens and the   30 rights that they actually enjoy, and, again, between the equality established by political codes and that which in fact exists among individuals. . . .

These differences have three main causes: inequality in wealth, inequality in status between the man whose means of subsistence are hereditary and the man whose means are dependent on the length of his life, or, rather, on that part of his life in which he is capable of work; and, finally, inequality in education.

We therefore need to show that these three sorts of real   40 inequality must constantly diminish without however disappearing altogether: for they are the result of natural and necessary causes which it would be foolish and dangerous to wish to eradicate. . . .

[As to education] we can teach the citizen everything that he needs to know in order to be able to manage his household, administer his affairs, and employ his labor and his faculties in freedom; to know his rights and to be able to exercise them; to be acquainted with his duties and fulfill them satisfactorily; to judge his own and other men's actions according to his own   50 lights and to be a stranger to none of the high and delicate feelings which honor human nature; not to be in a state of blind dependence upon those to whom he must entrust his affairs or the exercise of his rights; to be in a proper condition to choose and supervise them; to be no longer the dupe of those popular errors which torment man with superstitious fears and chimerical hopes; to defend himself against prejudice by the strength of his reason alone; and, finally, to escape the deceits of charlatans who would lay snares for his fortune, his health, his freedom of thought, and his conscience under the pretext of   60 granting him health, wealth, and salvation. . . .

The real advantages that should result from this progress, of which we can entertain a hope that is almost a certainty, can have no other term than that of the absolute perfection of the human race; since, as the various kinds of equality come to

work in its favor by producing ampler sources of supply, more extensive education, more complete liberty, so equality will be more real and will embrace everything which is really of importance for the happiness of human beings. . . .

Q In what ways does this reading illustrate the optimism of Enlightenment thought?

Q What, according to Condorcet, are the three main causes of social discord?

Enlightenment and the Rights of Women

While Condorcet was among the first moderns to champion the equality of the sexes, his efforts pale before the impassioned defense of women launched by Mary Wollstonecraft (1759–1797; Figure **24.7**). This self-educated British intellectual applied Enlightenment principles of natural law, liberty, and equality to forge a radical rethinking of the roles and responsibilities of women in Western society. In *A Vindication of the Rights of Woman*, Wollstonecraft attacked the persistence of the female stereotype (docile, domestic, and childlike) as formulated by misguided, misogynistic, and tyrannical males, who, as she complained, "try to secure the good conduct of women by attempting to keep them in a state of childhood." Calling for a "revolution of female manners," she criticized the "disorderly kind of education" received by women, who, owing to their domestic roles, learn "rather by snatches."

Figure 24.7 JOHN OPIE, *Mary Wollstonecraft*, ca. 1797. Oil on canvas, 29½ in. × 24½ in. The author of the cornerstone treatise for women's liberation, Wollstonecraft was reviled by one of her male contemporaries as "a hyena in petticoats."

Wollstonecraft emphasized the importance of reason in the cultivation of virtue, observing that, "it is a farce to call any being virtuous whose virtues do not result from the exercise of its own reason." She criticized women for embracing their roles in "the great art of pleasing [men]." The minds of women, she insisted, were enfeebled by "false refinement," sweet docility," and "slavish dependence."

Despite her high degree of critical acumen, however, Wollstonecraft seems to have been deeply conflicted by her own personal efforts to reconcile her sexual passions, her need for independence, and her free-spirited will. Her affair with an American speculator and timber merchant produced an illegitimate child and at least two attempts at suicide; and her marriage to the novelist William Godwin (subsequent to her becoming pregnant by him) proved no less turbulent. She died at the age of thirty-eight, following the birth of their daughter, the future Mary Shelley (see chapter 28). In contrast with her short and troubled life, Wollstonecraft's treatise has enjoyed sustained and significant influence; it stands at the threshold of the modern movement for female equality.

READING 24.7 From Wollstonecraft's *A Vindication of the Rights of Woman* (1792)

After considering the historic page, and viewing the living world with anxious solicitude, the most melancholy emotions of sorrowful indignation have depressed my spirits, and I have sighed when obliged to confess, that either nature has made a great difference between man and man, or that the civilization which has hitherto taken place in the world has been very partial. I have turned over various books written on the subject of education, and patiently observed the conduct of parents and the management of schools; but what has been the result?—a profound conviction that the neglected education of my fellow-creatures is the grand source of the misery I deplore; and that women, in particular, are rendered weak and wretched by a variety of concurring causes, originating from one hasty conclusion. The conduct and manners of women, in fact, evidently prove that their minds are not in a healthy state; for, like the flowers which are planted in too rich a soil, strength and usefulness are sacrificed to beauty; and the flaunting leaves, after having pleased a fastidious eye, fade, disregarded on the stalk, long before the season when they ought to have arrived at maturity.—One cause of this barren blooming I attribute to a false system of education, gathered from the books written on this subject by men who, considering females rather as women than human creatures, have been more anxious to make them alluring mistresses than affectionate wives and rational mothers and the understanding of the sex has been so bubbled by this specious homage, that the civilized women of the present century, with a few exceptions, are only anxious to inspire love, when they ought to cherish a nobler ambition, and by their abilities and virtues exact respect.

In a treatise, therefore, on female rights and manners, the works which have been particularly written for their improvement must not be overlooked; especially when it is asserted, in direct terms, that the minds of women are enfeebled by false refinement; that the books of instruction, written by men of genius, have had the same tendency as more frivolous productions; and that, in the true style of Mahometanism,[1] they are treated as a kind of subordinate beings, and not as a part of the human species, when improveable reason is allowed to be the dignified distinction which raises men above the brute creation, and puts a natural sceptre in a feeble hand.

Yet, because I am a woman, I would not lead my readers to suppose that I mean violently to agitate the contested question respecting the equality or inferiority of the sex; but as the subject lies in my way, and I cannot pass it over without subjecting the main tendency of my reasoning to misconstruction, I shall stop a moment to deliver, in a few words, my opinion.—In the government of the physical world it is observable that the female in point of strength is, in general, inferior to the male. This is the law of nature; and it does not appear to be suspended or abrogated in favour of woman. A degree of physical superiority cannot, therefore, be denied—and it is a noble prerogative! But not content with this natural preeminence, men endeavour to sink us still lower, merely to render us alluring objects for a moment; and women, intoxicated by the adoration which men, under the influence of their senses, pay to them, do not seek to obtain a durable interest in their hearts, or to become the friends of the fellow creatures who find amusement in their society. . . .

My own sex, I hope, will excuse me, if I treat them like rational creatures, instead of flattering their *fascinating* graces, and viewing them as if they were in a state of perpetual childhood, unable to stand alone. I earnestly wish to point out in what true dignity and human happiness consists—I wish to persuade women to endeavour to acquire strength, both of mind and body, and to convince them that the soft phrases, susceptibility of heart, delicacy of sentiment, and refinement of taste, are almost synonymous with epithets of weakness, and that those beings who are only the objects of pity and that kind of love, which has been termed its sister, will soon become objects of contempt.

Dismissing then those pretty feminine phrases, which the men condescendingly use to soften our slavish dependence, and despising that weak elegancy of mind, exquisite sensibility, and sweet docility of manners, supposed to be the sexual characteristics of the weaker vessel, I wish to shew that elegance is inferior to virtue, that the first object of laudable ambition is to obtain a character as a human being, regardless of the distinction of sex; and that secondary views should be brought to this simple touchstone. . . .

The education of women has, of late, been more attended to than formerly; yet they are still reckoned a frivolous sex, and ridiculed or pitied by the writers who endeavour by satire or instruction to improve them. It is acknowledged that they

1
10
20
30
40
50
60
70
80

---

[1] A reference to the widespread Christian misconception that Islam denied that women had souls.

spend many of the first years of their lives in acquiring a smattering of accomplishments; meanwhile strength of body and mind are sacrificed to libertine notions of beauty, to the desire of establishing themselves,—the only way women can rise in the world,—by marriage. And this desire making mere animals of them, when they marry they act as such children may be expected to act:—they dress; they paint, and nickname God's creatures.—Surely these weak beings are only fit for a seraglio! Can they be expected to govern a family with judgment, or take care of the poor babes whom they bring into the world?

If then it can be fairly deduced from the present conduct of the sex, from the prevalent fondness for pleasure which takes place of ambition and those nobler passions that open and enlarge the soul; that the instruction which women have hitherto received has only tended, with the constitution of civil society, to render them insignificant objects of desire—mere propagators of fools!—if it can be proved that in aiming to accomplish them, without cultivating their understandings, they are taken out of their sphere of duties, and made ridiculous and useless when the short-lived bloom of beauty is over, I presume that *rational* men will excuse me for endeavouring to persuade them to become more masculine and respectable. . . .

In the present state of society it appears necessary to go back to first principles in search of the most simple truths, and to dispute with some prevailing prejudice every inch of ground. To clear my way, I must be allowed to ask some plain questions, and the answers will probably appear as unequivocal as the axioms on which reasoning is built; though, when entangled with various motives of action, they are formally contradicted, either by the words or conduct of men.

In what does man's pre-eminence over the brute creation consist? The answer is as clear as that a half is less than the whole; in Reason.

What acquirement exalts one being above another? Virtue; we spontaneously reply.

For what purpose were the passions implanted? That man by struggling with them might attain a degree of knowledge denied to the brutes; whispers Experience.

Consequently the perfection of our nature and capability of happiness, must be estimated by the degree of reason, virtue, and knowledge, that distinguish the individual, and direct the laws which bind society: and that from the exercise of reason, knowledge and virtue naturally flow, is equally undeniable, if mankind be viewed collectively.

The rights and duties of man thus simplified, it seems almost impertinent to attempt to illustrate truths that appear so incontrovertible; yet such deeply rooted prejudices have clouded reason, and such spurious qualities have assumed the name of virtues, that it is necessary to pursue the course of reason as it has been perplexed and involved in error, by various adventitious circumstances, comparing the simple axiom with casual deviations. Men, in general, seem to employ their reason to justify prejudices, which they have imbibed, they can scarcely trace how, rather than to root them out. The mind must be strong that resolutely forms its own principles; for a kind of intellectual cowardice prevails which makes many

men shrink from the task, or only do it by halves. . . .

Many are the causes that, in the present corrupt state of society, contribute to enslave women by cramping their understandings and sharpening their senses. One, perhaps, that silently does more mischief than all the rest, is their disregard of order.

To do every thing in an orderly manner, is a most important precept, which women, who, generally speaking, receive only a disorderly kind of education, seldom attend to with that degree of exactness that men, who from their infancy are broken into method, observe. This negligent kind of guesswork, for what other epithet can be used to point out the random exertions of a sort of instinctive common sense, never brought to the test of reason? prevents their generalizing matters of fact—so they do to-day, what they did yesterday, merely because they did it yesterday.

This contempt of the understanding in early life has more baneful consequences that is commonly supposed; for the little knowledge which women of strong minds attain, is, from various circumstances, of a more desultory kind than the knowledge of men, and it is acquired more by sheer observations on real life, than from comparing what has been individually observed with the results of experience generalized by speculation. Led by their dependent situation and domestic employments more into society, what they learn is rather by snatches; and as learning is with them, in general, only a secondary thing, they do not pursue any one branch with that persevering ardour necessary to give vigour to the faculties, and clearness to the judgment. In the present state of society, a little learning is required to support the character of a gentleman; and boys are obliged to submit to a few years of discipline. But in the education of women, the cultivation of the understanding is always subordinate to the acquirement of some corporeal accomplishment; even while enervated by confinement and false notions of modesty, the body is prevented from attaining that grace and beauty which relaxed half-formed limbs never exhibit. Besides, in youth their faculties are not brought forward by emulation; and having no serious scientific study, if they have natural sagacity it is turned too soon on life and manners. . . .

Strengthen the female mind by enlarging it, and there will be an end to blind obedience; but, as blind obedience is ever sought for by power, tyrants and sensualists are in the right when they endeavour to keep women in the dark, because the former only want slaves, and the latter a play-thing. The sensualist, indeed, has been the most dangerous of tyrants, and women have been duped by their lovers, as princes by their ministers, whilst dreaming that they reigned over them. . . .

It appears to me necessary to dwell on these obvious truths, because females have been insulated, as it were; and, while they have been stripped of the virtues that should clothe humanity, they have been decked with artificial graces that enable them to exercise a short-lived tyranny. Love, in their bosoms, taking place of every nobler passion, their sole ambition is to be fair, to raise emotion instead of inspiring respect; and this ignoble desire, like the servility in absolute monarchies, destroys all strength of character. Liberty is the mother of virtue, and if women be, by their very constitution, slaves, and not allowed to breathe the sharp invigorating air of freedom, they must ever languish like exotics, and be reckoned beautiful flaws in nature. . . .

Make [women] free, and they will quickly become wise and virtuous, as men become more so; for the improvements must be mutual, or the injustice which one half of the human race are obliged to submit to, retorting on their oppressors, the **210** virtue of men will be worm-eaten by the insects whom he keeps under his feet.

Let men take their choice, man and woman were made for each other, though not to become one being; and if they will not improve women, they will deprave them!

— Q **What does Wollstonecraft mean by "a false system of education?"**

— Q **How does this system contribute to the plight of women?**

Enlightenment Literature

The Journalistic Essay

As the writings of Condorcet and Wollstonecraft suggest, social criticism assumed an important place in Enlightenment thought. Such criticism now also manifested itself in a new literary genre: the journalistic essay. Designed to address the middle-class reading public, prose essays and editorials were the stuff of magazines and daily newspapers.

The first daily emerged in London during the eighteenth century, although a weekly had been published since 1642. At this time, London, with a population of some three-quarters of a million people, was the largest European city, and England claimed the highest rate of literacy in Western Europe. With the rise of newspapers and periodicals, the "poetic" prose of the seventeenth century—characterized by long sentences and magisterial phrases (see Bacon's *Of Studies*, Reading 23.2)—gave way to a more informal prose style, one that reflected the conversational chatter of the *salons* and the cafés. Journalistic essays brought "philosophy out of the closets and libraries, schools and colleges, to dwell in clubs and assemblies, at tea-tables and in coffee houses," explained Joseph Addison (1672–1719), the leading British prose stylist of his day.

In collaboration with his lifelong friend Richard Steele (1672–1729), Addison published two London periodicals, the *Tatler* and the *Spectator*, which featured penetrating commentaries on current events and social behavior. The *Spectator* had a circulation of some 25,000 readers. Anticipating modern news magazines, eighteenth-century broadsheets and periodicals offered the literate public timely reports and diverse views on all aspects of popular culture. They provided entertainment even as they shaped popular opinion, and cultivated an urban chauvinism best expressed by Samuel Johnson: "When a man is tired of London, he is tired of life: for there is in London all that life can afford."

The Modern Novel

The most important new form of eighteenth-century literary entertainment was the *novel*. The novel first appeared in world literature in China and Japan. The oldest of the early Japanese novels, *The Tale of Genji*, was written by an unknown eleventh-century author known as Lady Shikibu Murasaki (see chapter 14). In China, where the history of the novel reached back to the twelfth century, prose tales of travel, love, and adventure were popular sources for operas and plays (see chapter 21). Neither Japanese nor Chinese prose fiction had any direct influence on Western forerunners of the genre, such as Cervantes' *Don Quixote* (see chapter 19).

In both the West and East Asia, the novel rose to prominence in part as a consequence of increasing urbanization and the emergence of a rising middle class seeking popular entertainment. Not referred to as "novels" until the end of the century, the earliest fictional portrayals of contemporary life were presented as "histories." The popular *Robinson Crusoe* (1719) by Daniel Defoe (1660–1731) took the form of a counterfeit historical document, whose full title was *The Life and Strange Surprising Adventures of Robinson Crusoe of York, Mariner; Who lived Eight and Twenty Years, all alone in an un-inhabited Island on the Coast of America, near the Mouth of the Great River of Oronoque; Having been cast on shore by Shipwreck, where-in all the Men Perished but himself. With an Account how he was at last as strangely deliver'd by Pyrates. Written by Himself*. This "autobiography," inspired by stories of real-life castaways in an age of sea voyages, appealed to readers as more true-to-life than the fantasy-laden stories of Defoe's predecessors, Cervantes and Rabelais.

Often considered the first English novel, Samuel Richardson's bestselling *Pamela, Or, Virtue Rewarded* (1740), was first conceived as a conduct book—a moralizing genre designed to instruct and entertain. Purported to be based on letters written by the main character, it told the tale of a young domestic servant who makes her way to upper-class society. Its immense popularity provoked sequels as well as satiric ridicule. The adventures of Henry Fielding's hero Tom Jones (in the novel *The History of Tom Jones, a Foundling*, 1749), which turn on improbable coincidences and dramatic reversals of fortune, bring to life the escapades of criminals and prostitutes. In early modern novels, with their graphic accounts of the personalities of lower- and middle-class people, the reading public discovered passions and sentiments much like their own. No wonder they appealed to the same individuals who enjoyed the spicy realism and journalistic prose of contemporary broadsheets.

Pope: Poet of the Enlightenment

If any single poet typified the spirit of the Enlightenment, it was surely Alexander Pope (1688–1744), the greatest English poet of the eighteenth century. Pope, a semi-invalid from the age of twelve, was a great admirer of Newton and a champion of the scientific method. He was also a staunch Neoclassicist who devotedly revived the wit and polish of the golden age Roman poets Virgil and Horace. Largely self-taught (in his time Roman Catholics were barred from attending English universities), Pope defended the value of education in Greek and Latin; his own love of the classics inspired him to produce new translations of Homer's *Iliad* and *Odyssey*. "A *little learning* is a dangerous thing," warned Pope in pleading for a broader and more thorough survey of the past.

Pope's poetry is as controlled and refined as a Poussin painting or a Bach fugue. His choice of the **heroic couplet** for most of his numerous satires, as well as for his translations of Homer, reflects his commitment to the fundamentals of balance and order. The concentrated brilliance and polish of each two-rhymed line bears out his claim that "True ease in writing comes from art, not chance,/As those move easiest who have learned to dance."

Pope's most famous poem was his *Essay on Man*. Like Milton's *Paradise Lost*, but on a smaller scale, the *Essay* tries to assess humankind's place in the universal scheme. But whereas Milton explained evil in terms of human will, Pope—a Catholic turned deist—envisioned evil as part of God's design for a universe he describes as "A mighty maze! but not without a plan." Like Leibniz (whom he admired), Pope insisted that whatever occurs in nature has been "programmed" by God as part of God's benign and rational order. Pope lacked the reforming zeal of the *philosophes*, but he caught the optimism of the Enlightenment in a single line: "Whatever is, is right." In the *Essay on Man*, Pope warns that we must not presume to understand the whole of nature. Nor should we aspire to a higher place in the great "chain of being." Rather, he counsels, "Know then thyself, presume not God to scan;/The proper study of Mankind is Man."

READING 24.8 From Pope's *Essay on Man*

(1733–1734)

Epistle I

IX   What if the foot, ordain'd the dust to tread,   1
Or hand, to toil, aspir'd to be the head?
What if the head, the eye, or ear repin'd[1]
To serve mere engines to the ruling Mind?
Just as absurd for any part to claim
To be another, in his gen'ral frame:
Just as absurd, to mourn the tasks or pains.
The great directing Mind of All ordains.
   All are but parts of one stupendous whole,
Whose body Nature is, and God the soul;   10
That, chang'd thro' all, and yet in all the same;
Great in the earth, as in th' ethereal frame;
Warms in the sun, refreshes in the breeze,
Glows in the stars, and blossoms in the trees,
Lives thro' all life, extends thro' all extent,
Spreads undivided, operates unspent;
Breathes in our soul, informs our mortal part,

As full, as perfect, in a hair as heart:
As full, as perfect, in vile Man that mourns,
As the rapt Seraph[2] that adores and burns: 20
To him no high, no low, no great, no small;
He fills, he bounds, connects, and equals all.

   X   Cease then, nor Order Imperfection name:
Our proper bliss depends on what we blame.
Know thy own point: This kind, this due degree
Of blindness, weakness, Heav'n bestows on thee.
Submit—In this, or any other sphere,
Secure to be as blest as thou canst bear:
Safe in the hand of one disposing Pow'r,
Or in the natal, or the mortal hour.   30
All Nature is but Art,[3] unknown to thee;
All Chance, Direction, which thou canst not see;
All Discord, Harmony not understood;
All partial Evil, universal Good:
And, spite of Pride, in erring Reason's spite,
One truth is clear, WHATEVER IS, IS RIGHT.

Epistle II

   I   Know then thyself, presume not God to scan;[4]
The proper study of Mankind is Man.
Plac'd on this isthmus of a middle state,[5]
A Being darkly wise, and rudely great: 40
With too much knowledge for the Sceptic side,
With too much weakness for the Stoic's pride,
He hangs between; in doubt to act, or rest;
In doubt to deem himself a God, or Beast;
In doubt his Mind or Body to prefer,
Born but to die, and reas'ning but to err;
Alike in ignorance, his reason such.
Whether he thinks too little, or too much:
Chaos of Thought and Passion, all confus'd;
Still by himself abus'd, or disabus'd;   50
Created half to rise, and half to fall;[6]
Great lord of all things, yet a prey to all;
Sole judge of Truth, in endless Error hurl'd:[7]
The glory, jest, and riddle of the world!

Q. **What aspects of this poem typify the spirit of the Enlightenment?**

Q. **What does Pope see as Man's limitations?**

---

[1] Complained.

[2] A member of the highest order of angels.
[3] Compare Hobbes: "Nature is the art whereby God governs the world."
[4] Investigate.
[5] Between the angels (above) and the animal kingdom (below). Compare Pico della Mirandola's view of human beings as creatures who partake of both earthly and celestial qualities and can therefore ascend or descend the great "chain of being" (chapter 16).
[6] See note 5.
[7] Cast back and forth.

LOOKING BACK

Liberty and Political Theory

- In political thought, Thomas Hobbes and John Locke advanced the idea of government based on a social contract between ruler and ruled.
- While Hobbes envisioned this contract as a bond between individuals who surrendered some portion of their freedom to a sovereign authority, Locke saw government as an agent of the people—bound to exercise the will of the majority.
- Locke's writing provided the intellectual foundation for the Enlightenment faith in reason as the sure guide to social progress.
- Jefferson and Montesquieu applied Locke's views on natural law to political theory and practice, the basics of which are enshrined in America's Declaration of Independence.

The Birth of Economic Theory

- In *An Inquiry into the Nature and Causes of the Wealth of Nations*, Smith set forth the "laws" of labor, production, and trade leading to the modern concepts of free enterprise and *laissez-faire* economics.

The *Philosophes*

- In Paris, the hub of intellectual activity, the *philosophes* gathered in *salons* to exchange views on morality, politics, science, and religion.
- Seeking a nonauthoritarian, secular morality, the *philosophes* challenged existing forms of intolerance, inequality, and injustice.

- The prime symbol of the Enlightenment zeal for knowledge was the *Encyclopédie*, produced by Diderot with the assistance of the *philosophes*.
- A zeal for the ordering of socially useful information inspired the production of dictionaries, biographies, and histories.

The Crusade for Progress

- The Enlightenment crusade for progress stemmed from an optimistic faith in the progressive improvement of humankind.
- The idea that human beings, free from the bonds of ignorance and superstition and operating according to the principles of reason, might achieve the good life here on earth inspired the philosophic optimism of Leibniz in Germany, the progressive theories of Beccaria in Italy, the visionary social reforms of Condorcet in France, and the defense of womankind by Wollstonecraft in England.

Enlightenment Literature

- The journalistic essay, a new literary genre, provided penetrating commentary on current events and social behavior, as popularized in the newspapers and periodicals of the day.
- The novel, which provided an expanding reading public with true-to-life characters drawn from everyday life, was the most important new form of literary entertainment.
- Alexander Pope's Neoclassical verses typified the spirit of the Age of Reason; his *Essay on Man* advanced an optimistic view of human beings as the enlightened inhabitants of an orderly and harmonious universe.

Glossary

heroic couplet a pair of rhymed iambic pentameter lines that reach completion in structure and in sense at the end of the second line

laissez-faire (French, "allow to act") a general policy of noninterference in the economy, defended by such classical economists as Adam Smith

philosophes (French, "philosophers") the intellectuals of the European Enlightenment

social contract an agreement made between citizens leading to the establishment of the state

Chapter

The Limits of Reason

ca. 1700–1800

". . . many authors have hastened to conclude that man is naturally cruel and needs civil institutions to make him peacable, whereas in truth nothing is more peacable than man in his primitive state."
Rousseau

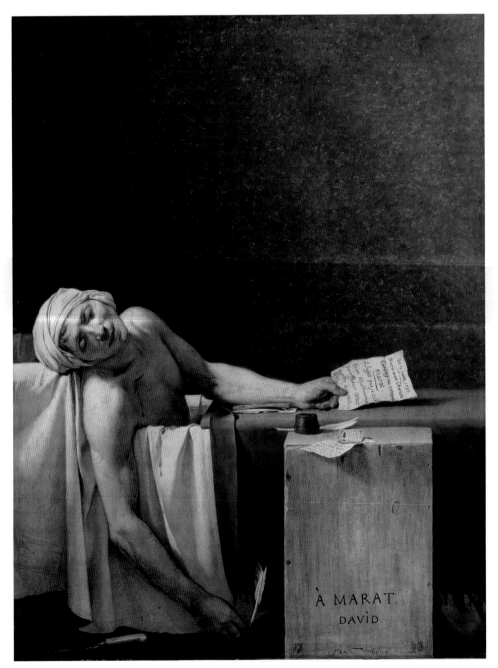

Figure 25.1 JACQUES-LOUIS DAVID, *The Death of Marat*, 1793. Oil on canvas, 65 × 50½ in. When, during the phase of the French Revolution known as the Reign of Terror, David's antiroyalist friend was murdered in his bathtub, the artist paid tribute to him with this unforgettable painting. Having visited Marat the day before he died, David recreated the event in realistic detail; however, he idealized the scene by bathing Marat in ethereal gold light, as was common to images of Christian martyrdom.

LOOKING AHEAD

Even that most enthusiastic champion of reason, Alexander Pope, acknowledged in his *Essay on Man* that human beings are "Born but to die, and reas'ning but to err"—that is, thinking creatures are finite and fallible. While generally committed to the belief in human perfectibility by way of reason, most Enlightenment thinkers realized that people are both imperfect and irrational. Reason is too frequently ignored or abandoned altogether. Perhaps the greatest obstacle to the promise of reason, however, lay in the hard realities of everyday urban life. In eighteenth-century Europe, where Enlightenment reformers exalted the ideals of human progress, there was clear evidence of ignorance, depravity, and despair, especially among those who felt the early effects of industrialization. Upon visiting the city of Paris, Henri Rousseau lamented its "dirty stinking streets, filthy black houses" and alleys filled with beggars. Indeed, outside the elegant drawing rooms of Paris and London, poverty, violence, and degradation prevailed.

Such conditions invited bitter attack, and none was more powerful than satire—the literary genre that engages humor to denounce human vice and folly. Satire became the intellectual weapon of the age, refined by the best thinkers of the time and devoured by the general public. Reform, however, would not be achieved exclusively by the pen. As the late eighteenth-century political revolutions in America and France proved, the musket would work to achieve what the pen had failed to secure. By the end of the eighteenth century, none of the age-old certainties were left unexamined: institutionalized religion, the autocratic rule of kings and despots, the agrarian way of life, the very social order—all fell under critical scrutiny and many came to crumble.

The Industrial Revolution

Early Industrialization

The Scientific Revolution of the seventeenth century encouraged the invention of new machinery and technologies that contributed to the Industrial Revolution of the following two centuries. Industrialization involved a process that transformed agrarian and handicraft-dominated economies into those involving machine-manufactured goods. The textile industry was the first to experience transformation. In England, the invention of the "flying shuttle" (a device that sped the weaving process), the "spinning jenny" (a multispooled spinning wheel), and the water-frame (a water-driven spinning machine) combined to revolutionize the production of textiles (see Science and Technology box).

The steam engine, inveafts; by the late eighteenth century, however, it served England's flourishing textile industry. By the middle of the nineteenth century, it was used for everything from sawmills to railroads (see chapter 27). Industrialization was also advanced by the technology of cast iron, a medium processed by the Chinese as early as the fourth century, but not known in Europe until the early eighteenth century, when carbon-based fuel (coke) was used to produce structural strength iron strong enough to support structures.

With industrialization came the construction of factories and the mass production (and consumption) of goods. Industrialization would have significant social and economic effects, both positive and negative, throughout the West (see chapter 27), but it was primarily in England that the consequences of an expanding factory system were first visible. Allied with unregulated capitalism, the English factory system often gave rise to dangerous working conditions and the exploitation of labor—mainly women and children. In many of London's factories, children tended the new machines for twelve- to fourteen-hour shifts, following which they were boarded in shabby barracks. And in the mines of Cornwall and County Durham, women and children were paid a pittance to labor like animals, pulling carts laden with coal. Some miners worked such long hours that they never saw the light of day.

The Transatlantic Slave Trade

In human terms, however, the most glaring evidence of the failure of the Enlightenment was the perpetuation of the slave trade, which, despite condemnation by many of the *philosophes*, flourished until the mid-nineteenth century. Begun by the Portuguese in the fifteenth century (see chapter 18), the transatlantic slave trade, by which millions of Africans were bought and shipped against their will to colonies in the "New World," reached its peak in the eighteenth century (Figure **25.2**). As England—lured by the lucrative sugar trade—became the leading player in the transatlantic traffic, some twelve million Africans—the exact number is much debated—were transported to work on sugar plantations in the West Indies and elsewhere in the Americas. British slave vessels were constructed in New England (notable for its outstanding timber), while nails, ropes, and anchors were provided by Liverpool. The slave trade was big business; one eighteenth-century merchant described it as "the hinge on which all trade of this globe moves." In order to supply this market, Africans—including African children—were frequently kidnapped by unscrupulous Africans, who profited handsomely by selling their captives to white slave traders. The fate of the African slave who survived the perilous "Middle Passage" between Africa and the Americas (it is estimated that roughly one-third perished in transit) was a life of unspeakable suffering.

A first-hand account of this inhumane system is central to the autobiographical narrative of Olaudah Equiano

Figure 25.2 Plan of the *Brookes*, a 320-ton British slave ship of the late eighteenth century.
Fig. 1 lengthwise cross-section of the ship;
Fig. 2 lower deck with stowage of 292 slaves, 130 of these being stowed under platforms as seen in Figs. 4 and 5;
Fig. 3 lower deck with platforms stowing an additional 130 slaves;
Figs. 6 and 7 half-deck with and without platforms. The *Brookes* was one of eighteen vessels examined in 1788 by a committee making recommendations to Parliament for the regulation of slave ships.

The legend in the upper right corner reads: "Note. The Brookes after the Regulation Act of 1788 was allowed to carry 454 Slaves. She could stow this number by following the rule adopted in this plate namely of allowing a space of 6 foot by 1 foot 4 inches to each man; 5 foot 10 inches by 1 foot 4 inches to each woman & 5 foot by 1 foot 2 inches to each boy, but so much space as this was seldom allowed even after the Regulation Act. It was proved by the confession of the Slave Merchant that before the above Act the Brookes has at one time carried as many as 609 Slaves. This was done by taking some out of Irons & locking them spoonwise, to use the technical term; that is by stowing one within the distended legs of the other."

(1745–1797), who was born in the West African kingdom of Benin and kidnapped and enslaved at the age of eleven. Both as a slave and after his release from slavery in 1766, Equiano traveled widely; during his stay in England (as one of only 30,000 black men and women in mid-eighteenth-century England), he mastered the English language and became an outspoken abolitionist (Figure **25.3**). The following excerpt from Equiano's autobiographic narrative recounts with dramatic simplicity the traumatic experience of an eleven-year-old child who was cruelly sold into bondage.

READING 25.1 From Equiano's *Travels* (1789)

That part of Africa known by the name of Guinea to which the trade for slaves is carried on extends along the coast above 3,400 miles, from the Senegal to Angola, and includes a variety of kingdoms. Of these the most considerable is the kingdom of Benin, both as to extent and wealth, the richness and cultivation of the soil, the power of its king, and the number and warlike disposition of the inhabitants. . . . This kingdom is divided into many provinces or districts, in one of the most remote and fertile of which, called Eboe, I was born in the year 1745, situated in a charming fruitful vale, named Essaka. The distance of this province from the capital of Benin and the sea coast must be very considerable, for I had never heard of white men or Europeans, nor of the sea, and our subjection to the king of Benin was little more than nominal; for every transaction of the government, as far as my slender observation extended, was conducted by the chiefs or elders of the place. . . . 1

My father, besides many slaves, had a numerous family of which seven lived to grow up, including myself and a sister who was the only daughter. As I was the youngest of the sons I became, of course, the greatest favourite with my mother and was always with her; and she used to take particular pains to form my mind. I was trained up from my earliest years in the art of war, my daily exercise was shooting and throwing javelins, and my mother adorned me with emblems[1] after the manner of our greatest warriors. In this way I grew up till I was turned the age of 11, when an end was put to my happiness in the following manner. Generally when the grown people in the neighbourhood were gone far in the fields to labour, the children assembled together in some of the neighbours' premises to play, and commonly some of us used to get up a tree to look out for any assailant or kidnapper that might come upon us, for they sometimes took those opportunities of our parents' absence to attack and carry off as many as they could seize. One day, as I was watching at the top of a tree in our yard, I saw one of those people come into the yard of our next neighbour but one to kidnap, there being many stout young people in it. Immediately on this I gave the alarm of the rogue and he was surrounded by the stoutest of them, who entangled him with cords so that he could not escape till some of the grown people came and secured him. But alas! ere long it was my fate to be thus attacked and to be carried off when none of 40

10

20

30

---

[1] Body decorations, such as scarification.

the grown people were nigh. One day, when all our people were gone out to their works as usual and only I and my dear sister were left to mind the house, two men and a woman got over our walls, and in a moment seized us both, and without giving us time to cry out or make resistance they stopped our mouths and ran off with us into the nearest wood. Here they tied our hands and continued to carry us as far as they could till night came on, when we reached a small house where the robbers halted for refreshment and spent the night. We were then unbound but were unable to take any food, and being quite overpowered by fatigue and grief, our only relief was some sleep, which allayed our misfortune for a short time. The next morning we left the house and continued travelling all the day. For a long time we had kept to the woods, but at last we came into a road which I believed I knew. I had now some hopes of being delivered, for we had advanced but a little way before I discovered some people at a distance, on which I began to cry out for their assistance: but my cries had no other effect than to make them tie me faster and stop my mouth, and then they put me into a large sack. They also stopped my sister's mouth and tied her hands, and in this manner we proceeded till we were out of the sight of these people. . . . It was in vain that we besought them not to part us; she was torn from me and immediately carried away, while I was left in a state of distraction not to be described. I cried and grieved continually, and for several days I did not eat anything but what they forced into my mouth. At length, after many days' travelling, during which I had often changed masters, I got into the hands of a chieftain in a very pleasant country. . . . 70

50

60

[Equiano describes his tenure with African masters; he is sold a number of times (during a period of six to seven months) before he is taken to the sea coast.]

The first object which saluted my eyes when I arrived on the coast was the sea, and a slave ship which was then riding at anchor and waiting for its cargo. These filled me with astonishment, which was soon converted into terror when I was carried on board. I was immediately handled and tossed up to see if I were sound by some of the crew, and I was now persuaded that I had gotten into a world of bad spirits and that they were going to kill me. Their complexions too differing so much from ours, their long hair and the language they spoke (which was very different from any I had ever heard) united to confirm me in this belief. Indeed such were the horrors of my views and fears at the moment that, if ten thousand worlds had been my own, I would have freely parted with them all to have exchanged my condition with that of the meanest slave in my own country. When I looked round the ship too and saw a large furnace or copper boiling and a multitude of black people of every description chained together, every one of their countenances expressing dejection and sorrow, I no longer doubted of my fate; and quite overpowered with horror and anguish, I fell motionless on the deck and fainted. When I recovered a little I found some black people about me, who I believed were some of those who had brought me on board and had been receiving their pay; they talked to me in order to cheer me, but all in vain. I asked them if we were not to be eaten by those white men with horrible looks, red faces, and loose hair.

80

90

Figure 25.3 *Olaudah Equiano*, ca. 1780.

feared that element the first time I saw it, yet nevertheless could I have got over the nettings I would have jumped over the side, but I could not; and besides, the crew used to watch us very closely who were not chained down to the decks, lest we should leap into the water: and I have seen some of these poor African prisoners most severely cut for attempting to do so, and hourly whipped for not eating. This indeed was often the case with myself. In a little time after, amongst the poor chained men I found some of my own nation,[3] which in a small degree gave ease to   **130** my mind. I inquired of these what was to be done with us; they gave me to understand we were to be carried to these white people's country to work for them. I then was a little revived, and thought if it were no worse than working, my situation was not so desperate: but still I feared I should be put to death, the white people looked and acted, as I thought, in so savage a manner; for I had never seen among my people such instances of brutal cruelty, and this not only shewn towards us blacks but also to some of the whites themselves. One white man in particular I saw, when we were permitted to be on deck,   **140** flogged so unmercifully with a large rope near the foremast that he died in consequence of it; and they tossed him over the side as they would have done a brute. This made me fear these people the more, and I expected nothing less than to be treated in the same manner. I could not help expressing my fears and apprehensions to some of my countrymen: I asked them if these people had no country but lived in this hollow place (the ship): they told me they did not, but came from a distant one. "Then," said I, "how comes it in all our country we never heard of them?" They told me because they lived so very far off. I then asked where were   **150** their women? had they any like themselves? I was told they had: "and why," said I, "do we not see them?" They answered, because they were left behind. . . . The stench of the hold while we were on the coast was so intolerably loathsome that it was dangerous to remain there for any time, and some of us had been permitted to stay on the deck for the fresh air; but now that the whole ship's cargo were confined together it became absolutely pestilential. The closeness of the place and the heat of the climate, added to the number in the ship, which was so crowded that each   **160** had scarcely room to turn himself, almost suffocated us. This produced copious perspirations, so that the air soon became unfit for respiration from a variety of loathsome smells, and brought on a sickness among the slaves, of which many died, thus falling victims to the improvident avarice, as I may call it, of their purchasers. This wretched situation was again aggravated by the galling of the chains, now become insupportable, and the filth of the necessary tubs, into which the children often fell and were almost suffocated. The shrieks of the women and the groans of the dying rendered the whole a scene of horror almost   **170** inconceivable. Happily perhaps for myself I was soon reduced so low here that it was thought necessary to keep me almost always on deck, and from my extreme youth I was not put in fetters. In this situation I expected every hour to share the fate of my companions, some of whom were almost daily brought upon deck at the point of death, which I began to hope would soon put an end to my miseries. Often did I think many of the inhabitants of

They told me I was not, and one of the crew brought me a small portion of spirituous liquor in a wine glass, but being afraid of him I would not take it out of his hand. One of the blacks therefore took it from him and gave it to me, and I took a little down my palate, which instead of reviving me, as they thought it would, threw   **100** me into the greatest consternation at the strange feeling it produced, having never tasted any such liquor before. Soon after this the blacks who brought me on board went off, and left me abandoned to despair.

I now saw myself deprived of all chance of returning to my native country or even the least glimpse of hope of gaining the shore, which I now considered as friendly; and I even wished for my former slavery in preference to my present situation, which was filled with horrors of every kind, still heightened by my ignorance of what I was to undergo. I was not long suffered to   **110** indulge my grief; I was soon put down under the decks, and there I received such a salutation in my nostrils as I had never experienced in my life: so that with the loathsomeness of the stench and crying together, I became so sick and low that I was not able to eat, nor had I the least desire to taste anything. I now wished for the last friend, death, to relieve me; but soon, to my grief, two of the white men offered me eatables, and on my refusing to eat, one of them held me fast by the hands and laid me across I think the windlass,[2] and tied my feet while the other flogged me severely. I had never experienced anything of this kind   **120** before, and although, not being used to the water, I naturally

---

[2] The device that works the ship's anchor.

[3] Ethnic group.

the deep much more happy than myself. I envied them the freedom they enjoyed, and as often wished I could change my condition for theirs. Every circumstance I met with served only to render my state more painful, and heighten my apprehensions and my opinion of the cruelty of the whites. One day they had taken a number of fishes, and when they had killed and satisfied themselves with as many as they thought fit, to our astonishment who were on the deck, rather than give any of them to us to eat as we expected, they tossed the remaining fish into the sea again, although we begged and prayed for some as well as we could, but in vain; and some of my countrymen, being pressed by hunger, took an opportunity when they thought no one saw them of trying to get a little privately; but they were discovered, and the attempt procured them some very severe floggings. One day, when we had a smooth sea and moderate wind, two of my wearied countrymen who were chained together (I was near them at the time), preferring death to such a life of misery, somehow made through the nettings and jumped into the sea: immediately another quite dejected fellow, who on account of his illness was suffered to be out of irons, also followed their example; and I believe many more would very soon have done the same if they had not been prevented by the ship's crew, who were instantly alarmed. Those of us that were the most active were in a moment put down under the deck, and there was such a noise and confusion amongst the people of the ship as I never heard before, to stop her and get the boat out to go after the slaves. However two of the wretches were drowned, but they got the other and afterwards flogged him unmercifully for thus attempting to prefer death to slavery. In this manner we continued to undergo more hardships than I can now relate, hardships which are inseparable from this accursed trade. . . . At last we came in sight of the island of Barbados, at which the whites on board gave a great shout and made many signs of joy to us. We did not know what to think of this, but as the vessel drew nearer we plainly saw the harbour and other ships of different kinds and sizes, and we soon anchored amongst them off Bridgetown. Many merchants and planters now came on board, though it was in the evening. They put us in separate parcels[4] and examined us attentively. They also made us jump,[5] and pointed to the land, signifying we were to go there. We thought by this we should be eaten by these ugly men, as they appeared to us; and when soon after we were all put down under the deck again, there was much dread and trembling among us, and nothing but bitter cries to be heard all the night from these apprehensions, insomuch that at last the white people got some old slaves from the land to pacify us. They told us we were not to be eaten but to work, and were soon to go on land where we should see many of our countrypeople. This report eased us much; and sure enough soon after we were landed there came to us Africans of all languages. We were conducted immediately to the merchant's yard, where we were all pent up together like so many sheep in a fold without regard to sex or age. . . . We were not many days in the merchant's custody before we were sold after their usual manner,

which is this: On a signal given, (as the beat of a drum) the buyers rush at once into the yard where the slaves are confined, and make choice of that parcel they like best. The noise and clamour with which this is attended and the eagerness visible in the countenances of the buyers serve not a little to increase the apprehensions of the terrified Africans, who may well be supposed to consider them as the ministers of that destruction to which they think themselves devoted. In this manner, without scruple, are relations and friends separated, most of them never to see each other again. I remember in the vessel in which I was brought over, in the men's apartment there were several brothers who, in the sale, were sold in different lots; and it was very moving on this occasion to see and hear their cries at parting. O, ye nominal Christians! might not an African ask you, Learned you this from your God who says unto you, Do unto all men as you would men should do unto you? Is it not enough that we are torn from our country and friends to toil for your luxury and lust of gain? Must every tender feeling be likewise sacrificed to your avarice? Are the dearest friends and relations, now rendered more dear by their separation from their kindred, still to be parted from each other and thus prevented from cheering the gloom of slavery with the small comfort of being together and mingling their sufferings and sorrows? Why are parents to lose their children, brothers their sisters, or husbands their wives? Surely this is a new refinement in cruelty which, while it has no advantage to atone for it, thus aggravates distress and adds fresh horrors even to the wretchedness of slavery. . . .

Q. **Which of the circumstances and conditions** described by Equiano strike you as most removed from the ideals of the *philosophes*?

As Equiano suggests, the "gloom of slavery" itself left slaves little opportunity for self-expression. It is therefore notable that one particular slave would become America's first black woman poet. Phillis Wheatley (1754?–1784) was kidnapped from Senegal and sold at auction in Boston at the age of seven. She was educated along with the children of her master, John Wheatley, and learned to read and write English, as well as Greek and Latin. Producing her first poem at the age of thirteen, Wheatley had difficulty publishing her collection of poems in America, where the authenticity of her work was held in doubt. Following interrogation by a panel of eighteen illustrious Bostonians, it was concluded that "Phillis, a young Negro Girl, who was but a few Years since, brought an uncultivated Barbarian from Africa" had indeed written the verses in question.

In 1773, Wheatley's *Poems on Various Subjects; Religious and Moral* was published in England (which country was more receptive than America to black authors); it soon won acclaim in both Europe and America. An encouragement to the work of other black writers, it became a landmark in black literary achievement. John Wheatley emancipated Phillis in 1773, giving her the opportunity to travel and continue writing. The poem that follows, written in heroic couplets—the favorite meter of Chaucer and

---

[4] Groups.
[5] In order to determine whether they were healthy.

Pope—is a terse and eloquent appeal to the Christian promise of equality before God, and the Enlightenment promise of reason.

READING 25.2 Wheatley's "On Being Brought from Africa to America" (1772)

'TWAS mercy brought me from my Pagan land,
Taught my benighted soul to understand
That there's a God, that there's a Saviour too:
Once I redemption neither sought nor knew.
Some view our sable[1] race with scornful eye,
"Their colour is a diabolic die."
Remember, *Christians*, Negros, black as *Cain*,
May be refin'd, and join the' angelic train.

Q How does the tone of Wheatley's poem differ from that of Equiano's narrative?

If slavery and industrialization in the West generated material conditions that were contrary to Enlightenment ideals, other factors served as serious obstacles to their realization. Ignorance, for example, the foundation for bias and (in many cases) unwitting prejudice, clouded the perceptions and judgments of some of the most educated *philosophes*. Diderot himself, who had no first-hand knowledge of the Muslim world, described Arabs (in his *Encyclopédie*) as "thievish and bellicose." Voltaire, who wrote a universal history that charted the customs of nations (including Russia and Africa), brought to his analysis an anti-Church, anti-Semitic, and anti-black bias.

Believing Africans to be intellectually inferior, America's leading Enlightenment thinker, Thomas Jefferson, defended the institution of slavery as a "necessary evil." His perception of African-American slaves was colored by prejudices that are shocking to modern sensibilities. In his *Notes on the State of Virginia*, Jefferson wrote:

> "Comparing [blacks] by their faculties of memory, reason, and imagination, it appears to me that in memory they are equal to the whites; in reason much inferior . . . I advance it . . . as a suspicion only, that the blacks, whether originally a distinct race, or made distinct by time and circumstances, are inferior to the whites in the endowments both of body and mind . . . This unfortunate difference of color, and perhaps of faculty, is a powerful obstacle to the emancipation of these people."

In maintaining such opinions, shared by most of his fellow *philosophes*, Jefferson provided an implicit rationale for enslaving Africans. Clearly, such thinkers were all too capable of finding rationalizations for policies in which political or social advantage for the privileged few overrode the ideals of liberty and equality. Thus slavery persisted in the Western hemisphere (and elsewhere) for nearly a century beyond the Age of Enlightenment.

Satire: Weapon of the Enlightenment

The discrepancies between the sordid realities of eighteenth-century life and the progressive ideas of the Enlightenment provoked indignant protests, and none so potent as those couched in humor. The eighteenth century was history's greatest age of satire. Satire, the genre that had served Juvenal in imperial Rome (see chapter 6) and Erasmus in the age of the Reformation (see chapter 19), now became the favorite weapon of social reformers, who drew attention to the vast contradictions between morals and manners, intentions and actions, and, more generally, between Enlightenment aspirations and contemporary degradation.

The Satires of Jonathan Swift

The premier British satirist of the eighteenth century was Jonathan Swift (1667–1745). Unlike the *philosophes*, this Dublin-born Anglican priest took a pessimistic view of human nature. He once confided (in a letter to the poet Alexander Pope) that he hated the human race, whose misuse of reason produced, in his view, an irredeemably corrupt society. Such negativism accompanied Swift's self-acclaimed "savage indignation." Yet Swift was not a man of despair, for no despairing personality could have produced such a profoundly moralizing body of literature. In 1726, he published his classic satire, *Gulliver's Travels*. At the simplest level, it is a story of travel and adventure that (somewhat like Equiano's true-to-life travels) describes the fortunes of a hero in imaginary lands peopled with midgets, giants, and other fabulous creatures. At a second, symbolic level, however, it is a social statement on the vagaries of human behavior. In one chapter, Gulliver visits the Lilliputians—"little people" whose moral pettiness and inhumanity seem to characterize humankind at its worst. In another, he meets noble horses whose rational behavior contrasts with the bestiality of their human-looking slaves, the Yahoos. An immediate popular sensation, *Gulliver's Travels* has become a landmark in fantasy literature and social satire.

Swift also wrote many pamphlets and letters protesting social and political ills. Among the most famous is an essay publicizing the wretched condition of the Irish peasants, who were exploited unmercifully by the British government. In his satirical treatise *A Modest Proposal*, Swift deals with the reality that many Irish peasants were too poor to feed their families; he proposes with deadpan frankness that Irish children should be bred and butchered for the English dining table, thus providing income for the poor and alleviating the miseries of all. While *Gulliver's Travels* attacks conditions that are universal and timeless, *A Modest Proposal* mocks a specific crisis of Swift's own time.

---

[1] Black or dark brown.

for Preventing the Children of Poor People in Ireland from Being a Burden to Their Parents or Country, and for Making Them Beneficial to the Public

It is a melancholy object to those who walk through this great [1] town[1] or travel in the country, when they see the streets, the roads, and cabin-doors, crowded with beggars of the female sex, followed by three, four, or six children, all in rags, and importuning every passenger for an alms.[2] These mothers, instead of being able to work for their honest livelihood, are forced to employ all their time in strolling, to beg sustenance for their helpless infants, who, as they grow up, either turn thieves for want of work, or leave their dear native country to fight. . . in Spain, or sell themselves to the Barbadoes.[3] [10]

I think it is agreed by all parties that this prodigious number of children, in the arms, or on the backs, or at the heels of their mothers, and frequently of their fathers, is in the present deplorable state of the kingdom a very great additional grievance; and therefore whoever could find out a fair, cheap, and easy method of making these children sound, useful members of the commonwealth, would deserve so well of the public as to have his statue set up for a preserver of the nation.

But my intention is very far from being confined to provide only for the children of professed beggars; it is of a much [20] greater extent, and shall take in the whole number of infants at a certain age, who are born of parents in effect as little able to support them as those who demand our charity in the streets.

As to my own part, having turned my thoughts for many years upon this important subject, and maturely weighed the several schemes of other projectors,[4] I have always found them grossly mistaken in their computation. It is true, a child, just dropped from its dam,[5] may be supported by her milk for a solar year with little other nourishment, at most not above the value of two shillings, which the mother may certainly get, or the value [30] in scraps, by her lawful occupation of begging; and it is exactly at one year old that I propose to provide for them in such a manner as instead of being a charge upon their parents or the parish, or wanting food and raiment[6] for the rest of their lives, they shall, on the contrary, contribute to the feeding and partly to the clothing of many thousands.

There is likewise another great advantage in my scheme, that it will prevent those voluntary abortions, and that horrid practice of women murdering their bastard children, alas too frequent among us, sacrificing the poor innocent babes, I [40] doubt, more to avoid the expense than the shame, which would move tears and pity in the most savage and inhuman breast.

The number of souls in this kingdom being usually reckoned one million and a half, of these I calculate there may be about two hundred thousand couple whose wives are breeders; from which number I subtract thirty thousand couple who are able to maintain their own children, although I apprehend there cannot be so many under the present distresses of the kingdom; but this being granted, there will remain an hundred and seventy thousand breeders. I again subtract fifty thousand for those women who [50] miscarry, or whose children die by accident or disease within the year. There only remain an hundred and twenty thousand children of poor parents annually born. The question therefore is, how this number shall be reared and provided for, which, as I have already said, under the present situation of affairs, is utterly impossible by all the methods hitherto proposed, for we can neither employ them in handicraft or agriculture; we neither build houses (I mean in the country) nor cultivate land; they can very seldom pick up a livelihood by stealing till they arrive at six years old, except where they are of towardly[7] parts, although [60] I confess they learn the rudiments[8] much earlier. . .

I am assured by our merchants that a boy or a girl before twelve years old is no saleable commodity, and even when they come to this age, they will not yield above three pounds, or three pounds and half-a-crown at most on the Exchange, which cannot turn to account either to the parents or kingdom, the charge of nutriment and rags having been at least four times that value. I shall now therefore humbly propose my own thoughts, which I hope will not be liable to the least objection.

I have been assured by a very knowing American of my [70] acquaintance in London, that a young healthy child well nursed is at a year old a most delicious, nourishing, and wholesome food, whether stewed, roasted, baked, or boiled, and I make no doubt that it will serve in a fricassee or a ragout.

I do therefore humbly offer it to public consideration that of the hundred and twenty thousand children already computed, twenty thousand may be reserved for breed, whereof only one fourth part to be males, which is more than we allow to sheep, [80] black cattle, or swine; and my reason is that these children are seldom the fruits of marriage, a circumstance not much regarded by our savages. Therefore one male will be sufficient to serve four females. That the remaining hundred thousand may at a year old be offered in sale to the persons of quality and fortune through the kingdom, always advising the mother to let them suck[9] plentifully in the last month, so as to render them plump and fat for a good table. A child will make two dishes at an entertainment for friends, and when the family dines alone, the fore or hind quarter will make a reasonable dish, and [90] seasoned with a little pepper or salt will be very good boiled on the fourth day, especially in winter.

I have reckoned, upon a medium,[10] that a child just born will weigh 12 pounds, and in a solar year if tolerably nursed will increase to 28 pounds.

I grant this food will be somewhat dear, and therefore very proper for landlords, who, as they have already devoured most of the parents, seem to have the best title to the children.

Infants' flesh will be in season throughout the year, but more

---

[1] Dublin.
[2] Charity.
[3] As slaves in the West Indies.
[4] Speculators.
[5] Just born.
[6] Clothing.

[7] Handsome.
[8] Fundamentals; first principles.
[9] To nurse at the breast.
[10] On an average.

plentiful in March, and a little before and after, for we are told [100]
by a grave author,[11] an eminent French physician, that fish being
a prolific diet, there are more children born in Roman Catholic
countries about nine months after Lent, than at any other season;
therefore reckoning a year after Lent, the markets will be more
glutted than usual, because the number of Popish infants is at
least three to one in this kingdom, and therefore it will have one
other collateral advantage, by lessening the number of Papists[12]
among us.

I have already computed the charge of nursing a beggar's
child (in which list I reckon all cottagers, labourers, and four- [110]
fifths of the farmers) to be about two shillings per annum, rags
included, and I believe no gentleman would repine to give ten
shillings for the carcass of a good fat child, which, as I have
said, will make four dishes of excellent nutritive meat, when he
has only some particular friend or his own family to dine with him.
Thus the squire will learn to be a good landlord, and grow
popular among his tenants, the mother will have eight shillings
for net profit, and be fit for work till she produces another child.

Those who are more thrifty (as I must confess the times
require) may flay the carcass; the skin of which, artificially [120]
dressed, will make admirable gloves for ladies, and summer
boots for fine gentlemen.

As to our city of Dublin, shambles[13] may be appointed for this
purpose in the most convenient parts of it, and butchers we may be
assured will not be wanting, although I rather recommend buying
the children alive, and dressing them hot from the knife, as we do
roasting pigs.

A very worthy person, a true lover of his country, and whose
virtues I highly esteem, was lately pleased, in discoursing on
this matter, to offer a refinement upon my scheme. He said, that [130]
many gentlemen of this kingdom having of late destroyed their
deer, he conceived that the want of venison might be well
supplied by the bodies of young lads and maidens, not exceeding
fourteen years of age, nor under twelve, so great a number of
both sexes in every country being now ready to starve, for want
of work and service, and these to be disposed of by their
parents if alive, or otherwise by their nearest relations.
But with due deference to so excellent a friend, and so
deserving a patriot, I cannot be altogether in his sentiments;
for as to the males, my American acquaintance assured me [140]
from frequent experience, that their flesh was generally tough
and lean, like that of our schoolboys, by continual exercise, and
their taste disagreeable, and to fatten them would not answer
the charge. Then as to the females, it would, I think with humble
submission, be a loss to the public, because they soon would
become breeders themselves. And besides, it is not improbable that
some scrupulous people might be apt to censure such a practice
(although indeed very unjustly), as a little bordering upon cruelty,
which, I confess, has always been with me the strongest objection
against any project, however so will intended. . . . [150]

I have too long digressed, and therefore shall return to my
subject. I think the advantages by the proposal which I have

made are obvious and many, as well as of the highest
importance.

For first, as I have already observed, it would greatly lessen the
number of Papists, with whom we are yearly over-run, being the
principal breeders of the nation, as well as our most dangerous
enemies, and who stay at home on purpose to
deliver the kingdom to the Pretender, hoping to take their [160]
advantage by the absence of so many good Protestants, who have
chosen rather to leave their country, than stay at home, and pay
tithes against their conscience, to an Episcopal curate.

Secondly, The poorer tenants will have something valuable of
their own, which by law may be made liable to distress, and
help to pay their landlord's rent, their corn and cattle being
already seized, and *money a thing unknown*.

Thirdly, whereas the maintenance of an hundred thousand
children, from two years old and upward, cannot be computed
at less than ten shillings a piece per annum, the nation's stock [170]
will be thereby increased fifty thousand pounds per annum, besides
the profit of a new dish, introduced to the tables of all gentlemen of
fortune in the kingdom who have any refinement in taste, and the
money will circulate among ourselves, the good being entirely of
our own growth and manufacture.

Fourthly, The constant breeders, beside the gain of eight
shillings sterling per annum, by the sale of their children, will be
rid of the charge of maintaining them after the first year.

Fifthly, This food would likewise bring great custom to
taverns, where the vintners will certainly be so prudent as to [180]
procure the best receipts for dressing it to perfection, and
consequently have their houses frequented by all the fine
gentlemen who justly value themselves upon their knowledge
in good eating; and a skilful cook, who understands how to
oblige his guests, will contrive to make it as expensive as
they please.

Sixthly, This would be a great inducement to marriage, which
all wise nations have either encouraged by rewards, or enforced
by laws and penalties. It would increase the care and
tenderness of mothers toward their children, when they were [190]
sure of a settlement for life, to the poor babes, provided in some
sort by the public, to their annual profit instead of expense. We
should see an honest emulation among the married women,
which of them could bring the fattest child to the market. Men
would become as fond of their wives, during the time of their
pregnancy, as they are now of their mares in foal, their cows in
calf, their sows when they are ready to farrow, nor offer to beat
or kick them (as is too frequent a practice) for fear of a miscarriage.

Many other advantages might be enumerated. For instance, [200]
the addition of some thousand carcasses in our exportation of
barrelled beef, the propagation of swine's flesh, and
improvement in the art of making good bacon, so much wanted
among us by the great destruction of pigs, too frequent at our
table, which are no way comparable in taste, or magnificence, to
a well-grown, fat yearling child, which roasted whole will
make a considerable figure at a Lord Mayor's feast, or any other
public entertainment. But this and many others I omit, being
studious of brevity.

Supposing that one thousand families in this city would be [210]
constant customers for infants' flesh, beside others who might
have it at merry-meetings, particularly at weddings and

---

[11] François Rabelais (see chapter 19).
[12] Roman Catholics, especially those who ardently support the pope.
[13] Slaughterhouses.

christenings, I compute that Dublin would take off annually about twenty thousand carcasses; and the rest of the kingdom (where probably they will be sold somewhat cheaper) the remaining eighty thousand.

I can think of no one objection, that will possibly be raised against this proposal, unless it should be urged that the number of people will be thereby much lessened in the kingdom. This I freely own, and it was indeed one principal   220
design in offering it to the world. I desire the reader to observe, that I calculate my remedy *for this one individual kingdom of Ireland, and for no other that ever was, is, or I think, ever can be upon earth.* Therefore let no man talk to me of other expedients: *Of taxing our absentees at five shillings a pound: Of using neither clothes, nor household furniture, except what is of our own growth and manufacture: Of utterly rejecting the materials and instruments that promote foreign luxury: Of curing the expensiveness of pride, vanity, idleness,*
and gaming[14] in our women: Of introducing a vein of parsimony,   230
prudence and temperance: Of learning to love our Country, wherein we differ even from Laplanders, and the inhabitants of Topinamboo[15]: Of quitting our animosities and factions, nor act any longer like Jews, who were murdering one another at the very moment their city was taken: Of being a little cautious not to sell our country and conscience for nothing: Of teaching landlords to have at least one degree of mercy toward their tenants. Lastly of putting a spirit of honesty, industry, and skill into our shopkeepers, who, if a resolution could now be taken to buy only our native goods,   240
would immediately unite to cheat and exact upon us in the price, the measure, and the goodness, nor could ever yet be brought to make one fair proposal of just dealing, though often and earnestly invited to it.

Q What aspects of Swift's proposal contribute to its effectiveness as a tool for political reform?

Voltaire and *Candide*

Swift's satires were an inspiration to that most scintillating of French *philosophes* and leading intellectual of French society, François Marie Arouet (1694–1778), who used the pen name Voltaire (Figure **25.4**). Born into a rising Parisian middle-class family and educated by Jesuits, Voltaire rose to fame as poet, playwright, critic, and as the central figure of the French *salons*. His visits to England instilled in him high regard for constitutional government, the principles of toleration, and the concepts of equality found in the writings of John Locke—all of which he championed in his writings. In his numerous pamphlets and letters, he attacked bigotry as man-made evil and injustice as institutional evil. On two separate occasions, his controversial

verse-satires led to his imprisonment in the Bastille (the French state prison).

More than any of the *philosophes*, Voltaire extolled the traditions of non-Western cultures: having read the works of Confucius in Jesuit translations, he esteemed the ancient teacher as a philosopher–sage. Voltaire was the first modern intellectual to assess the role of Russia in world society. In his *Essay on Manners*, a universal history that examines the customs of nations around the world, Voltaire gave thoughtful attention to the history of the Russian state. His fascination with Russia as a curious blend of Asian and European traditions became the basis for a lifelong pursuit of things Russian, including a long correspondence with Catherine the Great, who ruled as empress of Russia from 1762 to 1796.

Like most of the *philosophes*, Voltaire condemned organized religion and all forms of religious fanaticism. A declared deist, he compared human beings to mice who, living in the recesses of an immense ship, know nothing of its captain or its destination. Any confidence Voltaire might have had in beneficent Providence was dashed by the terrible Lisbon earthquake and tidal wave of 1755, which took the lives of more than 20,000 Portuguese. For Voltaire, the realities of natural disaster and human cruelty were not easily reconciled with the belief that a good God had created the universe or that humans were by nature rational—views basic to Enlightenment optimism.

Voltaire's satirical masterpiece, *Candide* (subtitled *Optimism*), addresses the age-old question of how evil can exist in a universe created and governed by the forces of good. A parody of the adventure romances

Figure 25.4 JEAN-ANTOINE HOUDON,
Voltaire in Old Age, 1781. Marble, height 20 in.

---

14 Gambling (the most popular pastime of the upper class).
15 A district in Brazil supposedly inhabited by savages.

and travel tales (Equiano and Swift both come to mind) in vogue in Voltaire's time, *Candide* relates the exploits of a naive and good-natured young man whose blissful life is daunted by a series of terrible (and hilarious) experiences. Initially, the youthful Candide (literally, "candid" or "frank") approaches life with the glib optimism taught to him by Dr. Pangloss (meaning "all tongue"), Voltaire's embodiment of Gottfried Wilhelm Leibniz (see chapter 24). But Candide soon discovers the folly of Leibniz's optimistic credo that "this is the best of [all] possible worlds." He experiences the horrors of war (the consequences of two equally self-righteous opposing armies), the evils of religious fanaticism (as manifested by the Spanish Inquisition), the disasters of nature (the Lisbon earthquake), and the dire effects of human greed (an affliction especially prevalent among the aristocracy and derived, according to Voltaire, from boredom). Experience becomes the antidote to the comfortable fatalism of Pope's "Whatever is, is right."

After a lifetime of sobering misadventures, Candide ends his days settled on a farm (in Turkey) in the company of his long-lost friends. (Not coincidentally, the aging Voltaire penned *Candide* while living on his farm retreat just outside Geneva.) "We must cultivate our garden," he concludes. This metaphor for achieving personal satisfaction in a hostile world relieves the otherwise devastating skepticism that underlies *Candide*. It is Voltaire's answer to blind optimism and to the foolish hope that human reason can combat evil.

Voltaire's genius, and the quality that separates his style from that of Swift, is his penetrating wit. Like the marksman's sword, Voltaire's satire is sharply pointed, precise in its aim, and devastating in its effect. With a sure hand, Voltaire manipulates the principal satirical devices: irony, understatement, and overstatement. Using irony—the contradiction between literal and intended meanings—he mocks serious matters and deflates lofty pretensions; he calls war, for instance, "heroic butchery" and refers to Paquetta's venereal disease as a "present" she received from "a very learned Franciscan." He exploits understatement when he notes, for example, that Pangloss "only lost one eye and one ear" (as the result of syphilis). And he uses overstatement for moral effect: the 350-pound baroness of Westphalia is "greatly respected"; thus corpulence—actually an indication of self-indulgence—becomes a specious sign of dignity and importance.

Voltaire's mock optimism, dispatched by Candide's persistent claim that this is "the best of all possible worlds" (even as he encounters repeated horrors), underscores the contradiction between the ideal and the real that lies at the heart of all satire. Although it was censored in many parts of Europe, *Candide* was so popular with the reading public that it went through forty editions in Voltaire's lifetime. A classic of Western satire, *Candide* has survived numerous adaptations, including a superb twentieth-century version as a comic operetta with lyrics by the American poet Richard Wilbur (b. 1921) and music by the American composer Leonard Bernstein (1918–1990).

READING 25.4 From Voltaire's *Candide, or Optimism* (1759)

Chapter 1

How Candide Was Brought Up in a Fine Castle, and How He Was Expelled From Thence

There lived in Westphalia,[1] in the castle of my Lord the Baron   1
of Thunder-ten-tronckh, a young man, on whom nature had
bestowed the most agreeable manners. His face was the index
to his mind. He had an upright heart, with an easy frankness;
which, I believe, was the reason he got the name of Candide.
He was suspected, by the old servants of the family, to be the
son of my Lord the Baron's sister, by a very honest gentleman
of the neighborhood, whom the young lady declined to marry,
because he could only produce seventy-one armorial
quarterings,[2] the rest of his genealogical tree having been   10
destroyed through the injuries of time.

The Baron was one of the most powerful lords in
Westphalia; his castle had both a gate and windows; and his
great hall was even adorned with tapestry. The dogs of his
outer yard composed his hunting pack upon occasion, his
grooms were his huntsmen, and the vicar of the parish was his
chief almoner. He was called My Lord by everybody, and
everyone laughed when he told his stories.

My Lady the Baroness, who weighed about three hundred
and fifty pounds, attracted, by that means, very great   20
attention, and did the honors of the house with a dignity that
rendered her still more respectable. Her daughter Cunegonde,
aged about seventeen years, was of a ruddy complexion, fresh,
plump, and well calculated to excite the passions. The Baron's
son appeared to be in every respect worthy of his father. The
preceptor, Pangloss,[3] was the oracle of the house, and little
Candide listened to his lectures with all the simplicity that was
suitable to his age and character.

Pangloss taught metaphysico-theologo-cosmoloonigology.[4]
He proved most admirably, that there could not be an effect   30
without cause; that, in this best of possible worlds,[5] my Lord
the Baron's castle was the most magnificent of castles, and my
Lady the best of Baronesses that possibly could be.

"It is demonstrable," said he, "that things cannot be
otherwise than they are: for things having been made for some
end, they must necessarily be for the best end. Observe well,
that the nose has been made for carrying spectacles; therefore
we have spectacles. The legs are visibly designed for
stockings, and therefore we have stockings. Stones have been
formed to be hewn, and make castles; therefore my Lord has   40
a very fine castle; the greatest baron of the province ought to

---

[1] A province in Germany.
[2] Genealogical degrees of noble ancestry; since each quartering represents one generation, the family "tree" is over 2000 years old—an obvious impossibility.
[3] The tutor's name is (literally) "all-tongue."
[4] In the original French version, the word *nigaud* ("booby") included in the elaborate title of this pompous-sounding discipline.
[5] One of many allusions in *Candide* to the philosophic optimism systematized by Leibniz and popularized by Pope (see chapter 24).

be the best accommodated. Swine were made to be eaten; therefore we eat pork all the year round: consequently, those who have merely asserted that all is good, have said a very foolish thing; they should have said all is the best possible."

Candide listened attentively, and believed implicitly; for he thought Miss Cunegonde extremely handsome, though he never had the courage to tell her so. He concluded, that next to the good fortune of being Baron of Thunder-ten-tronckh, the second degree of happiness was that of being Miss Cunegonde, the ⁵⁰ third to see her every day, and the fourth to listen to the teachings of Master Pangloss, the greatest philosopher of the province, and consequently of the whole world.

One day Cunegonde having taken a walk in the environs of the castle, in a little wood, which they called a park, espied Doctor Pangloss giving a lesson in experimental philosophy to her mother's chambermaid; a little brown wench, very handsome, and very docile. As Miss Cunegonde had a strong inclination for the sciences, she observed, without making any noise, the reiterated experiments that were going on before ⁶⁰ her eyes; she saw very clearly the sufficient reason of the Doctor, the effects and the causes; and she returned greatly flurried, quite pensive, and full of desire to be learned; imagining that she might be a sufficient reason for young Candide, who also, might be the same to her.

On her return to the castle, she met Candide, and blushed; Candide also blushed; she wished him good morrow with a faltering voice, and Candide answered her, hardly knowing what he said. The next day, after dinner, as they arose from table, Cunegonde and Candide happened to get behind the screen. ⁷⁰ Cunegonde dropped her handkerchief, and Candide picked it up; she, not thinking any harm, took hold of his hand; and the young man, not thinking any harm neither, kissed the hand of the young lady, with an eagerness, a sensibility, and grace, very particular; their lips met, their eyes sparkled, their knees trembled, their hands strayed.—The Baron of Thunder-ten-tronckh happening to pass close by the screen, and observing this cause and effect, thrust Candide out of the castle, with lusty kicks [to the behind]. Cunegonde fell into a swoon and as soon as she came to herself, was heartily cuffed on the ears ⁸⁰ by my Lady the Baroness. Thus all was thrown into confusion in the finest and most agreeable castle possible.

Chapter 2

What Became of Candide Among the Bulgarians⁶

Candide being expelled the terrestrial paradise, rambled a long while without knowing where, weeping, and lifting up his eyes to heaven, and sometimes turning them towards the finest of castles, which contained the handsomest of baronesses. He laid himself down, without his supper, in the open fields, between two furrows, while the snow fell in great flakes. Candide, almost frozen to death, crawled next morning to the neighboring village, which was called Waldber-ghoff-trarbk-dikdorff. ⁹⁰

---

⁶ Voltaire's name for the troops of Frederick the Great, king of Prussia, who, like their king, were widely regarded as Sodomites; the association between the name and the French *bougre* ("to bugger") is patent.

Having no money, and almost dying with hunger and fatigue, he stopped in a dejected posture before the gate of an inn. Two men, dressed in blue,⁷ observing him in such a situation, "Brother," says one of them to the other, "there is a young fellow well built, and of a proper height." They accosted Candide, and invited him very civilly to dinner.

"Gentlemen," replied Candide, with an agreeable modesty, "you do me much honor, but I have no money to pay my share."

"O sir," said one of the blues, "persons of your appearance and merit never pay anything; are you not five feet five ¹⁰⁰ inches high?"

"Yes, gentlemen, that is my height," returned he, making a bow.

"Come, sir, sit down at table; we will not only treat you, but we will never let such a man as you want money; men are made to assist one another."

"You are in the right," said Candide; "that is what Pangloss always told me, and I see plainly that everything is for the best."

They entreated him to take a few crowns, which he ¹¹⁰ accepted, and would have given them his note; but they refused it, and sat down to table.

"Do not you tenderly love—"

"O yes," replied he, "I tenderly love Miss Cunegonde."

"No," said one of the gentlemen; "we ask you if you do tenderly love the King of the Bulgarians?"

"Not at all," said he, "for I never saw him."

"How! he is the most charming of kings, and you must drink his health."

"O, with all my heart, gentlemen," and drinks. ¹²⁰

"That is enough," said they to him; "you are now the bulwark, the support, the defender, the hero of the Bulgarians; your fortune is made, and you are certain of glory." Instantly they put him in irons, and carried him to the regiment. They made him turn to the right, to the left, draw the ramrod, return the ramrod, present, fire, step double; and they gave him thirty blows with a cudgel. The next day, he performed his exercises not quite so badly, and received but twenty blows; the third day the blows were restricted to ten, and he was looked upon by his fellow-soldiers, as a kind of prodigy. ¹³⁰

Candide, quite stupefied, could not well conceive how he had become a hero. One fine Spring day he took it into his head to walk out, going straight forward, imagining that the human, as well as the animal species, were entitled to make whatever use they pleased of their limbs. He had not traveled two leagues, when four other heroes, six feet high, came up to him, bound him, and put him into a dungeon. He is asked by a Court-martial, whether he chooses to be whipped six and thirty times through the whole regiment, or receive at once twelve bullets through the forehead? He in vain argued that the will is free, and that ¹⁴⁰ he chose neither the one nor the other; he was obliged to make a choice; he therefore resolved, in virtue of God's gift called freewill, to run the gauntlet six and thirty times. He underwent this discipline twice. The regiment being composed of two thousand men, he received four thousand lashes, which laid open all his muscles and nerves, from the nape of the neck to

---

⁷ The color of the uniforms worn by the soldiers of Frederick the Great.

the back. As they were proceeding to a third course, Candide, being quite spent, begged as a favor that they would be so kind as to shoot him; he obtained his request; they hoodwinked him, and made him kneel; the King of the Bulgarians passing by, [150] inquired into the crime of the delinquent; and as this prince was a person of great penetration, he discovered from what he heard of Candide, that he was a young metaphysician, entirely ignorant of the things of this world; and he granted him his pardon, with a clemency which will be extolled in all histories, and throughout all ages. An experienced surgeon cured Candide in three weeks, with emollients prescribed by no less a master than Dioscorides.[8] His skin had already began to grow again, and he was able to walk, when the King of the Bulgarians gave battle to the King of the Abares. [160]

[Candide escapes from the Bulgarians and travels to Holland, where he encounters the ailing Pangloss. Surviving a tempest and a shipwreck, they arrive in Portugal.]

Chapter 6

How a Fine *Auto-da-Fé* [9] Was Celebrated to Prevent Earthquakes, and How Candide Was Whipped

After the earthquake, which had destroyed three-fourths of Lisbon, the sages of the country could not find any means more effectual to prevent a total destruction, than to give the people a splendid *auto-da-fé*. It had been decided by the university of Coimbra, that the spectacle of some persons burnt to death by a slow fire, with great ceremony, was an infallible antidote for earthquakes.

In consequence of this resolution, they had seized a [440] Biscayan, convicted of having married his godmother,[10] and two Portuguese, who, in eating a pullet, had stripped off the bacon.[11] After dinner, they came and secured Dr. Pangloss, and his disciple Candide; the one for having spoke too freely, and the other for having heard with an air of approbation. They were both conducted to separate apartments, extremely damp, and never incommoded with the sun.[12] Eight days after, they were both clothed with a gown[13] and had their heads adorned with paper crowns. Candide's crown and gown were painted with inverted flames, and with devils that had neither tails nor [450] claws; but Pangloss' devils had claws and tails, and the flames were pointed upwards. Being thus dressed, they marched in procession, and heard a very pathetic speech followed by fine music on a squeaking organ. Candide was whipped on the back in cadence, while they were singing; the Biscayan, and the two men who would not eat lard, were burnt; and Pangloss, though

it was contrary to custom, was hanged. The same day, the earth shook anew,[14] with a most dreadful noise.

Candide, affrighted, interdicted, astonished, all bloody, all panting, said to himself: "If this is the best of possible worlds, [460] what then are the rest? Supposing I had not been whipped now, I have been so, among the Bulgarians; but, Oh, my dear Pangloss; thou greatest of philosophers, that it should be my fate to see thee hanged without knowing for what! Oh! my dear Anabaptist! thou best of men, that it should be thy fate to be drowned in the harbor! Oh! Miss Cunegonde! the jewel of ladies, that it should be thy fate to have been outraged and slain!"

He returned, with difficulty, supporting himself, after being lectured, whipped, absolved, and blessed, when an old woman accosted him, and said: "Child, take courage, and follow me." [470]

Q **What attitudes, beliefs, and institutions does Voltaire attack in *Candide*?**

Q **How does Voltaire's *Candide* "reply" to Pope's *Essay on Man*?**

Satire in Chinese Literature

While literary satire drew enthusiastic audiences in the West, this genre also came into vogue elsewhere in the world. Following the Manchu conquest of China in the mid-seventeenth century, Chinese writers produced bitter fictional tales that satirized a wide variety of contemporary practices, including Buddhist rituals, commercial banditry, and homosexual unions.

One of the cruelest satires of the eighteenth century consisted of a collection of stories attacking the absurdities of the examination system by which talented individuals were brought into China's civil service. *The Scholars*, as the novel is titled, written around 1750 by Wu Jingzi (1701–1754), reflects Wu's failure to pass the highly competitive exams, which often brought pseudo-scholars to positions of great wealth and political power. The satire emphasized the unpopular and anti-Confucian truth that the morally unscrupulous often gain great prizes in the world, while the virtuous often go unrewarded.

Chinese satire was also effective in attacking some of the more socially inhibiting practices of traditional Chinese culture, such as female footbinding. Beginning in the eleventh century, upper-class Chinese parents bound the feet of their young daughters (thus breaking the arch and stunting the feet to half the normal size) in order to exempt them from common labor, hence making them more physically attractive as marriage partners to wealthy men.

Toward the end of the great age of Chinese prose fiction, the philologist Li Ruzhen (1763–1830) attacked this practice in a satire entitled *Flowers in the Mirror*. An adventure tale similar to *Gulliver's Travels* and *Candide*, *Flowers* is a series of loosely woven stories that recount the experiences

---

[8] A famous Greek physician of the first century C.E. whose book on medicine was for centuries a standard text.

[9] The public ceremony (literally, "act of faith") by which those found guilty of heresy were punished.

[10] A swipe at papal efforts to condemn as incestuous marriages in which the parties might be bound by family relation.

[11] Unwittingly revealing that they were secretly Jews—Jewish dietary laws prohibit the eating of pork. Under the pressure of the Spanish and Portuguese Inquisitions, many Iberian Jews had converted to Christianity.

[12] Prison cells.

[13] Yellow penitential garments worn by the confessed heretic.

[14] A second earthquake occurred in Lisbon on December 21, 1755.

of a voyager to many strange lands, including the Country of Two-Faced People, the Country of Long-Armed People, and the Country of Women. In the last of these fictional lands, the traditional roles of the sexes are reversed, and the ruling women of the country set upon the hero to prepare him as "royal concubine": they plait his hair, apply lipstick and powder to his face, pierce his ears, and, to his ultimate dismay, they bind his feet in the traditional Chinese manner. Li Ruzhen's blunt social criticism and his bold assertion of equal rights for women fell on deaf ears, for despite the fact that Manchu rulers censured footbinding, the custom continued in many parts of China until the early twentieth century.

READING 25.5 From Li Ruzhen's
Flowers in the Mirror (1828)

When Tang Ao heard that they had arrived at the Country of Women, he thought that the country was populated entirely by women, and was afraid to go ashore. But Old Tuo said, "Not at all! There are men as well as women, only they call men women, and women men. The men wear the skirts and take care of the home, while the women wear hats and trousers and manage affairs outside. If it were a country populated solely by women, I doubt that even Brother Lin here would dare to venture ashore, although he knows he always makes a good profit from sales here!" 10

"If the men dress like women, do they use cosmetics and bind their feet?" asked Tang Ao.

"Of course they do!" cried Lin, and took from his pocket a list of the merchandise he was going to sell, which consisted of huge quantities of rouge, face powder, combs and other women's notions. "Luckily I wasn't born in this country," he said. "Catch me mincing around on bound feet!"

When Tang Ao asked why he had not put down the price of the merchandise, Lin said, "The people here, no matter rich or poor, from the 'King' down to the simplest peasant, are all 20 mad about cosmetics. I'll charge them what I can. I shall have no difficulty selling the whole consignment to rich families in two or three days."

Beaming at the prospect of making a good profit, Lin went on shore with his list.

Tang Ao and Old Tuo decided to go and see the city. The people walking on the streets were small of stature, and rather slim, and although dressed in men's clothes, were beardless and spoke with women's voices, and walked with willowy steps. 30

"Look at them!" said Old Tuo. "They are perfectly normal-looking women. Isn't it a shame for them to dress like men?"

"Wait a minute," said Tang Ao. "Maybe when they see us, they think, 'Look at them, isn't it a shame that they dress like women'?"

"You're right. 'Whatever one is accustomed to always seems natural,' as the ancients say. But I wonder what the men are like?"

[Invited to sell his wares at the court of the "King," Lin visits the Palace.]

In a little time, Merchant Lin was ushered to a room upstairs where victuals of many kinds awaited him. As he ate, 40 however, he heard a great deal of noise downstairs. Several palace "maids" ran upstairs soon, and calling him "Your Highness," kowtowed to him and congratulated him. Before he knew what was happening, Merchant Lin was being stripped completely bare by the maids and led to a perfumed bath. Against the powerful arms of these maids, he could scarcely struggle. Soon he found himself being anointed, perfumed, powdered and rouged, and dressed in a skirt. His big feet were bound up in strips of cloth and socks, and his hair was combed into an elaborate braid over his head and decorated with pins. 50 These male "maids" thrust bracelets on his arms and rings on his fingers, and put a phoenix headdress on his head. They tied a jade green sash around his waist and put an embroidered cape around his shoulders.

Then they led him to a bed, and asked him to sit down.

Merchant Lin thought that he must be drunk, or dreaming, and began to tremble. He asked the maids what was happening, and was told that he had been chosen by the "King" to be the Imperial Consort, and that a propitious day would be chosen for him to enter the "King's" chambers. 60

Before he could utter a word, another group of maids, all tall and strong and wearing beards, came in. One was holding a threaded needle. "We are ordered to pierce your ears," he said, as the other four "maids" grabbed Lin by the arms and legs. The white-bearded one seized Lin's right ear, and after rubbing the lobe a little, drove the needle through it.

"Ooh!" Merchant Lin screamed.

The maid seized the other ear, and likewise drove the needle through it. As Lin screamed with pain, powdered lead was smeared on his earlobes and a pair of "eight-precious" 70 earrings was hung from the holes.

Having finished what they came to do, the maids retreated, and a black-bearded fellow came in with a bolt of white silk. Kneeling down before him, the fellow said, "I am ordered to bind Your Highness's feet."

Two other maids seized Lin's feet as the black-bearded one sat down on a low stool, and began to rip the silk into ribbons. Seizing Lin's right foot, he set it upon his knee, and sprinkled white alum powder between the toes and the grooves of the foot. He squeezed the toes tightly together, bent them down 80 so that the whole foot was shaped like an arch, and took a length of white silk and bound it tightly around it twice. One of the others sewed the ribbon together in small stitches. Again the silk went around the foot, and again, it was sewn up.

Merchant Lin felt as though his feet were burning, and wave after wave of pain rose to his heart. When he could stand it no longer, he let out his voice and began to cry. The "maids" had hastily made a pair of soft-soled red shoes, and these they put on both his feet.

"Please, kind brothers, go and tell Her Majesty that I'm a 90 married man," Lin begged. "How can I become her Consort? As for my feet, please liberate them. They have enjoyed the kind of freedom which scholars who are not interested in official careers enjoy! How can you bind them? Please tell your 'King' to let me go. I shall be grateful, and my wife will be very grateful."

But the maids said, "The King said that you are to enter his chambers as soon as your feet are bound. It is no time for talk of this kind."

When it was dark, a table was laid for him with mountains of meat and oceans of wine. But Merchant Lin only nibbled, and told the "maids" they could have the rest.

Still sitting on the bed, and with his feet aching terribly, he decided to lie down in his clothes for a rest.

At once a middle-aged "maid" came up to him and said, "Please, will you wash before you retire?"

No sooner was this said than a succession of maids came in with candles, basins of water and spittoon, dressing table, boxes of ointment, face powder, towels, silk handkerchiefs, and surrounded him. Lin had to submit to the motions of washing in front of them all. But after he had washed his face, a maid wanted to put some cream on it again.

Merchant Lin stoutly refused.

"But night time is the best time to treat the skin," the white-bearded maid said. "This powder has a lot of musk in it. It will make your skin fragrant, although I dare say it is fair enough already. If you use it regularly your skin will not only seem like white jade, but will give off a natural fragrance of its own. And the more fragrant it is, the fairer it will become, and the more lovely to behold, and the more lovable you will be. You'll see how good it is after you have used it regularly."

But Lin refused firmly, and the maids said, "If you are so stubborn, we will have to report this, and let Matron deal with you tomorrow."

Then they left him alone. But Lin's feet hurt so much that he could not sleep a wink. He tore at the ribbons with all his might, and after a great struggle succeeded in tearing them off. He stretched out his ten toes again, and luxuriating in their exquisite freedom, finally fell asleep.

The next morning, however, when the black-bearded maid discovered that he had torn off his foot-bandages, he immediately reported it to the "King," who ordered that Lin should be punished by receiving twenty strokes of the bamboo from the "Matron." Accordingly, a white-bearded "Matron" came in with a stick of bamboo about eight feet long, and when the others had stripped him and held him down, raised the stick and began to strike Lin's bottom and legs.

Before five strokes had been delivered, Lin's tender skin was bleeding, and the Matron did not have the heart to go on. "Look at her skin! Have you ever seen such white and tender and lovable skin? Why, I think indeed her looks are comparable to Pan An and Sung Yu!" the Matron thought to himself. "But what am I doing, comparing her bottom and not her face to them? Is that a compliment?"

The foot-binding maid came and asked Lin if he would behave from now on.

"Yes, I'll behave," Lin replied, and they stopped beating him. They wiped the blood from his wounds, and special ointment was sent by the "King" and ginseng soup was given him to drink.

Merchant Lin drank the soup, and fell on the bed for a rest. But the "King" had given orders that his feet must be bound again, and that he should be taught to walk on them. So with one maid supporting him on each side, Merchant Lin was marched up and down the room all day on his bound feet. When he lay down to sleep that night, he could not close his eyes for the excruciating pain.

But from now on, he was never left alone again. Maids took turns to sit with him. Merchant Lin knew that he was no longer in command of his destiny. . . .

Q What indignities are described in this satire?

Q What broader issues are suggested by the motif of role reversal?

The Visual Satires of William Hogarth

The visual counterpart of literary satire is found in the paintings and prints of the English artist William Hogarth (1697–1764). A master draftsman, Hogarth produced a telling visual record of the ills of eighteenth-century British society. Popular novels and plays provided inspiration for what Hogarth called his "modern moral subjects." He illustrated the novels of Defoe and Swift, including *Gulliver's Travels*, and executed a series of paintings based on John Gay's *Beggar's Opera*—a mock-heroic comedy that equated low-class crime with high-class corruption. The theater prompted many of the devices Hogarth used for pictorial representation: boxlike staging, lighting from below, and a wealth of "props." "I have endeavored," he wrote, "to treat my subjects as a dramatic writer: my picture is my stage, and men and women my actors."

Hogarth made engraved versions of his paintings and sold them (just as the volumes of Diderot's *Encyclopédie* were vended) by subscription. So popular were Hogarth's prints that they were pirated and sold without his authorization (a practice that continued even after Parliament passed the first copyright law in 1735). Especially successful were two series of prints based on his paintings. The first ("The Harlot's Progress") illustrates the misfortunes of a young woman who becomes a London prostitute; the second ("The Rake's Progress") depicts the comic misadventures of an antihero and ne'er-do-well named Tom Rakewell.

Following these, Hogarth published a series of six engravings entitled "Marriage à la Mode," which describes the tragic consequences of a marriage of convenience between the son of a poverty-stricken nobleman and the daughter of a wealthy and ambitious merchant. The first print in the series, *The Marriage Transaction*, shows the two families negotiating the terms of the matrimonial union (Figure **25.5**). The scene unfolds as if upon a stage: the corpulent Lord Squanderfield, victim of the gout (an ailment traditionally linked with rich food and drink), sits pompously in his ruffled velvet waistcoat, pointing to his family tree, which springs from the loins of William the Conqueror. Across the table, the wealthy merchant and father of the bride carefully peruses the financial terms of the marriage settlement. On a settee in the corner of the room, the pawns of this socially expedient match turn away from each other in attitudes of mutual dislike. The earl's son, young Squanderfield, sporting a beauty patch, opens

Figure 25.5 WILLIAM HOGARTH, *The Marriage Transaction*, from the "Marriage à la Mode" series, 1742–1746. Engraving, 15 × 18 in.

his snuffbox and vainly gazes at himself in a mirror, while his bride-to-be idly dangles her betrothal ring on a kerchief. She leans forward to hear the honeyed words of her future seducer, a lawyer named Lord Silvertongue. A combination of **caricature** (exaggeration of peculiarities or defects), comic irony, and symbolic detail, Hogarth's "stylish marriage" is drawn with a stylus every bit as sharp as Voltaire's pen.

Like Voltaire's Paris, Hogarth's London was not yet an industrial metropolis, but it was plagued by some of the worst urban conditions of the day. It lacked sewers, streetlights, and adequate law enforcement. A city of vast contrasts between rich and poor, it was crowded with thieves, drunks, and prostitutes, all of whom threatened the jealously guarded privileges of the rich. Hogarth represented mid-eighteenth-century London at its worst in the famous engraving *Gin Lane* (Figure **25.6**). This devastating attack on the combined evils of urban poverty and alcoholism portrays poor, ragged, and drunk men and women in various stages of depravity. Some pawn their possessions to support their expensive addictions (lower left); others commit suicide (upper right corner); and one pours gin down the throat of a babe-in-arms, following the common practice of using liquor and other drugs to quiet noisy infants (far right). In the center of the print is the figure of a drunken mother—her leg covered with syphilitic sores—who carelessly allows her child to fall over the edge of the stair rail.

Hogarth's visual satirization of gin addiction was a heroic attack on the social conditions of his time and on drug abuse in general. But even Parliament's passage of the Gin Law in 1751, which more than doubled the gin tax, did little to reduce the widespread use of this popular alcoholic beverage in eighteenth-century England. While Hogarth's prints failed to reduce the ills and inequities of his society, they remain an enduring condemnation of human hypocrisy, cruelty, vanity, and greed.

Rousseau's Revolt Against Reason

Jean-Jacques Rousseau, introduced in chapter 24 as a contributor to Diderot's *Encyclopédie*, was one of the Enlightenment's most outspoken critics. A playwright, composer, and educator, Rousseau took issue with some of the basic precepts of Enlightenment thought, including the idea that the progress of the arts and sciences might improve human conduct. Human beings may be good by nature, argued Rousseau, but they are ultimately corrupted by society and its institutions. "God makes all things good," he wrote; "man meddles with them and they become evil." Rousseau condemned the artificiality of civilized life and, although he did not advocate that humankind should return to a "state of nature," he exalted the "noble savage" as the model of the uncorrupted individual.

Rousseau's philosophy of the heart elevated the role of instinct over reason and encouraged a new appreciation of nature and the natural—principles that underlay the romantic movement of the early nineteenth century (see chapters 27 to 29). In the following excerpt from the *Discourse on the Origin of Inequality among Men* (1755), Rousseau gives an eloquent account of how, in his view, human beings came to lose their freedom and their innocence.

Figure 25.6 WILLIAM HOGARTH, *Gin Lane*, 1751. Engraving. Above the doorway of the Gin Shop on the lower left are the words, "Drunk for a penny, dead drunk for two pence, clean straw for nothing." (The straw provided bedding for the poor.)

READING 25.6 From Rousseau's *Discourse on the Origin of Inequality among Men* (1755)

The first man who, having enclosed a piece of land, thought   1
of saying "This is mine" and found people simple enough to
believe him, was the true founder of civil society. How many
crimes, wars, murders; how much misery and horror the human
race would have been spared if someone had pulled up the
stakes and filled in the ditch and cried out to his fellow men:
"Beware of listening to this impostor. You are lost if you forget
that the fruits of the earth belong to everyone and that the earth
itself belongs to no one!" But it is highly probable that by
this time things had reached a point beyond which they could   10
not go on as they were; for the idea of property, depending on
many prior ideas which could only have arisen in successive
stages, was not formed all at once in the human mind. It was
necessary for men to make much progress, to acquire much
industry and knowledge, to transmit and increase it from age
to age, before arriving at this final stage of the state of nature.
Let us therefore look farther back, and try to review from a single
perspective the slow succession of events and discoveries in
their most natural order.

Man's first feeling was that of his existence, his first   20
concern was that of his preservation. The products of the earth

furnished all the necessary aids; instinct prompted him to make
use of them. While hunger and other appetites made him
experience in turn different modes of existence, there was one
appetite which urged him to perpetuate his own species; and
this blind impulse, devoid of any sentiment of the heart,
produced only a purely animal act. The need satisfied, the two
sexes recognized each other no longer, and even the child meant
nothing to the mother, as soon as he could do without her.

Such was the condition of nascent[1] man; such was the life   30
of an animal limited at first to mere sensation; and scarcely
profiting from the gifts bestowed on him by nature, let alone was
he dreaming of wresting anything from her. But difficulties soon
presented themselves and man had to learn to overcome them.
The height of trees, which prevented him from reaching their
fruits; the competition of animals seeking to nourish themselves
on the same fruits; the ferocity of animals who threatened his
life—all this obliged man to apply himself to bodily exercises;
he had to make himself agile, fleet of foot,
and vigorous in combat. Natural weapons—branches of trees   40
and stones—were soon found to be at hand. He learned to
overcome the obstacles of nature, to fight when necessary
against other animals, to struggle for his subsistence even

---

[1] Early, developing.

against other men, or to indemnify[2] himself for what he was forced to yield to the stronger.

[Rousseau then describes how people devised a technology for hunting and fishing, invented fire, and developed superiority over other creatures.]

Instructed by experience that love of one's own wellbeing is the sole motive of human action, he found himself in a position to distinguish the rare occasions when common interest justified his relying on the aid of his fellows, and those even rarer occasions when competition should make him distrust them. In the first case, he united with them in a herd, or at most in a sort of free association that committed no one and which lasted only as long as the passing need which had brought it into being. In the second case, each sought to grasp his own advantage, either by sheer force, if he believed he had the strength, or by cunning and subtlety if he felt himself to be the weaker. . . .

. . . the habit of living together generated the sweetest sentiments known to man, conjugal love and paternal love. Each family became a little society, all the better united because mutual affection and liberty were its only bonds; at this stage also the first differences were established in the ways of life of the two sexes which had hitherto been identical. Women became more sedentary and accustomed themselves to looking after the hut and the children while men went out to seek their common subsistence. The two sexes began, in living a rather softer life, to lose something of their ferocity and their strength; but if each individual became separately less able to fight wild beasts, all, on the other hand, found it easier to group together to resist them jointly. . . .

To the extent that ideas and feelings succeeded one another, and the heart and mind were exercised, the human race became more sociable, relationships became more extensive and bonds tightened. People grew used to gathering together in front of their huts or around a large tree; singing and dancing, true progeny[3] of love and leisure, became the amusement, or rather the occupation, of idle men and women thus assembled. Each began to look at the others and to want to be looked at himself; and public esteem came to be prized. He who sang or danced the best; he who was the most handsome, the strongest, the most adroit[4] or the most eloquent became the most highly regarded, and this was the first step toward inequality and at the same time toward vice. From those first preferences there arose, on the one side, vanity and scorn, on the other, shame and envy, and the fermentation produced by these new leavens[5] finally produced compounds fatal to happiness and innocence.

As soon as men learned to value one another and the idea of consideration was formed in their minds, everyone claimed a right to it, and it was no longer possible for anyone to be refused consideration without affront. This gave rise to the first duties of civility, even among savages: and henceforth

every intentional wrong became an outrage, because together with the hurt which might result from the injury, the offended party saw an insult to his person which was often more unbearable than the hurt itself. Thus, as everyone punished the contempt shown him by another in a manner proportionate to the esteem he accorded himself, revenge became terrible, and men grew bloodthirsty and cruel. This is precisely the stage reached by most of the savage peoples known to us; and it is for lack of having sufficiently distinguished between different ideas and seen how far those peoples already are from the first state of nature that so many authors have hastened to conclude that man is naturally cruel and needs civil institutions to make him peaceable, whereas in truth nothing is more peaceable than man in his primitive state. Placed by nature at an equal distance from the stupidity of brutes[6] and the fatal enlightenment of civilized man, limited equally by reason and instinct to defending himself against evils which threaten him, he is restrained by natural pity from doing harm to anyone, even after receiving harm himself: for according to the wise Locke: "Where there is no property, there is no injury."

But it must be noted that society's having come into existence and relations among individuals having been already established meant that men were required to have qualities different from those they possessed from their primitive constitution. . . .

As long as men were content with their rustic huts, as long as they confined themselves to sewing their garments of skin with thorns or fishbones, and adorning themselves with feathers or shells, to painting their bodies with various colors, to improving or decorating their bows and arrows; and to using sharp stones to make a few fishing canoes or crude musical instruments; in a word, so long as they applied themselves only to work that one person could accomplish alone and to arts that did not require the collaboration of several hands, they lived as free, healthy, good and happy men. . . .

. . . but from the instant one man needed the help of another, and it was found to be useful for one man to have provisions enough for two, equality disappeared, property was introduced, work became necessary, and vast forests were transformed into pleasant fields which had to be watered with the sweat of men, and where slavery and misery were soon seen to germinate and flourish with the crops. . . .

Q What aspects of civilized life, according to Rousseau, weaken and corrupt society?

Rousseau was haunted by contradictions within the social order and within his own mind (he suffered acute attacks of paranoia during the last fifteen years of his life). The opening words of his treatise *The Social Contract* (1762), "Man is born free, and everywhere he is in chains," reflect his apprehension concerning the inhibiting role of institutional authority. In order to safeguard individual liberty, said Rousseau, people should form a contract among themselves. Unlike Hobbes, whose social contract

---

[2] Compensate.
[3] Offspring.
[4] Skillful.
[5] Significant changes.

[6] Beasts.

involved transferring absolute authority from the citizens to a sovereign ruler, or Locke, whose social contract gave limited power to the ruler, Rousseau defined the state as "the general will" of its citizens. "The general will alone," he explained, "can direct the State according to the object for which it was instituted, that is, the common good." Rousseau insisted, moreover, that whoever refused to obey the general will should be constrained to do so by the whole society; that is, all humans should "be forced to be free." "As nature gives each man absolute power over all his members," wrote Rousseau, "the social compact gives the body politic absolute power over all its members also." Such views might have contributed to newly developed theories of democracy, but they were equally effective in justifying totalitarian constraints leveled in the name of the people.

Rousseau and Education

Rousseau's wish to preserve the natural also led him to propose revolutionary changes in education. If society is indeed hopelessly corrupt, then let children grow up in accord with nature, argued Rousseau. In *Emile* (1762), his treatise on education, Rousseau advanced the hypothesis—unheard of in his time—that the education of a child begins at birth. He divided childhood development into five stages over a twenty-five-year span and outlined the type of rearing desirable for each stage.

"Hands-on" experience was essential to education, according to Rousseau, especially in the period just prior to the development of reason and intellect, which he placed between the ages of twelve and fifteen. "Nature provides for the child's growth in her own fashion, and this should never be thwarted. Do not make him sit still when he wants to run about, nor run when he wants to be quiet."

Rousseau also made a clear distinction between the education of men and that of women. Arguing that a woman's place was in the home and beside the cradle, he proposed for her a domestic education that cultivated modesty, obedience, and other virtues agreeable to her mate. Describing Emile's ideal mate, Rousseau writes, "Her education is in no way exceptional. She has taste without study, talents without art, judgment without knowledge. Her mind is still vacant but has been trained to learn; it is a well-tilled land only waiting for the grain. What a pleasing ignorance! Happy is the man destined to instruct her." Thus Rousseau's views on female education were less "enlightened" (by the standards of Mary Wollstonecraft, for one) than those advanced by Castiglione some 200 years earlier in *The Book of the Courtier* (see chapter 16). Nevertheless, *Emile* became a landmark in educational theory. Rousseau's unique approach to education—particularly his emphasis on the cultivation of natural inquisitiveness over and above rote learning—influenced modern teaching methods such as those developed by the Italian educator Maria Montessori (1870–1952). Ironically, however, Rousseau saw fit to put all five of his own children in a foundling hospital rather than raise them himself.

Kant's Mind/World Revolution

The German philosopher Immanuel Kant (1724–1804) was a defender of Enlightenment values; but he was also a critic of its view of reason as the ultimate means of understanding reality. In his essay, "An Answer to the Question, What is Enlightenment" (1784), he wrote, "Enlightenment is man's emergence from his self-imposed immaturity. Immaturity is the inability to use one's understanding without guidance from another." Rules, formulas, and traditional beliefs, he regarded as "shackles" that inhibit us from thinking for ourselves. "*Sapare Aude!*" ("Dare to know"), he proclaimed—that is, have the courage to think for yourself.

In the realm of philosophy, Kant fulfilled his own injunction, becoming one of the greatest philosophers of his time. His monumental work, the *Critique of Pure Reason*, published in 1781, attacked previous philosophic theories that held reason as the sole means of discovering the nature of reality. Taking issue with the theories of his predecessors, he argued that the manner in which one perceives the world depends on specific qualities in the perceiver's mind. The mind, according to Kant, is not a passive recipient of information (Locke's "blank slate"); rather, it participates in the process of knowing the world. Concepts such as time, space, and causality are innate conditions that organize experience. These intuitive forms, along with certain categories of thought (quantity, quality, relationship, and modality) exist in the mind from birth; they shape the data of the senses into a consistent picture of the world.

Kant claimed to have altered the relationship between mind and world as radically as Copernicus had changed the relationship between earth and sun. Shifting the focus of philosophic debate from the nature of objective reality to the question of cognition itself—the process by which the mind comprehends experience—he perceived the mind as not merely reflecting experience, but as organizing experience into a coherent pattern. The preeminence Kant gave to the role of the mind in constructing our idea of the world laid the basis for transcendental **idealism**, the doctrine that holds that reality consists of the mind and its forms of perception and understanding.

A giant in the field of modern ethics, Kant assessed the limits of reason with regard to morality. In contrast to Descartes and Locke, who held that knowledge was the key to intellectual advancement, Kant viewed knowledge as the vehicle of moral law. Recognizing that notions of good and evil differ widely in the world, Kant proposed a "supreme principle of morality," one that applied equally to all rational beings. In his *Critique of Practical Reason* (1788), he advanced a universal moral law, known as the "categorical imperative": we must act as if we could will that the maxim of our actions become the law for all humankind. The basis of this moral law is the recognition of our duty to act in ways justified by reasons so universal that they are good for all people at all times. It is not enough that our acts have good effects; it is necessary that we *will* the good. Kant's notion of "good will" is not identical with the Christian concept of mercy. Nor is it the same as Jesus' commandment: "Do to others as you would wish them do to you." In essence, ethical conduct is based not on love for humankind (which, after all, one may lack), but on the imperative to act rationally, a condition essential to human dignity.

The Revolutions of the Late Eighteenth Century

The American and French revolutions drew inspiration from the Enlightenment faith in the reforming power of reason. Both, however, demonstrated the limits of reason in the face of militant zeal.

The American Revolution

As early as 1776, North America's thirteen colonies had rebelled against the long-standing political control of the British government. In the Declaration of Independence (see chapter 24), Jefferson restated Locke's assertion that government must protect its citizens' rights to life, liberty, and property. The British government, however, in making unreasonable demands for revenues, threatened colonial liberty, igniting the passions of fervent populists who sought democratic reform. Following some seven years of armed conflict, several thousand battle deaths, and a war expense estimated at over $100 million, in 1783 the thirteen colonies achieved their independence. And, in 1789, they began to function under the Constitution of the United States of America. The British political theorist Thomas Paine (1737–1809) proclaimed that the revolution had done more to enlighten the world and diffuse a spirit of freedom among humankind than any event that had preceded it.

The French Revolution

The American Revolution did not go unnoticed in France. French intellectuals followed its every turn; the French government secretly aided the American cause and eventually joined in the war against Britain. However, the revolution that began on French soil in 1789 involved circumstances that were quite different from those in America. The French Revolution was, in the main, the product of two major problems: class inequality, and a serious financial crisis brought about by some 500 years of costly wars and royal extravagances (see chapter 21). In France, the lower classes sought to overturn long-standing social and political institutions and end upper-class privilege. With his nation on the verge of bankruptcy, King Louis XVI (1774–1792) sought new measures for raising revenue.

Throughout French history, taxes had fallen exclusively on the shoulders of the lower and middle classes, the so-called Third Estate. Almost four-fifths of the average peasant's income went to pay taxes, which supported the privileged upper classes. In a population of some twenty-five million people, the First Estate (the clergy) and the Second Estate (the nobility)—a total of only 200,000 citizens—controlled nearly half the land in France; yet they were exempt from paying taxes. Peasant grievances were not confined to matters of taxation: population growth and rising prices led to severe shortages of bread, the principal food of the lower classes.

When, in an effort to obtain public support for new taxes, Louis XVI called a meeting of the Estates General—its first in 175 years—the Third Estate withdrew. Declaring itself representative of the general will of the people, it formed a separate body claiming the right to approve or veto all taxation. This daring act set the revolution in motion. No sooner had the Third Estate proclaimed itself a national assembly than great masses of peasants and laborers began to riot throughout France.

On July 14, 1789, crowds stormed the Bastille and destroyed the visible symbol of the old French regime (Figure 25.7). Less than one month later, on August 4, the National Assembly—as the new body established by the Third Estate called itself—issued decrees that abolished the last remnants of medieval feudalism, including manorial

Figure 25.7 BRIFFAULT DE LA CHARPRAIS and **MME. ESCLAPART**, *The Siege of the Bastille, July 14, 1789*, 1791–1796. Engraving, 12 × 18¼ in.

courts, feudal duties, and church tithes. It also made provisions for a limited monarchy and an elected legislative assembly. The decrees of the National Assembly became part of a constitution, prefaced by the Declaration of the Rights of Man and Citizen. Modeled on the American Declaration of Independence, the preface listed among its seventeen articles due process of law, religious freedom, and taxation based on the ability to pay. The body of the document promised a constitutional monarchy, a uniform code of law, and free public education.

Not all of the "rights of man," applied equally to women. The right to vote, to sue for divorce, and to hold public office, were all withheld from women. In 1791, Olympe de Gouges (1748–1793), a butcher's daughter and a vocal advocate of women's rights, drafted a Declaration of the Rights of Woman and the Female Citizen. If a woman has the right to mount the scaffold, claimed de Gouges, "she must equally have the right to mount the rostrum." The declaration demanded equal political rights and responsibilities for women, the sex de Gouges described as "superior in beauty and courage." (Indeed, in October of 1789, 6000 courageous women had marched on Versailles to protest the lack of bread in Paris.) For the first time in history women constituted a collective revolutionary force, making demands for equal property rights, government employment for women, and equal educational opportunities—demands guaranteed by the Constitution of 1793 but lost less than two years later by the terms of a new constitution. Despite her tireless efforts, de Gouge's declaration was never passed into law.

While equality for women was not achieved in this era, in 1793, the Constitutional Convention voted to ban slavery in all French colonies. The decision was inspired in part by the impassioned appeals of the former Senegalese slave Jean-Baptiste Bellay (1746–1805; Figure **25.8**), one of three convention delegates from the French Caribbean island of Saint Domingue (present-day Haiti), where slaves under the leadership of Pierre-Dominique Toussaint-Louverture (1745–1803) had revolted two years earlier.

Enlightenment idealism, summed up in Rousseau's slogan "Liberty, Equality, Fraternity," had inflamed popular passions and inspired egalitarian reforms. Nevertheless, from the storming of the Bastille through the rural revolts and mass protests that followed, angry, unreasoning mobs controlled the course of the revolution. Divisions among the revolutionaries themselves soon led to a more radical phase of the revolution, called the Reign of Terror. This phase saw the failure of the existing government and sent Louis XVI and his queen, Marie Antoinette, to the guillotine. Between 1793 and 1794, over 40,000 people (including Olympe de Gouges) met their deaths at the guillotine. Others, members of the radical minority known as the Jacobins, met death by the hands of their ideological enemies. Jean-Paul Marat (1743–1793), a Jacobin hero and radical antiroyalist journalist, was assassinated in his bathtub, an event immortalized by his friend, the artist Jacques-Louis David (discussed in chapter 26). Shown in the wooden tub he bathed in to treat a skin condition, he holds the letter by which his assassin, the royalist extremist Charlotte Corday, gained entry to his chambers (see Figure 25.1). The painting, presented by David to the National Convention in October 1793, four months after Marat's death, became a highly celebrated image of patriotic martyrdom. Within eight months, however, David himself was imprisoned, as the Reign of Terror ended with the sweeping condemnation (and execution) of Jacobin extremists.

Finally, in 1794, a National Convention devised a system of government run by two legislative chambers and a five-man executive body of directors. One of these—Napoleon Bonaparte (1769–1821)—would turn France into a military dictatorship some five years later. If, indeed, the French Revolution defended the Enlightenment bastions of liberty and equality, its foundations of reason and rationality ultimately crumbled under the forces of extremism and violence. The radicals of this and many other world-historical revolutions to follow rewrote the words of the *philosophes* in blood.

Science and Technology

1752	Benjamin Franklin proves that lightning is a form of electricity
1783	the first parachute is used in France
1783	the French make the first manned hot-air balloon flight
1795	the Springfield flintlock musket is developed in the United States

Chronology

May 5, 1789	Meeting of the Estates General
July 14, 1789	Fall of the Bastille
August 26, 1789	Declaration of the Rights of Man and Citizen
October 1791	Legislative Assembly
September 1792	France declared a republic
January 1793	Louis XVI executed
1793–1794	Reign of Terror
1795–1799	Napoleon rules the Directory

Figure 25.8 ANNE-LOUIS GIRODET-TRIOSON, *Jean-Baptiste Bellay, Deputy from Santo Domingo*, 1797.
Bellay, who publicly advocated liberty for all black people, is depicted by Girodet, a student of David, in the
style of the aristocratic portrait (see chapter 21). Wearing the uniform of a member of the French National
Convention, Bellay stands before the bust of Guillaume-Thomas Raynal (1713–1796), an abolitionist and the
author of a political history of the trade between Europe and the West Indies.

LOOKING BACK

The Industrial Revolution

- The invention of new mechanical devices worked to transform Europe's agrarian and handicraft-dominated economy into one dominated by the technology of mass production.
- The steam engine, the technology of cast iron, and the factory system had major effects on social and economic life, the most immediate of which involved the exploitation of labor.

The Transatlantic Slave Trade

- The failure of the Enlightenment promise of social justice and reform was nowhere better illustrated than in the inhumane activities of the transatlantic slave trade.
- Olaudah Equiano's autobiography protested the trade in African slaves that persisted throughout the eighteenth century.

Satire: Weapon of the Enlightenment

- In England, the keenest critic of Enlightenment idealism was Jonathan Swift, whose classic satires, *Gulliver's Travels* and *A Modest Proposal*, attack the moral pettiness and inhumanity of humankind.
- In France, the acerbic writings of Voltaire described human folly as a universal condition. Voltaire's *Candide* remains the classic statement of comic skepticism in Western literature.
- The European masters of satire found their East Asian counterpart in Li Ruzhen, an outspoken and witty critic of outmoded Chinese traditions.
- Voltaire's contemporary William Hogarth brought the bitter invective of the satirists to the visual arts. His engravings exposed the social ills and class discrepancies of British society, even as they mocked universal human vices.

Rousseau's Revolt Against Reason

- Questioning the value of reason for the advancement of the human condition, Jean-Jacques Rousseau argued that society itself corrupts humankind. He rejected the artificiality of the wig-and-silk-stocking culture in which he lived and championed "man in his primitive state."
- Rousseau's treatises on social history, government, and education explored ways in which individuals might retain their natural goodness and remain free and self-determining.

Kant's Mind/World Revolution

- In Germany, the philosopher Immanuel Kant examined the limits of the mind in the process of knowing.
- He argued that human beings have knowledge of the world through certain innate capabilities of mind.
- Kant appealed to "good will" as the basis for moral action.

The Revolutions of the Late Eighteenth Century

- While Enlightenment ideals fueled armed revolt in both America and France, the revolutions themselves blazed with antirational sentiment.
- French intellectuals followed the events of the American Revolution closely; the French government secretly aided the American cause and eventually joined in the war against Britain.
- In France, on July 14, 1789, crowds stormed the Bastille and destroyed the visible symbol of the old French regime. Less than one month later, the National Assembly was formed. In 1794, following a Reign of Terror, the French established a governing legislative system and executive directory.
- Those who fired the cannons of revolt found reason inadequate to the task of effecting social and political reform. Operating according to the dictates of their passions and their will, they gave dramatic evidence of the limits of reason in creating a heaven on earth.

Glossary

caricature exaggeration of peculiarities or defects to produce comic or burlesque effects

idealism in philosophy, the theory that holds that reality consists of the mind and its ideas; transcendental (or critical) idealism is Kant's name for the doctrine that knowledge is a synthetic product of the logical self

Chapter

26

Eighteenth-Century Art, Music, and Society

ca. 1700–1820

"In the presence of this miracle of [ancient Greek] art, I forget the whole universe and my soul acquires a loftiness appropriate to its dignity."
Johann Joachim Winckelmann

Figure 26.1 JEAN-HONORÉ FRAGONARD, *The Swing*, 1768–1769. Oil on canvas, 32 × 25½ in. Cupid, depicted as a watchful garden sculpture (on the left), reacts to the amorous flirtations below by coyly putting his finger to his lips. Fragonard's deft brushstrokes render the surrounding foliage in delicate tones of gold, green, and blue.

LOOKING AHEAD

The dynamics of class and culture had a shaping influence on the arts of the eighteenth century. The Church and the royal courts remained the principal sources of artistic patronage, but a rising middle class presented opportunities for new audiences and contemporary subjects. While the arts of the era broadly reflect the intellectual ideals of the Enlightenment, they more closely mirror the tastes and values of different segments of society. No single style dominated the entire century, but three distinctive modes of expression emerged.

European aristocrats, who dominated artistic patronage between 1715 and 1750, found pleasure in an elegant and refined style known as the Rococo. Enlightenment reformers and members of the rising middle class favored genre paintings that described everyday life and the values of ordinary people. Genre painting became the visual equivalent of the popular novels, journalistic essays, and stage plays of the period. Toward the end of the century, the newly excavated ruins of ancient Greece and Rome inspired an archeological appreciation of antiquity and the rise of the Neoclassical style. Neoclassicism conveyed the rationalism and political idealism of reformers and revolutionaries in France and the young American republic.

In music, the eighteenth century witnessed a move away from the playful and delicate Rococo style to the formal precision of the classical symphony and the string quartet. An increased demand for secular entertainment called forth new types of instrumental music and a musical language that featured clarity and order. Despite their stylistic diversity, the arts shared a spirit of optimism and vitality that ensured their endurance beyond the Age of Enlightenment.

The Rococo Style

The Rococo style was born in France among members of the leisured nobility who had outlived Louis XIV. At Versailles and in the elegant urban townhouses (or *hôtels*, as they were called) of Paris, where the wealthy gathered to enjoy the pleasures of dancing, dining, and conversing, the Rococo provided an atmosphere of elegant refinement. The word "Rococo" derives from *rocaille*, French for the fancy rock- or shellwork that was commonly used to ornament aristocratic gardens and grottoes. Rococo interiors display the organic vitality of seashells, plants, and flowers. Rococo artists preserved the ornate and luxuriant features of the Baroque style, but they favored elements of play and intimacy that were best realized in works of a small scale, such as porcelain figurines, furniture, and paintings suitable for domestic quarters.

The Salon de la Princesse in the Hôtel de Soubise in Paris typifies the Rococo style (Figure **26.2**): its interior is airy and fragile by comparison with a Louis XIV *salon* (see Figure 21.10). Brilliant white walls accented with pastel tones of rose, pale blue, and lime replace the ruby reds and royal blues of the Baroque *salon*. The geometric regularity of the Baroque interior has given way to an organic medley of curves and countercurves, echoed in elegant mirrors and chandeliers. The walls,

Figure 26.2 GERMAIN BOFFRAND, Salon de la Princesse, Hôtel de Soubise, Paris, ca. 1740. Oval shaped, max. 33 × 26 ft. The Hôtel de Soubise, a fourteenth-century manor house, was remodeled in the early eighteenth century. Its oval *salons*, ornamented with gilded carvings and mirrors, look out onto gardens.

ornamented with gilded tendrils, playful cupids, and floral garlands, melt into sensuously painted ceiling vaults crowned with graceful moldings.

Rococo furnishings are generally more delicate than Baroque furnishings, and chairs are often fully upholstered—an innovation of the eighteenth century. Bureaus and tables may be fitted with panels of porcelain (Figure 26.3)—a Chinese technique that Marie Antoinette, the consort of Louis XVI, introduced at Versailles. Aristocratic women—Marie Antoinette in France, Catherine the Great in Russia, and Maria Theresa in Austria—were enthusiastic patrons of the Rococo style. Indeed, the Rococo may be said to reflect the distinctive influence of eighteenth-century women of taste.

Beyond the *salon*, the garden was the favorite setting for the leisured elite. Unlike Versailles' geometrically ordered parks, Rococo gardens imitated the calculated naturalism of the Chinese garden. They featured undulating paths that gave false impressions of scale and distance. They might include artificial lakes, small colonnaded temples, ornamental pagodas, and other architectural "follies." Both outdoors and in, the fascination with imported Chinese objects and motifs—which began as a fashion in Europe around 1720—promoted the cult of *chinoiserie* (see chapter 21).

Although the Rococo style originated in France, it reached spectacular heights in the courts of secular princes

Figure 26.3 MARTIN CARLIN (master 1766–1785), Lady's desk, ca. 1775. Decorated with Sèvres porcelain plaques; tulipwood, walnut, and hardwood veneered on oak, height 31⅞ in., width 25⅛ in., depth 16 in. Known as a *bonheur-du-jour*, this small writing desk was probably made for the Comtesse du Barry, Louise XV's mistress.

elsewhere in Europe. In Austria and the German states, it became the favorite style for the ornamentation of rural pilgrimage churches. The walls of Bavaria's Benedictine abbey church of Ottobeuren, designed by the German architect Johann Michael Fischer (1692–1766), seem to disappear beneath a riot of stucco "frosting" as rich and sumptuous as that on any wedding cake (Figure 26.4). The more restrained elegance of French Rococo interiors here erupts in a dazzling array of organic forms that sprout from the moldings and cornices like unruly flora. Shimmering light floods into the white-walled interior through oval windows, and pastel-colored frescoes turn ceilings and walls into heavenly antechambers. Illusionism reigns: wooden columns and stucco cornices are painted to look like marble; angels and cherubs, tendrils and leaves, curtains and clouds—all made of wood and stucco that have been painted and gilded—come to life as props in a theater of miracles. At Ottobeuren, the somber majesty of the Roman Baroque church has given way to a sublime vision of paradise that is also a feast for the senses.

Rococo Painting: Watteau

The pursuit of pleasure—a major eighteenth-century theme—dominates the paintings of the Rococo masters. The first of these, the Flemish-born Antoine Watteau (1684–1721) began his career by painting theatrical scenes. In 1717, he submitted to the Royal Academy of Painting and Sculpture his *Departure from the Island of Cythera* (Figure 26.5), a work that pays tribute to the fleeting joys of romantic love. The painting shows a group of fashionable men and women preparing to board a golden boat by which they will leave the island of Cythera, the legendary birthplace of Venus. They have made this outing—a *fête galante* (literally, "elegant entertainment")—in search of the goddess of love, whose rose-bedecked shrine appears at the far right. Amidst fluttering cupids, the pilgrims of love linger in pairs as they wistfully take leave of their florid hideaway. Watteau repeats the serpentine line formed by the figures in the delicate arabesques of the trees and rolling hills. He bathes the entire panorama in a misty, golden light.

Watteau's fragile forms and delicate colors, painted with feathery brushstrokes reminiscent of Rubens, evoke a mood of reverie and nostalgia. His doll-like men and women contrast sharply, however, with Rubens' physically powerful figures (see Figure 21.15) or, for that matter, with Poussin's idealized heroes (see Figure 21.13). Watteau's art conveys no moral or heroic message; rather, it explores the world of familiar but transitory pleasures. Not since the sixteenth-century artists Giorgione and Titian had any painter indulged so deeply in the pleasures of nature or the voluptuous world of the senses.

Among Watteau's attractive smaller works are the drawings he executed in the new medium of **pastel**. Invented at the beginning of the eighteenth century, pastel crayons or chalks, which produced soft textures and light tones, were an ideal medium for the swift and spontaneous sketch and the portrait likeness.

Figure 26.4 **JOHAN MICHAEL FISCHER**, interior, Benedictine abbey church, Ottobeuren, Bavaria, 1736–1766. Painted and gilded wood and stucco.

Figure 26.5 ANTOINE WATTEAU, *Departure from the Island of Cythera*, 1717. Oil on canvas, 4 ft. 3 in. × 6 ft. 4 in. Apprenticed to a stage designer in his early career, Watteau drew the subject of this painting from a popular play, *Les Trois Cousins*, written by Florent Dancourt, and performed in Paris in 1709. In the play, the central character invites her friends to visit the island birthplace of Venus, where a single man or woman might find a wife or husband.

Boucher

If Watteau's world was wistful and poetic, that of his contemporary François Boucher (1703–1770) was sensual and indulgent. Boucher, a specialist in designing mythological scenes, became head of the Gobelins tapestry factory in 1755 and director of the Royal Academy ten years later. He was First Painter to King Louis XV (1715–1774) and a good friend of the king's favorite mistress, Jeanne Antoinette Poisson, the Marquise de Pompadour (1721–1764). A woman of remarkable beauty and intellect—she owned two telescopes, a microscope, and a lathe that she installed in her apartments in order to carve cameos—Madame de Pompadour influenced state policy and dominated fashion and the arts at Versailles for almost twenty years.

With the idyllic *Venus Consoling Love*, Boucher flattered his patron by portraying her as the goddess of love (Figure **26.6**). Surrounded by attentive doves and cupids, the nubile Venus relaxes on a bed of sumptuous rose and blue satin robes nestled in a bower of leafy trees and windswept grasses. Boucher delighted in sensuous contrasts of flesh, fabric, feathers, and flowers. His girlish women, with their unnaturally tiny feet, rosebud-pink nipples, and wistful glances, were coy symbols of erotic pleasure.

Figure 26.6 FRANÇOIS BOUCHER, *Venus Consoling Love*, 1751. Oil on canvas, 3 ft. 6¼ in. × 33¾ in. Boucher is said to have established the erotic female nude as a Rococo genre.

Figure 26.7 Sèvres porcelain potpourri vase, mid-eighteenth century. Gondola-shaped body, scrolled handles, 4-lobed cover, height 14⅛ in., length 14½ in., width 8 in. This vase, purchased by Madame de Pompadour, is one of the finest products of the Sèvres porcelain factory, which she sponsored and patronized.

Boucher designed sets and costumes for the Royal Opera and motifs for tapestries and porcelains. From the Sèvres porcelain factory, located near Paris and founded by Madame de Pompadour, came magnificent porcelains ornamented with gilded wreaths, arabesque cartouches, and playful cupids floating on fleecy clouds (Figure 26.7). Outside of France, as well, in Germany and Austria, porcelain figurines of shepherds and shepherdesses advertised the eighteenth-century enthusiasm for the pastoral life.

Vigée-Lebrun

Fashion and fashionableness—public expressions of self-conscious materialism—were major themes of Rococo art. Marie-Louise-Elizabeth Vigée-Lebrun (1775–1842), one of only four women elected to the Royal Academy, produced refined portrait paintings for an almost exclusively female clientele. The favorite painter of Queen Marie Antoinette, she produced some 800 paintings in the course of her career. Most of these were glamorous likenesses that paid tribute to the French fashion industry: plumed headdresses and low-cut velvet gowns bedecked with lace and ribbons turned their subjects into conspicuous ornaments. (The size of women's billowing skirts required them to turn sideways in order to pass through an open door.)

Vigée-Lebrun's portrait of Marie Antoinette and her children (Figure 26.8) is no exception. However, the elegant formality of the aristocratic portrait is humanized here by the presence of the queen's sweet-faced eldest daughter (at her right), the lively baby on her lap, and her son, Louis-Joseph, who points to the empty cradle—drawing attention to the recent death of the queen's youngest child. In this painting, the artist casts Marie Antoinette in a manner reminiscent of the allegorical figure of Abundance; she is the embodiment of motherhood—a role designed, perhaps, to offset her public image of royal extravagance.

In response to the upper-class infatuation with pastoral and idyllic themes, Vigée-Lebrun also painted portraits of more modestly dressed women in muslin skirts and straw hats. Unlike Boucher, she did not cast her subjects as goddesses, but imparted to them a chic sweetness and artless simplicity. These talents earned her the equivalent of over $200,000 a year and allowed her an independence uncommon among eighteenth-century women.

Fragonard

Jean-Honoré Fragonard (1732–1806), the last of the great Rococo artists, was the undisputed master of translating the art of seduction into paint. Working shortly before the French Revolution, he captured the pastimes of a waning aristocracy, especially the pleasures of courtship and flirtation. In 1766, a wealthy aristocrat, the Baron of Saint Julien, commissioned Fragonard to paint a scene that showed his mistress seated on a swing being pushed by a friendly clergyman. *The Swing* depicts the frivolous encounter which takes place in a garden bower filled with frothy trees, Classical statuary, and delicate light. The young woman, dressed in yards of satin and lace, kicks her tiny shoe into the air in the direction of a statue of Cupid, while her lover, hiding in the bushes below, peers delightedly beneath her billowing skirts (see Figure 26.1). Whether or not the young lady is aware of her lover's presence, her coy gesture and the irreverent *ménage à trois* (lover, mistress, and cleric) contribute to a theme of erotic intrigue common to popular comic operas and pornographic novels—the latter developed as a genre in eighteenth-century France. Although Fragonard immortalized the union of wealth, privilege, and pleasure enjoyed by the upper classes of the eighteenth century, he captured a spirit of sensuous abandon that has easily outlived the particulars of time, place, and social class.

Rococo Sculpture

The finest examples of eighteenth-century sculpture are small in scale, intimate in mood, and almost entirely lacking in dramatic urgency and religious fervor. Intended for the boudoir or the drawing room, Rococo sculpture usually depicted elegant dancers, wooing couples, or other lighthearted subjects. The French sculptor Claude Michel, known as Clodion (1738–1814), who worked almost exclusively for private patrons, was among the favorite Rococo artists of the late eighteenth century. His *Intoxication of Wine* revived a Classical theme—a celebration honoring Dionysus, the Greek god of wine and fertility (Figure 26.9). Flushed with wine and revelry, the **satyr** (a semibestial woodland creature symbolic of Dionysus) wildly embraces a **bacchante**, an attendant of Dionysus. Clodion made the piece in terracotta, a clay medium that requires rapid modeling, thus inviting the artist to capture a sense of spontaneity. Rococo painters sought similar effects through the use of loose and rapid brushstrokes and by sketching with pastels. The expressive impact of *The Intoxication of Wine* belies its tiny size—it is just under 2 feet high.

Rococo Music

By the middle of the eighteenth century, the Rococo (or *galant*) style began to challenge the popularity of Bach and Handel. Rococo composers abandoned the intricate counterpoint and dense textures of the Baroque in favor of light and graceful melodies organized into short, distinct suites bear playful titles based on women's names, parlor games, or human moods or attributes, such as Languor, Coquetry, and Jealousy. "Le Croc-en-jambe" ("*donner un croc-en-jambe*" means "to trip up" or "to play a dirty trick"), for example, is itself a tripping, lighthearted piece. Couperin's suites were written for solo instruments or for orchestral ensembles that accompanied such dances as the courante, the minuet, and the sarabande, all of which were performed in fashionable eighteenth-century *salons*. Embroidered with florid *agréments*, Couperin's music shares the lighthearted spirit and fragile elegance of the Rococo style in the visual arts.

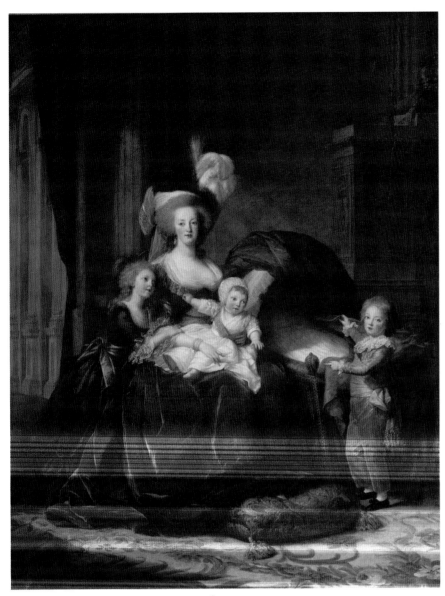

Figure 26.8 MARIE-LOUISE-ELIZABETH VIGÉE-LEBRUN, *Queen Marie Antoinette and Her Children*, 1787. Oil on canvas, 108¼ × 84¼ in. The artist's travels in the Low Countries allowed her to study the works of Rubens and van Dyck, whose painterly style she greatly admired.

Figure 26.9 CLODION (Claude Michel), *The Intoxication of Wine*, ca. 1775. Terracotta, height 23¼ in.

phrases. As with Rococo art, Rococo music was delicate in effect, thin in texture, and natural in feeling. These qualities graced the works of the French composer François Couperin (1668–1733).

Couperin, a contemporary of Bach, wrote in both the Baroque and Rococo styles, as did many composers of the early eighteenth century. In 1716, Couperin published one of the most important musical treatises of the period, *The Art of Playing the Clavecin*, which offers precise instructions for keyboard fingering and for the execution of musical ornaments known as *agréments*. The Rococo preference for intimate forms of expression cast in miniature is reflected in Couperin's suites for harpsichord (in French, *clavecin*). The individual sections of these

♪ See Music Listening Selections at end of chapter.

Eighteenth-Century Genre Painting

Many of the *philosophes* found the works of Boucher, Clodion, and other Rococo artists intellectually trivial and morally degenerate. Diderot, for example, denounced Rococo boudoir imagery and demanded an art that made "virtue attractive and vice odious." He argued that art should seek "to move, to educate, to improve us, and to induce us to virtue." Artists favored by rationalist critics like Diderot avoided the indulgent themes and frivolous diversions of the Rococo. They focused instead on scenes of everyday life and behavior among the middle and lower classes. Genre painting, introduced earlier, in our treatment of Brueghel (see chapter 19), reflected the growing interest in middle-class tastes and values, as well as the popular fascination with the "modern moral subjects" that dominated the contemporary novel, the journal, and the theater.

Greuze

Jean-Baptiste Greuze (1725–1805), Diderot's favorite artist, exalted the natural virtues of ordinary people. His genre paintings brought to life moralizing subjects: *The Father Reading the Bible to His Children, The Well-Beloved Mother,* and *The Effects of Drunkenness.* In the manner of

Science and Technology

1775	the flush toilet is patented in Britain
1777	steam heat is used in France for the first time since the Roman era
1779	the first bicycles appear in Paris

Hogarth (whose works Greuze admired), he chose engaging narratives that illustrated an unfolding story. With their obsessive attention to realistic detail and their intimate treatment of human vice and virtue, Greuze's canvases had much in common with the popular novels of the time.

Greuze's *Village Betrothal* (Figure **26.10**) of 1761 could easily have been an illustration of a scene from one of these novels or a play. It tells the story of an impending marriage among hard-working, simple-living rustics: the father, who has just given over the dowry to the humble groom, blesses the couple; the mother laments losing a daughter; while the other members of the household, including the hen and chicks (possibly a symbol of the couple's prospective

Figure 26.10 JEAN-BAPTISTE GREUZE, *Village Betrothal,* 1761. Oil on canvas, 3 ft. 10½ in. × 3 ft.

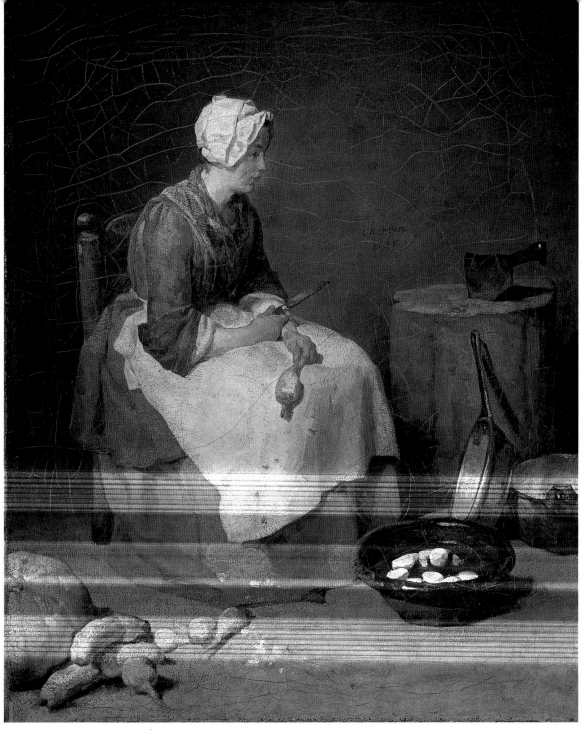

Figure 26.11 **JEAN-BAPTISTE-SIMÉON CHARDIN**, *The Kitchen Maid*, 1738. Oil on canvas, 18⅛ × 14¾ in.

progeny), look on approvingly. Greuze shunned the intellectualism of Poussin, the sensuality of Fragonard, and the satirical acrimony of Hogarth. His melodramatic representations appealed to common emotion and sentiment. Understandably, they were among the most popular artworks of the eighteenth and nineteenth centuries.

Chardin

The art of Greuze's contemporary, Jean-Baptiste-Siméon Chardin (1699–1779), was less openly sentimental. He painted humble still lifes and genre scenes showing nurses, governesses, and kitchen maids at work (Figure **26.11**). Unlike Greuze, who illustrated his moral tales as literally as possible, Chardin avoided explicit moralizing and anecdotal themes. Yet Chardin's paintings bear a deep concern for commonplace humanity, and they convey an implicit message—that of the ennobling dignity of work and the virtues of domesticity. The forthright qualities of Chardin's subjects are echoed in his style: his figures are simple and monumental, and his compositions reveal an uncanny sense of balance reminiscent of the works of de Hooch and Vermeer. Each object seems to assume its proper and predestined place in the composition. Executed in mellow, creamy tones, Chardin's paintings evoke a mood of gentility and gravity.

Greuze and Chardin brought painting out of the drawing room and into the kitchen. Their canvases were in such high demand that they were sold widely in engraved copies. Ironically, while Chardin's subjects were humble and commonplace, his patrons were often bankers, foreign ambassadors, and royalty itself—Louis XV owned at least two of Chardin's paintings.

Not all eighteenth-century genre paintings contained the unstated moral meanings found in Chardin's works. Some, like the study of a man scraping chocolate, by an anonymous Spanish artist (Figure **26.12**), offer an unidealized record of common labor. Kneeling before a heated grinding stone (introduced into Spain from the Americas), a young man scrapes a large slab of chocolate, a luxury brought from the Americas to Europe in the sixteenth century. His efforts will produce patties of chocolate seen in the foreground, as well as a grated chocolate paste (contained in the large bowl) that was the main ingredient for hot chocolate—a favorite drink among all social classes in Europe.

Figure 26.12 *A Man Scraping Chocolate*, Spain, ca. 1680–1780. Oil on canvas, 41 × 28 in. The *metate*, a type of grinding stone, was used by natives of Mexico and Guatemala to grind corn and chocolate. Like chocolate itself, it was brought to Europe by Spanish conquistadors.

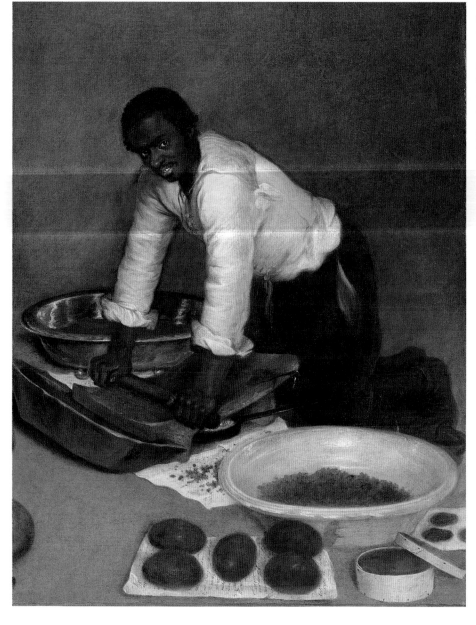

Eighteenth-Century Neoclassicism

By mid-century, yet another style came to dominate the arts: Neoclassicism—the self-conscious revival of Greco-Roman culture—belonged to a tradition that stretched from the Early Renaissance through the age of Louis XIV. During the seventeenth century, Poussin and other artists of the European academies (see chapter 21) had resurrected the Classical ideals of clarity, simplicity, balance, and restraint, as configured in the Grand Manner of Raphael and other High Renaissance masters. During the eighteenth century, however, the long-standing respect for antiquity was infused by an important new development: the scientific study of Classical ruins.

In 1738, the king of Naples sponsored the first archeological excavations at Herculaneum, one of the two Roman cities in southern Italy buried under volcanic ash by the eruption of Mount Vesuvius in 79 C.E. The excavations at Pompeii would take place in 1748. These enterprises, followed by European archeological expeditions to Greece and Asia Minor in 1750, inspired scholars to assemble vast collections of Greek and Roman artifacts (Figure **26.13**). Both the Louvre and the Vatican became museum repositories for the treasures of these expeditions, now available to artists, antiquarians, and the general public. For the first time in history, one was able to make clear distinctions between the artifacts of Greece and those of Rome. The result was a more archeologically correct Neoclassicism than any that had previously existed.

Figure 26.13 GIOVANNI PAOLO PANINI (copy after), *Picture Gallery (Roma Antica)*, 1691–1765. Pen and black ink with brush and gray wash and watercolor over graphite on ivory laid paper, 17¼ × 27⅝ in. Art collecting paralleled the rise of the academies in the seventeenth century. In the eighteenth century, Classical antiquities and depictions of famous Classical monuments were found in picture galleries and private collections, alongside paintings by the old masters, copies after such works (note the *Laocoön* on the right), and portable examples of contemporary art.

Winckelmann

Shortly after the first English expeditions to Athens, the German scholar Johann Joachim Winckelmann (1717–1768) began to study Greek and Roman antiquities. He published an eloquent assessment of these objects in a magnificently illustrated *History of Ancient Art* (1764). These and other of Winckelmann's texts offered a critical analysis of ancient art objects. Widely circulated, they established Winckelmann as the "father of modern art historical scholarship."

Although Winckelmann himself never visited Greece, he was infatuated with Hellenic and Hellenistic sculpture. He argued that artists of his time could become great only by imitating the ancient Greeks, in whose best works he discovered "a noble simplicity and a quiet grandeur." Of his favorite ancient statue, the *Apollo Belvedere* (see Figures 5.31 and 26.16, left), he proclaimed, "In the presence of this miracle of art, I forget the whole universe and my soul acquires a loftiness appropriate to its dignity." Winckelmann's reverence for antiquity typified the eighteenth-century attitude toward Classicism as a vehicle for the elevation of human consciousness. Here, finally, was the ideal mode of expression for the Enlightenment program of reason, clarity, and order—a style that equated beauty with goodness, virtue, and truth. Winckelmann's publications became an inspiration for artists and aesthetes all over Europe. In Britain, Sir Joshua Reynolds (1723–1792), the painter and founder of the Royal Academy of Arts in London, lectured on the Grand Manner; his *Discourses* were translated into French, German, and Italian. The lofty vision of a style that captured the nobility and dignity of the Greco-Roman past fired the imagination of intellectuals across Western Europe and America.

Piranesi

Since Renaissance times, Rome had been a favorite destination for well-educated tourists and artists. But during the eighteenth century, Rome and its monuments came under new scrutiny. Architects studied the monuments of antiquity, and artists made topographic sketches, often reproduced in copper engravings that were sold cheaply—in the manner of modern-day postcards. In 1740 the Venetian architect and engineer Giovanni Battista Piranesi (1720–1778) established himself in Rome as a printmaker. Piranesi's engravings of Rome were widely bought and appreciated (see Figure 20.14), while his studies of Roman monuments, with their precisely rendered technical details and inscriptions, exerted considerable influence on French and English architects of his time (Figure **26.14**). Piranesi's later works—nightmarish visions of dungeons inspired by the Roman sewer system—abandoned all Classical canons of objectivity and emotional restraint. Nevertheless, with European artists more eager than ever to rediscover antiquity through the careful study of its remains, the Neoclassical revival was under way.

Neoclassical Architecture

The Classical revival of the eighteenth century was unique in its accuracy of detail and its purity of design. Neoclassical architects made careful distinctions between Greek and Roman buildings and between the various Renaissance and post-Renaissance styles modeled upon antiquity. They took inspiration from simple geometric shapes—spheres, cubes, and cylinders—to provide a new, more abstract and austere Classicism. They rejected the illusionistic theatricality of the Baroque style with its broken pediments, cartouches, and ornamental devices. They also turned their backs on the stucco foliage, cherubic angels, and "wedding-cake" fantasies of the Rococo. The

ideal Neoclassical exterior was free of frivolous ornamentation, while its interior consisted of clean and rectilinear walls, soberly accented with engaged columns or pilasters, geometric motifs, and shallow niches that might house copies of antique statuary (see Figure 26.16).

The leading French Neoclassical architect, Jacques-Germain Soufflot (1713–1780), traveled to Italy and Greece to study ancient monuments. Commissioned by Louis XV to design the church of Sainte Geneviève, honoring the patron saint of Paris (Figure **26.15**), Soufflot took inspiration from the Pantheon, which he had studied firsthand as a student at the French Academy in Rome. While the portico of the church is indebted to the Pantheon, its strict central plan, with four shallow domes covering each of the arms, followed an architectural tradition perfected by Bramante and Michelangelo at Saint Peter's in Rome. Saint Geneviève's massive dome, supported entirely on pillars, rises over the crossing in a manner that looks back to Saint Paul's in London (see Figure 22.3).

Clearly, Soufflot did not slavishly imitate any single landmark structure; rather, he selected specific features from some of history's greatest architectural monuments and combined them with clarity and reserve. During the French Revolution, when radicals rededicated many

Figure 26.14 GIOVANNI BATTISTA PIRANESI, *The Pantheon*, from *Views of Rome*, ca. 1748–1778. Etching. The towers flanking the portico, which were added in the seventeenth century when the Pantheon functioned as a church, have since been removed.

Figure 26.15 JACQUES-GERMAIN SOUFFLOT, Sainte Geneviève (renamed the "Panthéon" during the French Revolution), Paris, 1757–1792.

churches as "temples of reason," Sainte Geneviève was renamed "the Panthéon"; inspired by the building that once honored the Roman gods, it would entomb the "gods" of the Enlightenment, including Voltaire and Rousseau.

Some of the purest examples of the Classical revival are found in late eighteenth-century English country homes. The interiors of these sprawling symbols of wealth and prestige reflect close attention to archeological drawings of Greek and Roman antiquities. Kedleston Hall in Derbyshire, England, designed by the Scottish architect Robert Adam (1728–1792), is a pristine synthesis of geometric shapes and Greco-Roman motifs (Figure **26.16**).

Figure 26.16 ROBERT ADAM, Marble Hall, Kedleston Hall, Derbyshire, England, 1763–1777. (Note copy of the *Apollo Belvedere* in niche at left.) 67 × 42 ft., height 40 ft.

Figure 26.17 **ANTONIO CANOVA**, *Pauline Borghese as Venus*, 1808. Marble, life-sized. Canova's idealized portrait of Napoleon's sister was intended for private viewing rather than for public display. While depicted here as a goddess, Pauline was notorious for her numerous illicit affairs and her self-indulgent habits—she was said to insist on being carried to the bath by her servants.

In such estates as this, the Neoclassical spirit touched everything from sculpture (Figure 26.17) and furniture to tea services and tableware. Among the most popular items of the day were the ceramics of the English potter Josiah Wedgwood (1730–1795). Wedgwood's wares were modeled on Greek and Roman vases and embellished with finely applied, molded white clay surface designs (Figure 26.18).

The austerity and dignity of Neoclassicism made it the ideal style for public monuments and offices of state. In Paris, Berlin, and Washington D.C., Neoclassical architects borrowed Greek and Roman temple designs for public and private buildings, especially for banks, where the modern-day gods of money and materialism replaced the ancient deities. In some instances (such as Soufflot's Panthéon), the spirit of revival produced daring architectural hybrids. In England, for instance, the Scottish architect James Gibbs (1682–1754) designed churches that combined a Classical portico with a Gothic spire (Figure 26.19). This scheme, which united the Baroque love of dramatic contrast with the Neoclassical rule of perfect symmetry, became extremely popular in America, primarily in the Congregational churches built across New England.

Figure 26.18 **WEDGWOOD & SONS**, copy of Portland vase (No. 7) with stand, ca. 1790. Black and white jasperware, height 10 in. The Portland Vase is a Roman cameo glass vase that dates from the first century B.C.E. Excavated in the sixteenth century, it came into the hands of William Cavendish-Bentinck, the third duke of Portland, in the late eighteenth century, at which time it became an inspiration to makers of glass and porcelain wares. The identity of the reclining woman is much disputed; she has been identified as Ariadne, as Hecuba, and as Octavia, the wife of Mark Anthony.

Figure 26.19 **JAMES GIBBS**, Saint Martin-in-the-Fields, London, 1721–1726.

Neoclassicism in America

A tour of the city of Washington in the District of Columbia will convince any student of the impact of Neoclassicism on the architecture of the United States. The Neoclassical movement in America did not originate, however, in the capital city, whose major buildings date only from the nineteenth century, but rather among the founding fathers. One of the most passionate devotees of Greco-Roman art and life was the Virginia lawyer and statesman Thomas Jefferson (1743–1826), introduced in chapter 24. Farmer, linguist, educator, inventor, self-taught architect, musician, and politician, the man who served as third president of the United States was an eighteenth-century *uomo universale* (see Figure 24.3). Jefferson was a student of ancient and Renaissance treatises on architecture and an impassioned apostle of Neoclassicism. He understood that a nation's buildings not only create a national image, but affect social conduct and human aspiration. In 1786, he designed the Virginia State Capitol, using as his model the ancient Roman Maison Carrée (see Figure 26.30).

Jefferson's tightly organized and geometrically correct plan for the campus of the university of Virginia reflects the basic sympathy between Neoclassical design and the

MAKING CONNECTIONS

Figure **26.20** The Pantheon, Rome, ca. 118–125 C.E.

For the design of his country estate at Monticello (near Charlottesville, Virginia), and for the university of Virginia, America's first state university, Jefferson drew on that most admired of all Roman imperial monuments, the Pantheon (Figure **26.20**). In the Rotunda, which housed the original university library, he constructed the ancient Roman temple at two-thirds of its original size (Figure **26.21**). Considerably smaller than Soufflot's "Panthéon," the Rotunda is also purer in form. It is faithful to the design of the Roman temple and is unadorned, except for its Corinthian (rather than Doric) columns.

Figure **26.21** Thomas Jefferson, The Rotunda, University of Virginia, Charlottesville, Virginia, 1822–1826.

Figure 26.22 Great Seal of the United States.

rationalist ideals of the Enlightenment. The "academical village," as Jefferson described it, was a community of the free-thinking elite—exclusively white, wealthy, and male, yet it provided both a physical and a spiritual model for nonsectarian education in the United States.

The young American nation drew on the heritage of the ancients (and especially the history of the Roman Republic) to symbolize its newly forged commitment to the ideals of liberty and equality. The leaders of the American Revolution regarded themselves as descendants of ancient Roman heroes. Like the humanists of Renaissance Italy, some even adopted Latin names. On the Great Seal of the United States, the Latin phrase "E pluribus unum" ("out of many, one") and the bundle of arrows in the grasp of the American eagle (suggesting the Roman *fasces*: a bundle of rods surrounding an ax—the ancient symbol for power and authority) identified America as heir to republican Rome (Figure 26.22).

Neoclassical Sculpture

Neoclassical sculptors heeded the Enlightenment call for an art that perpetuated the memory of illustrious men. Jean-Antoine Houdon (1741–1828), the leading portrait sculptor of Europe, immortalized in stone the features of his contemporaries. Reviving a tradition that had reached its high-water mark among the ancient Romans, Houdon's portrait busts met the popular demand for achieving a familiar likeness. Houdon had a special talent for catching characteristic gestures and expressions: Diderot, shown without a wig, surveys his world with inquisitive candor (see Figure 24.4), while the aging Voltaire addresses us with a grim and knowing smile (see Figure 25.4). While visiting America, Houdon carved portraits of Jefferson (see Figure 24.3), Franklin, and other "virtuous men" of the republic. His life-sized statue of George Washington renders the first president of the United States as country gentleman and eminent statesman (Figure 26.23). Resting his hand on a columnar *fasces*, the poised but slightly potbellied Washington recalls (however faintly) the monumental dignity of the Greek gods and the Roman emperors.

Figure 26.23 JEAN-ANTOINE HOUDON, *George Washington*, 1786–1796. Marble, life-size.

Figure 26.24 JACQUES-LOUIS DAVID, *The Oath of the Horatii*, 1784. Oil on canvas, 10 ft. 10 in. × 14 ft. One of the Horatii sisters, pictured at the right, had been engaged to marry a Curati warrior. Legend has it that when her brother returned triumphant and found her weeping over her lover's demise, he stabbed her to death.

While Houdon invested Neoclassicism with a strong taste for Realism, most of his contemporaries preferred to idealize the human form. Such was the case with the Italian-born sculptor Antonio Canova (1757–1822). Considered the greatest sculptor of his generation, he received frequent commissions for portraits and multifigured burial tombs. In 1802, Napoleon invited Canova to Paris, where the artist glorified the French ruler in a colossal freestanding nude image of Napoleon as Mars, the Roman god of war. Napoleon also commissioned Canova to portray his sister, Pauline Borghese. Canova's life-sized marble portrait of Pauline is a sublime example of Neoclassical refinement and restraint (see Figure 26.17). Canova casts Pauline in the guise of a reclining Venus. Perfectly proportioned, she shares the flawless elegance of Classical statuary and Wedgwood reliefs. In contrast to the vigorously carved surfaces of Baroque sculpture (recall, for instance, Bernini's *Ecstasy of Saint Teresa*, Figure 20.3), Canova's figure is smooth and neutral—even stark. A comparison of

Canova's *Pauline Borghese as Venus* with Clodion's *Intoxication of Wine* (see Figure 26.9) is also revealing: both depend on Classical themes and models, but whereas Clodion's piece is intimate, sensuous, and spontaneous, Canova's seems remote, controlled, and reserved. Its aesthetic distance is intensified by the ghostlike whiteness of the figure and its "blank" eyes—eighteenth-century sculptors were unaware that Classical artists painted parts of their statues to make them look more lifelike.

Neoclassical Painting and Politics: The Art of David

During the last decades of the eighteenth century, as the tides of revolution began to engulf the indulgent lifestyles of the French aristocracy, the Rococo style gave way to a sober new approach to picture-making. The pioneer of this style was the French artist Jacques-Louis David (1748–1825). David's early canvases were executed in the Rococo style of his teacher and distant cousin, Boucher. But after winning the coveted Prix de Rome, which took him to study in the foremost city of antiquity, David found his place among the Classicists. In 1784 he completed one of the most influential paintings of the late eighteenth century: *The Oath of the Horatii* (Figure **26.24**). The piece was commissioned by the French king some five years before the outbreak of the revolution; ironically, however, it would become a symbol of the very spirit that toppled the royal crown.

The Oath of the Horatii illustrates a dramatic event recorded in the first book of Livy's *History of Rome*: amidst a military contest for control of central Italy, the three sons of Horatius Proclus volunteer to meet the champions of the treacherous Curatii family in a win-or-die sword battle that will determine the future of Rome. Two of the Horatii brothers die in combat, but the third returns victorious, having killed all three of his opponents. In France, this historic legend, symbolic of the spirit of patriotism leading up to the French Revolution, became especially popular as the subject of a play by the French dramatist Pierre Corneille (1606–1684). David captured the spirit of the story in a single potent image: resolved to pursue their destiny as defenders of liberty, the Horatii lift their arms in a dramatic military salute. If David's subject matter was revolutionary, so was his style: geometric order, hard-edged contours, and somber colors—features that recalled the art of David's favourite artist, Poussin—replaced the sensuous curves, amorphous forms, and pastel tones of Rococo art. Bathed in golden light, the heroic figures stand along the strict horizontal line of the picture plane. The figure of the warrior on

the far left forms a rigid triangle that is subtly repeated throughout the composition—in the arches of the colonnade, for instance, and in the group of grieving women. Austere, realistic, and Neoclassically precise—witness the archeologically correct helmets, sandals, and swords—the *Oath* exalted sober simplicity and serious drama over and above the playful and luxuriant spirit of the Rococo.

David's painting was an immediate success: people lined up to see it while it hung in the artist's studio in Rome, and the city of Paris received it enthusiastically when it arrived there in 1785. The huge canvas (over 10 by 14 feet) came to be perceived as a clear denunciation of aristocratic pastimes. It proclaimed the importance of reason and the intellect over and above feeling and sentiment, and it defended the ideals of male heroism and self-sacrifice in the interest of one's country.

Three years after painting *The Oath of the Horatii*, David conceived the smaller but equally popular *Death of Socrates* (Figure **26.25**). The scene is a fifth-century B.C.E. Athenian prison. It is the moment before Socrates, the father of Greek philosophy, drinks the fatal hemlock. Surrounding Socrates are his students and friends, posed in various expressions of lament, while the apostle of reason himself—illuminated in the style of Caravaggio—rhetorically lifts his hand to heaven. Clarity and intellectual control dominate the composition: figures and objects are arranged as if plotted on a grid of lines horizontal and vertical to the picture plane. This ideal geometry,

Figure 26.25 **JACQUES-LOUIS DAVID**, *The Death of Socrates*, 1787. Oil on canvas, 4 ft. 3 in. × 6 ft. 5¼ in.

Figure 26.26A JEAN-AUGUSTE-DOMINIQUE INGRES, *The Apotheosis of Homer*, 1827. Oil on canvas, 12 ft. 8 in. × 16 ft. 10¾ in.

Figure 26.26B Plan of *The Apotheosis of Homer*, 1827. Following Emilio Radius, *L'opera completa di Ingres*, the following figures are identified:

1 Virgil	22 Shakespeare
2 Raphael	23 La Fontaine
3 Sappho	24 Tasso
4 Euripides	25 Mozart
5 Demosthenes	26 Poussin
6 Sophocles	27 Corneille
7 Herodotus	28 Racine
8 Orpheus	29 Molière
9 Pindar	30 Glück
10 Hesiod	31 Apelles
11 Plato	32 Phidias
12 Socrates	
13 Pericles	
14 Michelangelo	
15 Aristotle	
16 Aristarchus	
17 Alexander the Great	
18 Dante	
19 Iliad	
20 Odyssey	
21 Aesop	

a metaphor for the ordering function of reason, complements the grave and noble message of the painting: reason guides human beings to live and, if need be, to die for their moral principles. In *The Death of Socrates*, as in *The Oath of the Horatii*, David put Neoclassicism at the service of a morality based on Greco-Roman Stoicism, self-sacrifice, and stern patriotism.

Ingres and Academic Neoclassicism

David's most talented pupil was Jean-Auguste-Dominique Ingres (1780–1867). The son of an artist–craftsman, Ingres rose to fame with his polished depictions of Classical history and mythology and with his accomplished portraits of middle- and upper-class patrons. He spent much of his career in Italy, where he came to prize (as he himself admitted), "Raphael, his century, the ancients, and above all the divine Greeks." Ingres shunned the weighty Realism of David in favor of the purity of line he admired in Greek vase painting, in the published drawings of the newly unearthed Classical artifacts, and in engraved book illustrations for the works of Homer and Hesiod.

Commissioned to paint a ceiling mural for the Louvre, Ingres produced a visual testament to Europe's esteem for its Classical heritage. The monumental *Apotheosis of Homer* shows the ancient Greek bard enthroned amidst forty-six notables of Classical and modern times; Homer is "deified" with a laurel crown bestowed by a winged figure of Victory (Figure **26.26A**). Surrounding the poet is an academic assembly that includes Plato, Dante, Raphael, Poussin, Racine, and other Western "luminaries"

(thirty of whom are identified in Figure **26.26B**). Ingres' iconic figure occupies the apex of the compositional pyramid; at his feet are the allegorical figures of his epics, the *Iliad* and the *Odyssey*, while behind him is a Neoclassical temple façade, not unlike that of "La Madeleine," which was then under construction in Paris (see Figure 26.29). Both in composition and in conception, the *Apotheosis* looks back to Raphael (see *The School of Athens*, Figure 17.28), but Ingres has brought self-conscious rigor to his application of the Neoclassical principles of clarity and symmetry.

Late in his career, Ingres turned his nostalgia for the past to more exotic themes. Intrigued, for instance, by Turkish culture (publicized by Napoleon's campaigns in Syria and North Africa), he painted languorous harem women, such as *La Grande Odalisque* (Figure **26.27**). A revisualization of both Titian's *Venus of Urbino* (see Figure 17.41) and Canova's *Pauline Borghese as Venus* (see Figure 26.17), Ingres' nude turns in a self-consciously seductive manner: both away from and toward the beholder. The firm contours and polished brushstrokes are typically Neoclassical; but Ingres rejected Neoclassical canons of proportion by elongating the limbs in the tradition of the Italian mannerists (see, for instance, Figure 20.5). The "incorrect" anatomy of the figure drew strong criticism from Ingres' contemporaries, who claimed that his subject had three too many vertebrae. Nevertheless (or perhaps because of its bold departures from both real and ideal norms), *La Grande Odalisque* remains one of the most arresting images of womanhood in Western art.

Figure 26.27 JEAN-AUGUSTE-DOMINIQUE INGRES, *La Grande Odalisque*, 1814. Oil on canvas, 2 ft. 11¼ in. × 5 ft. 3¾ in. While criticized for depriving his female nudes of "bone and muscle," Ingres was celebrated for the exquisite perfection of his drawing, his subtle modeling, and his appreciation of antiquity. He was among the first artists to introduce exotic details of the East—the peacock fan, inlaid footstool, and embroidered turban—into his paintings.

Kauffmann and Academic Neoclassicism

Well into the eighteenth century, the painting of large-scale historical, mythological, and religious subjects was dominated by male artists. Talented females, such as Maria van Oosterwyck (see Figure 23.6) and Judith Leyster (see Figure 23.14), confined themselves to still-life subjects and portrait painting, genres considered of lesser importance among academicians. Nevertheless, the Italian-trained Angelica Kauffmann (1741–1807), like Artemisia Gentileschi (see Figure 20.10), established a glowing reputation as a skilled painter of historical subjects. Kauffmann, the daughter of a Swiss artist who schooled her in music, history, and the visual arts, was one of the founding members of England's Royal Academy of Arts, to which she contributed many critically successful paintings based on Classical subjects. Commissioned to paint portrait likenesses of her contemporaries (including Johann Winckelmann) during her sojourns in Rome, Florence, and London, she also became one of the most sought-after and highly paid portrait painters of her day.

Kauffmann's history subjects, many of which served as models for wall and ceiling designs in the Neoclassical interiors of Robert Adam (see Figure 26.16), reveal her familiarity with the figure types found in the wall-paintings of Pompeii and Herculaneum, her love of lyrical linear compositions, and her skillful, fluent brushwork. These features are especially apparent in the painting, *Zeuxis Selecting Models for His Painting of Helen of Troy* (Figure 26.28), in which the Greek artist is shown (as described by ancient historians) choosing the finest features of his various female models, so as to combine them in an idealized image of Helen of Troy. Kauffmann herself may have served as the model for the figure at the far right.

Neoclassicism under Napoleon

While Neoclassicism was the "official" style of the French Revolution, it soon became the vehicle of French imperialism. Under the leadership of Napoleon Bonaparte (1769–1821), the imagery of Classical Greece and republican Rome was abandoned for the more appropriate imagery of Augustan Rome. Like the Roman emperors, Napoleon used the arts to magnify his greatness. He appointed David to commemorate his military achievements, and he commissioned architects to redesign Paris in the spirit of

Figure 26.28 ANGELICA KAUFFMANN, *Zeuxis Selecting Models for His Painting of Helen of Troy*, ca. 1765. The only female painter of her time to produce historical narratives, Kauffmann was commissioned to decorate Saint Paul's in London and the walls of country homes designed by Robert Adam. Esteemed by artists and writers throughout Europe, she was a founding member of Britain's Royal Academy of Arts.

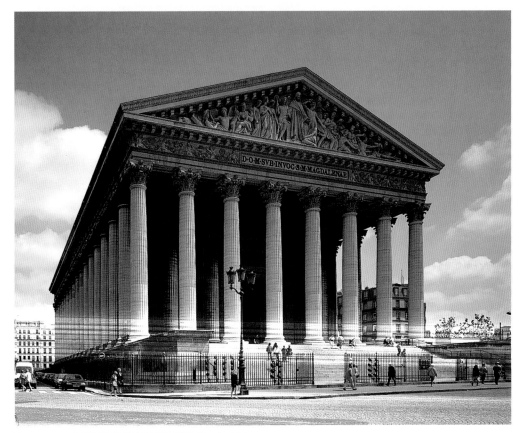

Figure 26.29 ALEXANDRE-PIERRE VIGNON, Church of Saint Mary Magdalene ("La Madeleine"), Paris, 1807–1842. Length 350 ft., width 147 ft., height of podium 23 ft. Following the fall of Napoleon and the return of the monarchy, the Catholic king Louis XVIII rededicated the church to Mary Magdalene.

In 1806, Alexandre-Pierre Vignon (1763–1828) was commissioned to redesign the church of Saint Mary Magdalene (called "La Madeleine") as a Roman temple dedicated to the glory of the French army (Figure **26.29**). Originally dedicated to the saint, it was to become one of the monumental secular temples of Paris. Fifty-two Corinthian columns, each 66 feet tall, surround the temple, which rises on a 23-foot-high podium, like a gigantic version of the small Roman temple known as the Maison Carrée in Nîmes (Figure **26.30**). Vignon's gloomy interior—a nave crowned with three domes—falls short of reflecting the majesty of the exterior, despite his use of the Corinthian and Ionic orders in the decorative scheme.

Figure 26.30 Maison Carrée, Nîmes, France, 16 B.C.E.

ancient Rome. Paris became a city of straight, wide avenues and huge, impressive squares. Imaginary axes linked the Classically inspired monuments raised to honor the emperor, and older buildings were remodeled in the new Empire style.

Napoleon was also instrumental in reviving that best-known symbol of Roman imperialism: the triumphal arch. The Arc du Carrousel, which stands adjacent to the Louvre, is faithful to its Roman model, the Arch of Constantine in Rome. And the grandest of Paris' triumphal arches, which occupies the crossing of twelve avenues at the end of the famous Avenue des Champs-Elysées (Figure 26.31), closely resembles the Arch of Titus in the Roman Forum (see Figure 6.21). The 164-foot-high commemorative monument—which was dedicated to the French army—was larger than any arch built in ancient times. Napoleon would become one of the nineteenth century's most celebrated romantic heroes (see chapter 28), but the monuments he commissioned for Paris were stamped unmistakably with the Classical spirit.

Eighteenth-Century Western Music

The eighteenth century was as rich in music as it was in the visual arts. Music filled the courts and concert halls, the latter as a response to a rising popular demand for public recitals. The eighteenth-century concert hall was small by modern standards. Its lights were rarely dimmed during performances and audiences were not expected to wait until the end of each piece to applaud. Often they showed their enthusiasm by applauding after a movement, insisting that it be repeated—a practice that is very much out of favor in our own time. Religious compositions were still in demand, but church music was overshadowed by the vast amounts of music composed for secular entertainment. Composers sought the patronage of wealthy aristocrats, at whose courts they often served. At the same time, composers wrote music for amateur performance and for the concert hall. While opera remained the favorite vocal form, instrumental music began to free itself from religious and ceremonial functions.

During the eighteenth century certain distinctive characteristics converged to set Western musical culture apart from that of the rest of the world. These included the idea that harmony is proper and essential to music, that a musical composition should be the original product of a single composer, and that a piece of music should be rehearsed and performed in much the same manner each time it is played. Such standards, which emphasize order and formality over spontaneity and improvisation, would come to characterize *classical* music—that is, "serious" or "art" music as distinct from the more ephemeral "popular" or "folk" music.

Classical Music

The term "classical" is also used more narrowly to describe a specific musical style that prevailed in the West between approximately 1760 and 1820. The music of this era shares

Science and Technology

1680s	the earliest form of the clarinet is invented in Germany
1700	the French coin the term acoustics to describe the science of sound

the essential features of Neoclassical art: symmetry, order, and formal restraint. Unlike Neoclassical art and architecture, however, classical music had little to do with the heritage of Greece and Rome, for European composers had no surviving evidence of Greek and Roman music and, therefore, no antique musical models to imitate. Nevertheless, classical music would develop its own unique model for clarity of form and purity of design. Classical composers, most of whom came from Germany and Austria, wrote homophonic compositions with easy-to-grasp melodies, which are repeated or developed within a definitive formal structure. The liberation of melody from Baroque polyphony was anticipated by the light and graceful nature of French Rococo music (discussed earlier in this chapter).

While classical composers retained the fast/slow/fast contrasts of Baroque instrumental forms, they rid their compositions of many Baroque features. They replaced, for instance, the abrupt changes from loud to soft with more gently graduated contrasts. They eliminated the unflagging rhythms and ornate embellishments of Baroque polyphony in favor of clear-cut musical phrases. While counterpoint continued to play an important role in classical music, the intricate webs of sound (as heard, for example, in Bach's fugues) gave way to a new harmonic clarity. In short, classical music developed formal attributes that reflect the Enlightenment quest for reasoned clarity and the Neoclassical commitment to balance and purity of design.

The Birth of the Symphony Orchestra

Eighteenth-century instrumental music served as secular entertainment in public theaters and in the *salons* of courtly residences. The most important instrumental grouping to emerge at this time was the orchestra. The eighteenth-century Bohemian composer Johann Stamitz (1717–1757), who settled in the south German town of Mannheim in the 1740s, organized what is thought to have been one of the earliest forms of the classical orchestra. It consisted of groups of related instruments, each with its own character or personality. The **strings**, made up of violins, violas, cellos, and double basses, formed the nucleus of the orchestra, since they were the most melodious and lyrical of the instrumental families. The **woodwinds**, consisting of flutes, oboes, clarinets, and bassoons, specialized in mellow harmonies. The **brass** section, made up of trumpets and French horns (and, by the end of the century, trombones), added volume and resonance. Lastly the **percussion** section, using kettledrums (also known as timpani), functioned as rhythm markers (Figure 26.32).

Figure 26.31 JEAN-FRANÇOIS THÉRÈSE CHALGRIN AND OTHERS, Arc de Triomphe, Paris, 1806–1836. Height 164 ft.

Stamitz's orchestra was small by modern-day standards. It included some thirty-five pieces, many of which were still rudimentary: brass instruments lacked valves, and the clarinet was not perfected until roughly 1790. The piano, which was invented around 1720, remained until 1775 more closely related to the clavichord than to the modern grand piano. During the last quarter of the century, however, as the piano underwent technical refinement, it came to be the favorite solo instrument.

As musical instruments became more sophisticated, the orchestra, capable of an increasingly expressive and subtle range of sounds, grew in size and popularity. The eighteenth-century orchestra was led by a musician (often the composer himself) who played part of the composition on the clavier or keyboard instrument located at the place now occupied by the conductor's podium. The string section was seated to the right and left, while the other instruments were spread across the middle distance, in a pattern that has persisted to this day.

To facilitate the conductor's control over the music, the orchestra used a **score**, that is, a record of musical notation that indicates every sound to be played by each instrument. Each musical part appeared in groups of five-line staffs that enabled the conductor to "view" the composition as a whole. Separate parts were written out for each instrument as well. In the eighteenth century, both instrumentation and methods of scoring became standardized. Scores included a time signature, which indicated the number of beats per measure; a key signature, which noted the number of sharps or flats in the specified key; and abbreviations of the Italian words that indicated the dynamics of specific passages: *f* for *forte* ("loud") and *p* for *piano* ("soft"). Interpretive directions, such as *scherzando* ("sprightly") and *affettuoso* ("with feeling"), signified the intentions of the composer as to how a musical passage should be performed. All these notational devices served the principle of formality that governed eighteenth-century music and Western musical composition in general.

Classical Instrumental Compositions

Classical composers wrote music for a variety of instrumental groupings. The largest of these was the orchestral form known as the **symphony**. The Italian word *sinfonia* was used during the seventeenth century to describe various kinds of instrumental pieces; but, by the mid-eighteenth century, the word came to mean an independent instrumental composition for full orchestra. In addition to the symphony, three other instrumental genres dominated the classical era: the **concerto**, a composition featuring one or more solo instruments and an orchestra; the **string quartet**, a piece for two violins, a viola, and a cello; and the **sonata**, a composition for an unaccompanied keyboard instrument or for another instrument with keyboard accompaniment.

Although the concerto and the sonata originated earlier (see chapter 23), they now took on a new formality. Indeed, all four instrumental forms—the symphony, the classical concerto, the string quartet, and the classical sonata—assumed the same formal structure: they were

Figure 26.32 The classical symphony orchestra.

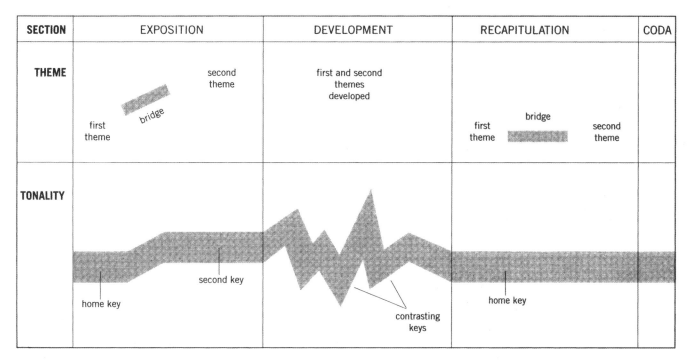

SECTION	EXPOSITION	DEVELOPMENT	RECAPITULATION	CODA
THEME	first theme bridge second theme	first and second themes developed	first theme bridge second theme	
TONALITY	home key second key	contrasting keys	home key	

Figure 26.33 Sonata form.

divided into three or four sections, or movements, each of which followed a specific tempo, or musical pace. The first movement was played *allegro* or in fast tempo; the second *andante* or *largo*, that is, in moderate or slow tempo; the third movement (usually omitted in concertos) was written in dance tempo (usually in three-quarter time); and the fourth was again *allegro*.

For the organization of the first and last movements, classical composers used a special form known as **sonata form** (or **sonata allegro** form; Figure 26.33). This calls for the division of the movement into three parts: the exposition, the development, and the recapitulation. In the exposition, the composer "exposes," or introduces, a theme in the "home" key, then contrasts it with a second theme in a different key. Musical effect is based on the tension of two opposing key centers. In the development, the composer moves to further contrasting keys, expanding and altering the themes stated in the exposition. Finally, in the recapitulation, the themes from the exposition are restated, both now in the home key, resolving the earlier tension. A **coda** ("tail") is often added as a definitive end piece.

Also popular among classical composers was the form known as **theme and variations**, which might appear as an independent piece or as a musical idea within the movement of a symphony, string quartet, or sonata. As the name suggests, theme and variations features a basic musical idea that is repeated in a number of ways, that is, by changes in rhythm, harmony, melody, and so on. Already evident in Late Renaissance and Baroque music, this form was employed inventively in classical compositions that gave each variation of the theme its own identity.

Classical composers frequently deviated from sonata form, but they looked to it to provide the "rules" of musical design—the architectural guidelines, so to speak, for musical composition. Just as Neoclassical artists and writers favored clear definitions and an Aristotelian "beginning, middle, and end," so classical composers delighted in the threefold balance of the sonata form, the repetition of simple harmonies, and the crisp phrasing of bright, free-flowing melodies.

The Development of the Classical Style: Haydn

The classical style owes its development to the Austrian composer Franz Joseph Haydn (1732–1809). Of peasant birth, Haydn was recruited at the age of eight to sing in the choir of Saint Stephen's Cathedral in Vienna. As a young man, he taught music and struggled to make a living. In 1761, at the age of twenty-nine, he became musical director to the court of the powerful and wealthy Hungarian nobleman Prince Paul Anton Esterházy, who was also an accomplished musician. The magnificent Esterházy country estate (modeled on Versailles) included two theaters—one for opera and one for puppet plays—and two richly appointed concert halls. There, for almost thirty years, Haydn took charge of all aspects of musical entertainment: he composed music, trained choristers, oversaw the repair of instruments, and rehearsed and conducted an orchestra of some twenty-five musicians. At the princely court, Haydn produced music for various instrumental groups. Tailoring his creative talents to suit special occasions and the tastes of his wealthy patron, he wrote operas, oratorios, solo concertos, sonatas, overtures, and liturgical music. But his most original works were those whose forms he himself helped to develop: the classical symphony and the string quartet.

The "father of the symphony," as Haydn is often called, wrote 104 symphonies and 84 string quartets. The string quartet, a concentrated instrumental form, met the need for elite entertainment in a small room or chamber—hence the term "chamber music." Unlike the symphony, the string quartet requires close attention to the fine points of musical discourse between the instruments. Unfortunately, such works are today often performed in huge music halls, rather than in the intimate surroundings for which they were intended.

After the death of Prince Esterházy in 1790, Haydn was invited to perform in London, where he composed his last twelve symphonies. In the London symphonies, which he wrote for an orchestra of some sixty players, he explored an expanded harmonic range and a wealth of dramatic effects. For some of the symphonies he used folk melodies as basic themes, inventively repeating key fragments in different parts of the piece. Among the most memorable of the London symphonies is the *Symphony No. 94*. It is known as the "Surprise Symphony" because Haydn introduced an unexpected *fortissimo* ("very loud") instrumental crash on a weak beat in the second movement of the piece. Tradition has it that the blaring chord, occurring amidst a soft and folklike melody, was calculated to waken a drowsy audience—London concerts often lasted well past midnight. It was also designed to entice them to anticipate the next jarring "surprise," which never occurs.

Haydn brought a lifetime of musical experience to his last works. Their witty phrasing and melodic effects made his symphonies enormously popular. Haydn's music was so popular, in fact, that eighteenth-century publishers often sold compositions falsely attributed to him. A celebrity in his old age, "Papa Haydn" (as he was affectionately called) was one of the first musicians to attain the status of a culture hero during his own lifetime.

The Genius of Mozart

The foremost musical genius of the eighteenth century—and, some would say, of all time—was Haydn's younger contemporary and colleague, Wolfgang Amadeus Mozart (1756–1791). A child prodigy, Mozart wrote his first original composition at the age of six and his first symphony at the age of eight. His ability to sight read, improvise, and transpose music, to identify the pitch of any sound, and to transcribe flawlessly whole compositions that he had heard only once, remains unequaled in the history of music. During his brief life, Mozart produced a total of some 650 works, including 41 symphonies, 60 sonatas, 23 piano concertos, 70 string quartets, and 20 operas. (These were catalogued and numbered in the late nineteenth century by Ludwig von Köchel, hence the "K." numbers used to identify Mozart's compositions.)

Wolfgang, the son of a prominent composer, was born in Salzburg, Austria. With his father, Leopold, and his sister Nannerl, he toured Europe, performing hundreds of public and private concerts before he was thirteen (Figure **26.34**). He often performed his own pieces, particularly his

piano concertos, which constitute some of his most important musical contributions. Unlike Haydn, Mozart did not invent any new forms. However, he brought to the instrumental genres of his time unparalleled melodic inventiveness. He borrowed melodies from popular dance tunes and transformed them into elegant compositions appropriate for garden parties, weddings, and balls. One such piece is the Serenade No. 13 in G Major, K. 525, also known as "Eine kleine Nachtmusik" ("A Little Night Music"), a work for small string orchestra. While light and buoyant, it is structured (as is evident in the recorded excerpt) according to the formal divisions of the sonata form: exposition, development, and recapitulation. Mozart incorporated popular melodies into his symphonies as well, three of which (K. 543, K. 550, and K. 551) were written in a six-week period in 1788. These pieces remain among the most eloquent examples of the classical symphonic form.

After leaving the service of the archbishop of Salzburg in 1781, Mozart sought appointments in the aristocratic courts of Europe, but he never received adequate patronage and had difficulty supporting himself and his family. Throughout his life, he was excessively concerned with money; when he died in Vienna at the age of thirty-six, he was buried in a pauper's grave.* During the last six years of his life, Mozart wrote four of his finest operas, receiving commissions for all but the first. These works are among the best loved in the Western operatic repertory: *Le nozze di Figaro* (*The Marriage of Figaro*, 1786), *Don Giovanni* (1787), *Così fan tutte* (*Thus Do All Women*, 1790), and *Die Zauberflöte* (*The Magic Flute*, 1791).

The *Marriage of Figaro* is an example of **opera buffa**, a type of comic opera that developed in Italy during the eighteenth century as a short, humorous entertainment. Formerly inserted between the acts of a serious play or opera, these **intermezzos** made use of stock, comic types such as the clever servant, the miser, and the fool. Like the playwright Molière (see chapter 21), Mozart transformed the stock characters of the Italian *opera buffa* into believable personalities—psychologically complex and often comical. Sharing Molière's view that wealth and status are accidents of fortune and may have little to do with personal worth, Mozart used his characters to level a pointed attack on the decadence of the European aristocracy. The central intrigue of *Figaro*, for example, involves the maid Susanna and her fiancé, the valet Figaro, in a plot to outwit their master Count Almaviva, who seeks to seduce Susanna. In an era dominated by aristocratic privilege, and one that still honored the feudal claim to "first-night rights" over a female servant, *The Marriage of Figaro* was unique: it championed the wit and ingenuity of the lower class (and especially the females of that class) over the self-serving arrogance of the nobility. And while such a theme might seem less than controversial today, it stirred heated

---

♪ See Music Listening Selections at end of chapter.

* For a fascinating interpretation of Mozart's life, see the play *Amadeus* by Peter Shaffer (New York: Harper and Row, 1981) and the Academy Award-winning film version of the play produced in 1984.

Figure 26.34 LOUIS CARMONTELLE, *The Mozarts in Concert: Leopold, Wolfgang (age seven), and Nannerl*, 1764. Engraving.

debate in Mozart's time—Napoleon called the play by Pierre-Augustin Beaumarchais (1732–1799), on which the opera was based, "revolution already in action." Certainly Mozart was more interested in music than in political reform—he agreed to temper Beaumarchais' scolding satire by way of Lorenzo da Ponte's Italian libretto. But his scorn for the upper classes—perhaps stemming from his own personal difficulties with aristocratic patrons—is readily apparent in the piece.

Politics aside, the enduring beauty of *The Marriage of Figaro* lies in its lyrical force and its expressive ingenuity. In the aria "Dove sono," the wife of the philandering count laments the loss of her husband's affections; she nevertheless holds out the hope of love's return. As this aria suggests, Mozart had a special talent for shaping personalities by way of music. While the characters in the operas of Monteverdi and Lully were allegorical stick figures, Mozart's appeal to us as real human beings. They convey a wide range of human expression, from grief and despair to hope and joy. Mozart's vocal music is never sentimental; it retains the precision and clarity of the classical style and invests it with unparalleled melodic grace. Only by listening to Mozart's

music can one appreciate the reason why Haydn called him "the greatest composer known to me either in person or by name."

Beethoven: The Early Years

Generally considered the third of the great classical composers, Ludwig van Beethoven (1770–1827) spanned the era between the classical and Romantic styles in music. Born in Bonn, in northern Germany, Beethoven spent the greater part of his life in Vienna, where he studied briefly with Haydn. His earliest works, mainly keyboard pieces composed between 1782 and 1792, reveal his debt to Mozart, as well as his facility with classical form and style.

Between 1793 and 1803, his first years in Vienna, Beethoven made his name as a virtuoso pianist, a composer of piano pieces, and a master of the string quartet. By 1799, however, he began to break with the more formal aspects of classical music. By the turn of the century, his compositions, which include the first two of his nine symphonies, would anticipate the tension and vigor, the emphasis on rhythm rather than melody, and the forceful instrumental language that would stretch classical form, and, ultimately, move in a new direction (see chapter 29).

See Music Listening Selections at end of chapter.

LOOKING BACK

The Rococo Style

- The fashionable Rococo style reflected the tastes of the European aristocracy. Notable for ornamental delicacy, intimacy, and playful elegance, this style dominated the *salons* of Paris and the courts and churches of Austria and Germany.
- In France, Watteau, Boucher, Vigée-Lebrun, Fragonard, and Clodion produced art that evoked a world of physical pleasure and sensuous delight.

Eighteenth-Century Genre Painting

- Encouraged by the *philosophes'* demand for an art of moral virtue, Greuze and Chardin produced genre paintings that gave dignity to the life and work of ordinary individuals.
- Genre paintings, especially those of Greuze and Chardin, were among the most popular images of the eighteenth century, collected by middle- and upper-class patrons.

Eighteenth-Century Neoclassicism

- Archeological investigations in Greece and southern Italy encouraged new interest in Greco-Roman artifacts and produced a more accurate picture of Classical culture than had been available previously.
- In Europe Neoclassicism influenced all the arts, from Adam's English country houses and Soufflot's "Panthéon" to the portraits of Houdon and Canova, and the ceramics of Wedgwood.
- In America Neoclassicism was best expressed in the architectural achievements of Thomas Jefferson.
- Just as the French Revolution swept away the old regime, so Neoclassicism replaced the Rococo style. As Jacques-Louis David's stirring pictorial recreations of Greek and Roman history invoked a message of self-sacrifice and moral purpose, Neoclassicism came to symbolize the ideals of reason and liberty.

- During the reign of Napoleon, Neoclassicists drew on the arts of imperial Rome to glorify the French capital, Paris, and the emperor himself.

Eighteenth-Century Western Music

- The period between approximately 1760 and 1820 witnessed the birth of the orchestra and the development of the classical forms of Western instrumental music.
- Classical music was characterized by order, symmetry, and intellectual control—features similar to those admired by Neoclassical writers, painters, sculptors, and architects.
- Composers used the sonata form to govern the composition of the symphony, the string quartet, the sonata, and the concerto.
- Franz Joseph Haydn shaped the character of the classical symphony and the string quartet; Mozart moved easily between light musical genres and classical instrumental forms, investing both with extraordinary melodic grace.

- In his operas as well as his symphonies, Mozart achieved a balance between lyrical invention and formal clarity that brought the classical style to its peak.

Music Listening Selections

CD Two Selection 8 Couperin, "Le Croc-en-jambe" from Ordre No. 22, harpsichord, 1730.

CD Two Selection 9 Haydn, Symphony No. 94 in G Major, "Surprise," second movement, excerpt, 1791.

CD Two Selection 10 Mozart, Serenade No. 13 in G Major, K. 525, "Eine kleine Nachtmusik," first movement, excerpt, 1787.

CD Two Selection 11 Mozart, *Le nozze di Figaro*, "Dove sono" aria, 1786.

Glossary

allegro (Italian, "cheerful") a fast tempo in music

andante (Italian, "going," i.e., a normal walking pace) a moderate tempo in music

bacchante a female attendant or devotee of Dionysus

brass a family of wind instruments that usually includes the French horn, trumpet, trombone, and tuba

coda (Italian, "tail") passage added to the closing section of a movement or musical composition in order to create the sense of a definite ending

concerto see Glossary, chapter 23; the classical concerto, which made use of *sonata form*, usually featured one or more solo instruments and orchestra

fête galante (French, "elegant entertainment") a festive diversion enjoyed by aristocrats, a favored subject in Rococo art

fortissimo (Italian, "very loud") a directive indicating that the music should be played very loud; its opposite is *pianissimo* ("very soft")

intermezzo a short dramatic entertainment, with music, inserted between the acts of a play or opera

largo (Italian, "broad") a very slow tempo; the slowest of the conventional tempos in music

opera buffa a type of comic opera usually featuring stock characters

pastel a crayon made of dry powdered color and a gum binder, used for drawing

percussion a group of instruments that are sounded by being struck or shaken, used especially for rhythm

satyr a semibestial woodland creature symbolic of Dionysus

score the musical notation for all of the instruments or voices in a particular composition; a composite from which the whole piece may be conducted or studied

sonata a composition for an unaccompanied keyboard instrument or for another instrument with keyboard accompaniment; see also Glossary, chapter 23

sonata form (or **sonata allegro form**) a structural form commonly used in the late eighteenth century for the first and fourth movements of symphonies and other instrumental compositions

string quartet a composition for four stringed instruments, each of which plays its own part

strings a family of instruments that usually includes the violin, viola, cello, and double bass (which are normally bowed); the harp, guitar, lute, and zither (which are normally plucked) can also be included, as can the viol, a bowed instrument common in the sixteenth and seventeenth centuries and a forerunner of the violin family

symphony an independent instrumental composition for orchestra

theme and variations a form employing a basic musical idea that is repeated with changes in rhythm, harmony, melody, dynamics, or tone color

woodwinds a family of wind instruments, usually consisting of the flute, oboe, clarinet, and bassoon

Picture Credits

The author and publishers wish to thank the following for permission to use copyright material. Every effort has been made to trace or contact copyright holders, but if notified of any omissions, Laurence King Publishing would be pleased to insert the appropriate acknowledgement in any subsequent edition of this publication.

Chapter 20

Figure
20.1 © The National Gallery, London.
20.2 National Palace, Mexico City, Dagli Orti. The Art Archive.
20.3 Altar of Cornaro Chapel, Santa Maria della Vittoria, Rome. © 1990 Scala—Ministero Beni e Att. Culturali.
20.4 Altar wall, Sistine Chapel, Vatican Museums, Rome. Nippon Television, Tokyo.
20.5 Uffizi Gallery, Florence. © 1996 Scala—Ministero Beni e Att. Culturali.
20.6 San Giorgio Maggiore, Venice. © 1990 Scala, Florence.
20.7 Refectory, Santa Maria delle Grazie, Milan. © 2002 Scala, Florence.
20.8 Courtesy of the Toledo Museum of Art, Ohio. Purchased with funds from the Libbey Endowment, Gift of Edward Drummond Libbey.
20.9 Santa Maria del Popolo, Rome. © 1990 Scala, Florence.
20.10 Uffizi Gallery, Florence.
20.11 © Mimmo Jodice/CORBIS.
20.12 Galleria Borghese, Rome. © 2000, Photo Scala, Florence, courtesy of the Ministero Beni e Att. Culturali.
20.13 © Vincenzo Pirozzi, Rome. fotopirozzi@inwind.it.
20.14 Kunstbibliothek, Berlin.
20.15 Saint Peter's, Rome. © 1990 Photo Scala, Florence.
20.16 Foto Marburg.
20.17 © Vincenzo Pirozzi, Rome. fotopirozzi@inwind.it.
20.18 Scala, Florence.
20.19 © Araldo de Luca, Rome.
20.20 © 1990 Photo Scala, Florence.
20.21 Nave ceiling, Sant'Ignazio, Rome. Scala, Florence.
20.22 Courtesy of the Municipal Museum, Turin, Italy.

Chapter 21

21.1 © 1994 Photo Scala, Florence.
21.2 Louvre, Paris. Photo R.M.N.—© Gérard Blot.
21.3 Musée de Versailles.
21.4 Chateau de Versailles et de Trianon. Photo R.M.N.—© Gérard Blot.
21.5 Chateau de Versailles et de Trianon.
21.6 Photo: James Austin, Cambridge, U.K.
21.7 Musée de Versailles. © Paul M. R. Maeyaert, El Tossal, Spain.
21.8 The Metropolitan Museum of Art, New York. Harris Brisbane Dick Fund, 1930 (30–22.32[53]).
21.9 Musée de Versailles. Lauros/Giraudon/Bridgeman Art Library.
21.10 Musée de Versailles. Lauros/Giraudon/Bridgeman Art Library.
21.11 Musée de Versailles. © Paul M. R. Maeyaert, El Tossal, Spain.
21.12 Musée de Versailles. © Photo R.M.N., Paris.

21.13 Louvre, Paris. Photo R.M.N.—© René-Gabriel Ojéda.
21.14 National Gallery, London.
21.15 Alte Pinakothek, Munich.
21.16 Bibliothèque Nationale, Paris.
21.17 Topkapi Sarayi Museum, Istanbul.
21.18 Philadelphia Museum of Art. The Joseph Lees Williams Memorial Collection.
21.19 © E. Böhm, Mainz.
21.20 The Chester Beatty Library, Dublin.
21.21 Courtesy of the Freer Gallery of Art, Smithsonian Institution, Washington, D.C. (42.15V).
21.22 Courtesy of the British Library, London.
21.23 © Doranne Jacobson International Images.
21.24 AKG Images, London/Jean-Louis Nou.
21.25 National Palace Museum, Beijing.
21.27 Gavin Hellier/Robert Harding World Images, London.
21.28 Courtesy of the Freer Gallery of Art, Smithsonian Institution, Washington, D.C. (42.20).
21.29 Ashmolean Museum, Oxford, Department of Eastern Art.
21.30 Courtesy of the Freer Gallery of Art, Smithsonian Institution, Washington, D.C. (F61.12).
21.31 The Art Institute of Chicago.
21.32 Imperial Palace Museum, Beijing.
21.33 Nezu Institute of Fine Art, Tokyo.
21.34 The Art Archive / Tokyo National Museum / Laurie Platt Winfrey.
21.35 © 1997, The Art Institution of Chicago, All Rights Reserved. Clarence Buckingham Collection, 1928.1056.
21.36 Kurt and Millie Gitter Collection.

Chapter 22

22.1 Image courtesy of the Board of Trustees, National Gallery of Art, Washington.
22.2 National Gallery, London.
22.3 Courtesy Saint Paul's Cathedral.
22.5 Hermitage Museum, Saint Petersburg, Russia/Bridgeman Art Library, London.
22.6 From Richard Phipps and Richard Wink, Invitation to the Gallery. Copyright © 1987 Wm. C. Brown Publishers, Dubuque, Iowa. All rights reserved. Reprinted by permission.
22.7 Rijksmuseum, Amsterdam.
22.9 William H. Scheide Library, Princeton University.
22.10 AKG-images, London/Werner Unfug.

Chapter 23

23.1 Städel Museum / Artothek.
23.2 Science Photo Library.
23.3 National Gallery, London.
23.4 Réunion des Musées Nationaux / Art Resource, NY.
23.5 The J. Paul Getty Museum, Los Angeles. Credit: © The J. Paul Getty Museum.
23.6 Kunsthistorisches Museum, Vienna.
23.7 © 2009 Board of Trustees, National Gallery of Art, Washington, D.C. Andrew W. Mellon Collection.
23.8 © The Cleveland Museum of Art 1998. Gift of the Hanna Fund (1951.355).
23.9 © 2009 Board of Trustees, National Gallery of Art, Washington, D.C. Andrew W. Mellon Collection.
23.10 Mauritshuis, The Hague.

23.12 © 2009 Board of Trustees, National Gallery of Art, Washington, D.C. The Widener Collection, 1962.
23.13 Reproduced by permission of the Trustees, the Wallace Collection, London.
23.14 © 2009 Board of Trustees, National Gallery of Art, Washington, D.C. Gift of Mr. and Mrs. Robert Woods Bliss.
23.15 Rijksmuseum, Amsterdam.
23.16 Mauritshuis, The Hague.
23.17 The Metropolitan Museum of Art, New York. The Crosby Brown Collection of Musical Instruments, 1889 (89.4.2363).

Chapter 24

24.1 Scala/Art Resource, NY.
24.2 © National Portrait Gallery, London.
24.3 Library of Congress, Washington, D.C.
24.4 The Metropolitan Museum of Art, New York. Gift of Mr. and Mrs. Charles Wrightsman, 1974 (1974.291).
24.5 Thomas J. Watson Library, The Metropolitan Museum of Art, New York.
24.6 Columbus Museum of Art, Ohio. Bequest of Frederick W. Schumacher.
24.7 © National Portrait Gallery, London.

Chapter 25

25.1 © Musées Royaux des Beaux-Arts de Belgique, Bruxelles.
25.2 Library of Congress.
25.4 Musée de Versailles. © Corbis/Bettmann, London.
25.5 © The Trustees of the British Museum.
25.6 © The Trustees of the British Museum.
25.7 Pierpont Morgan Library, New York. Bequest of Gordon N. Ray, GNR 78 (plate #16). Art Resource, New York.
25.8 © RMN / Réunion des Musées Nationaux.

Chapter 26

26.1 © By kind permission of the Trustees of the Wallace Collection, London.
26.2 © 1990, Photo Scala, Florence.
26.3 The Metropolitan Museum of Art, New York. Gift of Samuel H. Kress Foundation, 1958 (58.75.49).
26.4 Vanni/Art Resource, New York.
26.5 Louvre, Paris. Photo: R.M.N., © Gérard Blot.
26.6 © 2009 Board of Trustees. National Gallery of Art, Washington, D.C. Chester Dale Collection.
26.7 The Metropolitan Museum of Art, New York. Gift of Samuel H. Kress Foundation, 1958 (58.75.88 a, b, c).
26.8 © RMN / Réunion des Musées Nationaux.
26.9 The Metropolitan Museum of Art, New York. Bequest of Benjamin Altman, 1913 (14.40.687).
26.10 Louvre, Paris. © Photo Josse, Paris.
26.11 © 2009 Board of Trustees, National Gallery of Art, Washington, D.C. Samuel H. Kress Collection.
26.12 North Carolina Museum of Art, Raleigh. Gift of Mr and Mrs Benjamin Cone, 1969 (69.20.1).
26.13 The Art Institute of Chicago, Gift of Emily Crane Chadbourne, 1955.745. Photo by Robert Lifson. Reproduction, The Art Institute of Chicago.
26.14 © The Trustees of the British Museum.
26.15 Réunion des Musées Nationaux / Art Resource, NY.
26.16 © NTPL/Madia Mackenzie.

26.17 Galleria Borghese, Rome. © 1999, Photo Scala, Florence—courtesy of the Ministero Beni e Att. Culturali.

26.18 Courtesy Museum of Fine Arts, Boston. Gift of Dr. Lloyd E. Hawes.

26.19 © Angelo Hornak, London.

26.20 Photo: R. Liebermann.

26.21 Photo: Ralph Thompson. Albert and Shirley Small Special Collections Library, University of Virginia.

26.22 Courtesy of the Bureau of Printing and Engraving, U.S. Treasury Department.

26.23 The Library of Virginia.

26.24 Louvre, Paris. Photo: © Photo Josse, Paris.

26.25 The Metropolitan Museum of Art, New York. Catharine Lorillard Wolfe Collection. Wolfe Fund, 1931 (31.45).

26.26 Louvre, Paris. Photo R.M.N.—© René-Gabriel Ojéda.

26.27 Louvre, Paris. Photo: © 1990, Photo Scala, Florence.

26.28 The Annmary Brown Memorial, Brown University, Providence, Rhode Island.

26.29 © Paul M. R. Maeyaert, El Tossal, Spain.

26.30 © Paul M. R. Maeyaert, El Tossal, Spain.

26.31 © Paul M. R. Maeyaert, El Tossal, Spain.

26.32 From Carter Harmon, A Popular History of Music. Copyright © 1956 by Carter Harmon. Used by permission of Dell Books, a division of Bantam Doubleday Dell Publishing Group, Inc.

26.34 © The Trustees of the British Museum.

Literary Credits

The author and publishers wish to thank the following for permission to use copyright material. Every effort has been made to trace or contact copyright holders, but if notified of any omissions or errors, Laurence King Publishing would be pleased to insert the appropriate acknowledgement in any subsequent edition of this publication.

Chapter 20

READING

20.1 (p. 3): From *The Spiritual Excercises of St. Ignatius of Loyola*, translated by Louis J. Puhl, SJ (Newman Press, 1951). Reprinted by permission of Loyala Press.

20.3 (p. 5): From *The Poems of Richard Crashaw*, edited by L.C. Martin (Oxford University Press, 1957).

(p. 12): From *New Revised Standard Version Bible with Apocryphal/Deutorocanical Books* (HarperCollins Study Bible, 1991), copyright © 1989 by the National Council of the Churches of Christ in the USA.

Chapter 21

21.1 (p. 38): From *The Maxims of La Rochefourcauld*, translated by Louise Kronenberger (Random House, 1959).

21.2 (p. 39): From Molière, *Le Bourgois Gentilhomme (The Tradesman Turned Gentleman)*, translated by Curtis Hidden Page (modernized by the author) (G.P. Putnam's, 1908).

(p. 59): Matsuo Basho, five haikus from *An Introduction to Haiku* by Harold G. Henderson (Doubleday, 1958), copyright © 1958 by Harold G. Henderson. Used by permission of Doubleday, a division of Random House, Inc.

Chapter 22

22.1 (p. 64): "Twenty-Third Psalm" from *Douay Bible*, reprinted from *The College Survey of English Literature*, Shorter Edition, by Alexander Witherspoon (Harcourt Brace Jovanovich, 1951); "Twenty-Third Psalm" from *Authorised Version of the Bible (The King James Bible)* (Cambridge University Press).

22.4 (p. 66): John Milton, from *Paradise Lost: A Norton Critical Edition*, Second Edition, edited by Scott Elledge (W.W. Norton, 1993), copyright © 1993, 1975 by W. W. Norton & Company, Inc.

Chapter 23

23.1 (p. 80): Sir Francis Bacon, from "Novum Organum" from *The Complete Works of Francis Bacon*, translated by James Spedding (modernized by the author) (Longman, 1960).

23.2 (p. 81): Sir Francis Bacon, from "Of Studies" from *The Complete Works of Francis Bacon*, translated by James Spedding (modernized by the author) (Longman, 1960).

23.3 (p. 82): René Descartes, from "Discourse on Method" from *Descartes Selections*, edited by Ralph M. Eaton (Scribner, 1927), © 1927 Charles Scribner's Sons, © renewed 1955.

Chapter 24

24.5 (p. 106): Denis Diderot, from the "Encyclopédie" from *Diderot's Selected Writings*, edited by L.G. Crocker and D. Coltman (Macmillan, 1966), © 1966 by Macmillan Publishing Company.

24.6 (p. 109): Antoine Nicolas de Condorcet, from *Sketch for a Historical Picture of the Progress of the Human Mind*, translated by June Barraclough (Weidenfeld & Nicolson, 1955), copyright © 1955 George Weidenfeld & Nicolson Ltd. Reprinted by permission of The Orion Publishing Group.

Chapter 25

25.1 (p. 119): Olaudah Equiano, from Equiano's *Travels*, edited by Paul Edwards (Heinemann Educational Books, 1970).

25.2 (p. 122): Phillis Wheatley, "On Being Brought from Africa to America" from *The Poems of Phillis Wheatley*, edited an with an introduction by Julian D. Mason, Jr (University of North Carolina Press, 1989), copyright © 1966 by the University of North America Carolina Press, renewed 1989. Used by permission of the publisher.

25.4 (p. 126): Voltaire, from "Candide" from *The Best Known Works of Voltaire*, (with notes by G.K. Fiero, modernized and edited by G.K. Fiero) (Blue Ribbon Books, 1927).

25.5 (p. 129): Li Ruzhen, from *Flowers in the Mirror*, translated by Lin Tai-yi (University of California Press, 1965).

25.6 (p. 132): Jean-Jacques Rousseau, from *Discourse on the Origin of Inequality among Men*, translated by Maurice Cranston (Viking Penguin, 1984), copyright by Maurice Cranston.

Index

Numbers in **bold** refer to figure numbers. Text excerpts are indicated by (quoted).

A

Abbas, Shah 45, 46, 59
absolutism 25, 37, 44–5, 46, 51–2, 54, 56–7, 62
academies
    French 31–2, 37, 54
    Royal Academy of Art, London 143, 144, 149, 160
acoustics 162
Adam, Robert 160
    Kedleston Hall, Derbyshire 151, **26.16**
Adams, Abigail: letter 103 (quoted)
Adams, John 103
Addison, Joseph 113
Advancement of Learning, The (Bacon) 81
Africa: slavery 106–7, 117–22
Agony in the Garden, The (El Greco) 10, **20.8**
Agra, India: Taj Mahal 50, **21.24**
agréments 145
air pump 78, 81, **23.2**
Akbar, Emperor 46, 47, 48, 49, 59
Alberti, Leon Battista: Santa Maria Novella, Florence 17, **20.18**
Alceste (Lully) **21.8**
Alembert, Jean Le Rond d' 106
allegro 165, 169
Amadeus (Shaffer) 164n
Amati family 93
American Revolution 100, 117, 135, 155
Americas
    Jesuits in 2, 4
    slave trade 117–22
    see also United States of America
Amsterdam, Netherlands 70, 84, 92
Anabaptists 70
Anatomy Lesson of Dr. Nicolaes Tulp, The (Rembrandt) 92, **23.16**
andante 165, 169
Answer to the Question: What is Enlightenment?, An (Kant) 134
anthropology 98
Apocrypha: *Book of Judith* 12 (quoted)
Apollo Attended by the Nymphs (Girardon) 32, **21.12**
Apollo Belvedere 151, **26.16**
Apotheosis of Homer (Ingres) 159, **26.26A, 26.26B**
Apotheosis of Saint Ignatius (Pozzo) 18, **20.21**
Arc de Triomphe, Paris (Chalgrin and others) 162, **26.31**
Arc du Carrousel, Paris 162
Arcadian Shepherds (Poussin) 34, **21.13**
architecture
    American 153, 154–5
    Baroque 13, 14–18, 27–8, 62, 69
    British 69, 153
    Chinese 52–4
    French 25–31, 140–1, 150–1, 160–2
    Italian 14–18, 62
    Mogul 48–50
    Neoclassical 150–3, 154–5, 161–2
    Persian 46
    Rococo 140–1

Argis, Antoine-Gaspart Boucher d': *Encyclopédie* article on natural law 106 (quoted)
arias 21, 23
Aristotle 77, 78, 80
Art of Fugue, The (Bach) 95
Art of Playing the Clavecin, The (Couperin) 145
Asai Ruyoi: *The Tale of the Floating World* 57 (quoted)
Assembly in a Salon (Lavréince, N.) **24.1**
astronomy 18, 69, 77–8, 90, 98
Augustinian order 4

B

bacchantes 144, 169
Bach, Johann Sebastian 72, 73–4, 94, **22.9**
    The Art of Fugue 95
    Brandenburg Concertos 94–5
    preludes 73
    Well-Tempered Clavier 93
Bacon, Francis 79–80, 81, 84
    The Advancement of Learning 81
    Novum Organum 79, 80 (quoted), 81 (quoted), 84, 95
    Of Studies 81 (quoted), 113
Baldacchino (Bernini) 15, **20.15**
ballet 30, 37–8, 60
Ballet de la Nuit 37, **21.16**
balloon flight, first 136
barometer, mercury 78, 81
Baroque style 2, 10, 25–27, 28, 62, 74
    architecture 13, 14–18, 27–8, 62, 69
    literature 64–9
    music and opera 19–22, 72–4, 77, 93–5, 162
    painting 11–12, 35, 85–92
    sculpture 10–11, 13–14
Bastille, Storming of the 135, 136, **25.7**
Bavaria: Ottobeuren abbey (Fischer) 141, **26.4**
bayonets, attached 25
Beaumarchais, Pierre-Augustin 168
Beccaria, Cesare de: *On Crimes and Punishments* 108
Beethoven, Ludwig van 168
Beggar's Opera (Gay) 130
Beijing, China 55, 56
    Forbidden City 52–4, **21.25–21.27**
Bellay, Jean-Baptiste 136, **25.8**
Bernini, Gianlorenzo 13–15, 29
    David 13–14, **20.12**
    The Ecstasy of Saint Teresa 5, 14, 156, **20.3, 20.13**
    Fountain of the Four Rivers 13, **20.11**
    Saint Peter's, Rome
        Baldacchino 15, **20.15**
        colonnade and *piazza* 14–15, **20.14**
Bernstein, Leonard: *Candide* 126
Bible 62, 72, 73, 78
    Book of Judith 12 (quoted)
    Douay 62–4, 64 (quoted)
    King James 62–4, 64 (quoted), 72
Bichitr: *Jahangir Preferring a Sufi Shaikh to Kings* 48, **21.21**
bicycles 146
Bird's-Eye View of the Capital (Xu Yang) 52, **21.25**
blank verse 66
blood pressure 110
blood, circulation of the 78, 79
Bodin, Jean 98
Boffrand, Germain: Salon de la Princesse, Hôtel de

Soubise 140–1, **26.2**
Borch, Gerard ter: *The Suitor's Visit* 88–9, **23.9**
Borghese, Pauline: sculpture by Canova 153, 156, **26.17**
Borromini, Francesco: San Carlo alle Quattro Fontane, Rome 17–18, **20.19, 20.20**
Boucher, François 143, 156
    Venus Consoling Love 143, **26.6**
Bourgeois Gentilhomme, Le (Molière) 38–9, 39–44 (quoted)
Brandenburg Concertos (Bach) 94–5
brass instruments 162, 164, 169
Britain 62
    architecture 69, 153
    Civil War 62, 66, 68, 98
    "Glorious Revolution" 62, 68, 100, 103
    literature 62, 113–4, 122–5 *see also* poetry (below)
    music 72–3, 94
    painting and prints 130–1
    philosophers 84–5, 103–5
    poetry 5, 64–9, 113–4, 121, 122
    political theorists 98–102, 135
    satire 122–5, 130–1
    textile industry 117
    theater 69
Bruno, Giordano 78
Buddhism 5
    Zen 58
Buffon, Georges Louis Leclerc, Comte de 108
burins 71, 75

C

calculating machine 81
calculus 79, 82, 85, 107
calipers 86
calligraphy 58
Calvinism 70, 102
camera obscura 90, **23.11**
Candide (Voltaire) 125–6, 126–8 (quoted)
Candide (Wilbur and Bernstein) 126
Canova, Antonio 153, 156
    Pauline Borghese as Venus 153, 156, **26.17**
Cantata No. 80 73
    Passion According to Saint Matthew 74
cantatas 73, 75
    Cantata No. 80 (Bach) 73
Cao Xueqin: *The Dream of the Red Chamber (The Story of the Stone)* 56
capitalism 117
Capuchins 3
Caravaggio (Mighelangelo Merisi) 11–12, 13, 34, 71
    The Crucifixion of Saint Peter 11–12, **20.9**
    The Supper at Emmaus 11, **20.1**
caricature 131, 138
Carlin, Martin: lady's desk 141, **26.3**
Carmontelle, Louis: *The Mozarts in Concert* **26.34**
carpets
    French 30
    Persian 46, 48, **21.18**
Cartesian philosophy 82, 96
cartouches 17, 23
Cartwright, Edward 117
cast iron 117
Castiglione, Baldassare: *The Book of the Courtier* 134
Catherine II ("the Great"), of Russia 101, 125, 141

Mogul dynasty 25, 45, 46–8, 50, 59, **Map 21.1**
  architecture 48–50
  gardens 49
  manuscripts 47–8, **21.20**
  painting 47–8
Molière (Jean-Baptiste Poquelin) 38, 56, 166
  Le Bourgeois Gentilhomme 38–9, 39–44 (quoted)
Mongols 51
Montesquieu, Charles Louis de Secondat 102, 103, 106
  The Spirit of the Laws 102
Montessori, Maria 134
Monteverdi, Claudio 21–2
  Orfeo 21
Monticello, Charlottesville, Virginia (Jefferson) 154
mosques
  Imperial Mosque, Isfahan 46, **21.19**
  Red Fort, Old Delhi 49
movements (music) 94, 96, 165
Mozart, Leopold 166, **26.34**
Mozart, Nannerl 166, **26.34**
Mozart, Wolfgang Amadeus 166–8, **26.34**
  Così fan tutti 166
  Don Giovanni 166
  "Eine kleine Nachtmusik" 166
  The Magic Flute 166
  The Marriage of Figaro 166–8
  Mozarts in Concert, The (Carmontelle) **26.34**
Mumtaz Mahal 50
music and musical instruments
  Austria *see* Haydn, Joseph; Mozart, Wolfgang Amadeus
  Baroque 19–22, 72–4, 77, 93–5, 162
  British 72–3, 94
  Chinese 56
  classical 140, 162–5
  Dutch 86, 88–9, 90
  French 37, 94, 145
  German 72–3, 162, 168 *see also* Bach, Johann Sebastian
  Italian 21–2, 93, 94
  Neoclassical 37
  Rococo (*galant* style) 140, 144–5, 162
  symphonies 140, 164–5, 166, 169
  symphony orchestras 162–4
Muslims 2, 25, 44, 46, 50–1, 60

N
Napoleon Bonaparte 136, 156, 159, 160–2
natural law 98, 104, 105, 106, 110
  Encyclopédie article on (d'Argis) 106–7 (quoted)
"natural philosophy" 81, 85
Neoclassicism 32, 34, 113, 140, 148, 165
  architecture 150–3, 154–5, 161–2
  literature 38
  music 37
  painting 156–60
  porcelain 153
  sculpture 32, 153, 155–6
Netherlands 4, 62, 70, 86, 88
  Delftware 55
  music 86, 88–9, 90
  see also Dutch art
New England, USA: churches 153
newspapers 98, 105, 113
Newton, Isaac 85, 90, 98, 113
  Principia Mathematica 85, 98, 104, 107, 108

Nîmes: Maison Carée 161, **26.30**
No plays 57
Notes on the State of Virginia (Jefferson) 122 (quoted)
novels 98, 140
  Chinese 56, 113
  English 113, 130
Novum Organum (Bacon) 79, 80 (quoted), 81 (quoted), 84, 95

O
Oath of the Horatii, The (David) 157, **26.24**
objets d'art 30, 60
oboes 93, 94, 162, 169
Odyssey (Homer) 114, 159
Of Civil Government (Locke) 100, 101–2 (quoted), 103 (quoted)
Of Studies (Bacon) 81 (quoted), 113
Ogata Korin: *Irises at Yatsuhashi* 57, **21.33**
Olivier, Pietro Domenico: *The Theatro Regio, Turin* **20.22**
"On Being Brought from Africa to America" (Wheatley) 122 (quoted)
On Crimes and Punishments (Beccaria) 108
On Government (Locke) 100
On the Revolution of the Heavenly Spheres (Copernicus) 77, 95
Oosterwyck, Maria van 86, 160
  Vanitas Still Life 86, **23.6**
opera 72, 162, 166
  China 56
  France 30, 37
  Italy 21–2, 72
  see also Mozart, Wolfgang Amadeus
opera buffa 166, 169
Opie, John: *Mary Wollstonecraft* 110, **24.7**
optics 77, 79, 85, 90
oratorios 72–3, 74, 75, **22.8**
orchestras 37, 74, 94, 145, 162–4, **26.32**
Orfeo (Monteverdi) 21
organs 73, 93, **22.10**
Ottobeuren, Bavaria: abbey (Fischer) 141, **26.4**
Ottoman Empire 25, 44–5, 50, 51, 59, **Map 21.1**
  ceremonial canteen 45, **21.17**
overtures 21, 23
  French 37

P
Paine, Thomas 135
painting
  academic 32–4
  Baroque 10–12, 37, 85–92
  Chinese 54
  Dutch 34, 70, 85–91 *see also* Rembrandt van Rijn
  British 130–1
  Flemish 36–7
  French 31, 32–4, 35, 141–5, 146–8, 156–9
  Italian 5–9, 11–12
  Japanese 57, 58
  Mannerist 5–10
  Neoclassical 156–60
  Rococo 141–5
  Spanish 10, 35–6, 148 *see also* Greco, El
Palestrina, Giovanni di 19
  Pope Marcellus Mass 19
Panini, Giovanni Paolo: *Picture Gallery (Roma Antica)* 148, **26.13**

Pantheon (Church of Sainte Geneviève) (Soufflot) 150–1, 153, **26.15**
Pantheon, Paris (Soufflot) 150–1, 153, **26.15**
Pantheon, Rome 150, 154, **26.14**, **26.20**
Pantheon, The (Piranesi) 150, **26.14**
Paracelsus, Philippus Ambrosius 77
parachute, first 136
Paradise Lost (Milton) 66–9 (quoted), 69, 73, 74
Paradise Regained (Milton) 66
Paris 105, 117, 157, 160–2
  Arc de Triomphe (Chalgrin and others) 162, **26.31**
  Arc du Carrousel 162
  Hôtel de Soubise (Boffrand) 140–1, **26.2**
  La Madeleine (Vignon) 159, 161, **26.29**
  Louvre 25, 28, 31, 148, **21.6**
Parmigianino: *Madonna of the Long Neck* 8, **20.5**
Pascal, Blaise 81, 84
  Pensées 84
Passion According to Saint Matthew (Bach) 74
pastel 141, 144, 169
Peacock Throne 50
Peking *see* Beijing
Pensées (Pascal) 84
percussion instruments 162, 169
periodicals, English 113
Perrault, Charles: Louvre 28, **21.6**
Persia (Iran)
  architecture 46, **21.19**
  carpets 46, 48, **21.18**
  Safavid dynasty 25, 44, 50, **Map 21.1**
perspective, linear 55
Phèdre (Racine) 38
Philip II, King of Spain 10, 19, 70
Philip IV, King of Spain 35, 37, **21.1**
philosophes 105, 106, 108, 114, 115, 117, 125, 146
philosophy and philosophers 77, 81
  British 84–5
  French 81–3, 106, 108–9, 131–4
  German 134–5 *see also* Leibniz, Gottfried
  Italian 108
  "natural philosophy" 81, 85
physics 77, 78, 85, 107
pianos 164, 166
piazza 14, 23
Picture Gallery (Roma Antica) (Panini) 148, **26.13**
Pietism 62
pietra dura 50, 60
Piranesi, Giovanni Battista 149–50
  The Pantheon 150, **26.14**
pizzicato 21, 23
plants, classification of 108
Plato 83, 159
poetry
  African-American 121–2
  British 5, 64–9, 113–4, 121, 122
  Japanese 58–9
  metaphysical 64, 65
political theorists
  British 98–102, 135
  French 98, 102
  USA 102–3
polychoral music 21, 23
Pompadour, Jeanne Antoinette Poisson, Marquise de 143, 144, **26.6**, **26.7**
Pompeii, Italy 148, 160
Ponte, Lorenzo da 168
Pope Marcellus Mass (Palestrina) 19

Pope, Alexander 85, 113–4, 122
Essay on Man 114 (quoted), 117
porcelain 30, 141
Chinese 54, **21.29**
Imari ware 57
Sèvres 144, **26.3, 26.7**
Porta, Giacomo della: Il Gesù, Rome 15–17,
20.17
Portland vase (Wedgwood copy) 153, **26.18**
Portrait of a Family Making Music (de Hooch)
88, **23.8**
portraiture 77, 160
American 35
aristocratic 35, 36, 37
Chinese 56
Dutch 70, 85, 90–2
in England 37
French 35, 144
Japanese 57, **21.35**
Mogul 48
Spanish 35–6
see also Houdon, Jean-Antoine
Portugal 4, 117, 125, 126
Poussin, Nicolas 32–4, 36, 89, 148, 157, 159
Arcadian Shepherds 34, **21.13**
Pozzo, Andrea: *Apotheosis of Saint Ignatius* 18,
20.21
preludes 73, 75, 93
Principia Mathematica (Newton) 85, 98, 104, 107,
108
Protestantism 2, 62, 70, 73 *see also* Anabaptists;
Calvinism; Puritans
protozoa 79, 81
Ptolemy 77
Purcell, Henry 94
Puritans 62, 66, 69

Q
Qing dynasty 25, 51–2, 53, 59, 108
ceramics 54, **21.28, 21.29**
dragon robe 55, **21.31**
literature 56
Quesnay, François 106

R
Racine, Jean 38, 159
Phèdre 38
"Rake's Progress, The" (Hogarth) 130
Rape of the Daughters of Leucippus (Rubens)
36–7, **21.15**
Raphael 32, 148, 159
rationalism 81, 83, 108, 140, 146, 155
reasoning
deductive 82, 96
inductive 77, 79, 82, 96
recitatives 21, 23
"Red Fort" (Shahjahanabad), Delhi 49–50, **21.22,
21.23**
refrigeration 81
Rejoicing at the Birth of Prince Salim in 1569
(manuscript illustration) 48, **21.20**
Rembrandt van Rijn 70–1, 74, 91
The Anatomy Lesson of Dr. Nicolaes Tulp
92, **23.16**
Christ Preaching "Hundred-Guilder Print" 71,
22.1, 22.7
etchings 71
The Return of the Prodigal Son 70–1, **22.5**

Self-Portrait as Saint Paul 92, **23.15**
Renaissance 21, 77, 93, 154
reproduction, theory of human 79
"Republicanism" 103
Return of the Prodigal Son, The (Rembrandt)
70–1, **22.5**
revolutions
American 100, 117, 135, 155
French 25, 100, 105, 108, 117, 135–6, 144,
150–1, 156, 157, **25.1, 25.7**
"Glorious" 62, 68, 100, 103
Reynolds, Sir Joshua 149
Discourses 149
Richardson, Samuel 113
Rigaud, Hyacinthe: *Portrait of Louis XIV* 35, **21.2**
ritornello 94, 96
Robinson Crusoe (Defoe) 113
Rococo style 140, 157
architecture and interiors 140–1
gardens 141
music 140, 144–5, 162
painting 141–5
porcelain 141, 143
sculpture 144
Roman Catholic Church *see* Catholic Church
Rome, Italy 5, 7, 149
Cornaro Chapel, Santa Maria della Vittoria
14, **20.13**
Fountain of the Four Rivers (Bernini) 13, **20.11**
Il Gesù 15–17, **20.16, 20.17**
Pantheon 150, 154, **26.14, 26.20**
Saint Peter's 69
Baldacchino (Bernini) 15, **20.15**
colonnade and *piazza* (Bernini) 14–15, **20.14**
San Carlo alle Quattro Fontane (Borromini)
17–18, **20.19, 20.20**
Sant'Ignazio (Pozzo fresco) 18, **20.21**
Sistine Chapel: *The Last Judgement*
(Michelangelo) 7–8, **20.4**
Rotunda, University of Virginia (Jefferson)
154, **26.21**
Rousseau, Jean-Jacques 106, 117, 131, 133–4, 136
dictionary of music 108
Discourse on the Origin of Inequality among Men
132–3 (quoted)
Emile 134
The Social Contract 133
Royal Academy of Art, London 143, 144, 149, 160
Royal Society of London for Improving Natural
Knowledge 69, 80, 95
Rubens, Peter Paul 36
Rape of the Daughters of Leucippus 36–7, **21.15**
Ruysch, Rachel 86

S
Safavid dynasty 25, 44, 50, 59, **Map 21.1**
Saint Mark's Cathedral, Venice 21, 94
Saint Martin-in-the-Fields, London (Gibbs)
153, **26.19**
Saint Mary Magdalene, Paris (Vignon) 159, 161,
26.29
Saint Paul's Cathedral, London (Wren) 64, 69,
22.3, 22.4
Saint Peter's, Rome 69
Baldacchino (Bernini) 15, **20.15**
colonnade and *piazza* (Bernini) 14–15, **20.14**
Sainte Geneviève, Paris (Soufflot) 150–1, 153,
26.15

salons 30, 31, 60, 145
Parisian 105, 113, 125, **24.1**
Samson (Handel) 72
samurai 56–7, 58
San Carlo alle Quattro Fontane, Rome
(Borromini) 17–18, **20.19, 20.20**
Santa Maria Novella, Florence (Alberti)
17, **20.18**
sarabandes 94, 145
satire 114, 117, 122
in British art 130–1
in British literature 122–5
in Chinese literature 128–30
in French literature 125–8
satyrs 144, 169
Scholars, The (Wu Jingzi) 128
science
discoveries and inventions 25, 47, 77, 78, 79,
81, 84, 105, 110, 117, 136, 146, 152
and religion 81, 83–4
Scientific Revolution 2, 18, 77–9, 85, 108, 117
and art 85–6, 90
scores, musical 162, 169
sculpture
Baroque 10–11, 13–14
Neoclassical 32, 153, 155–6
Rococo 144
*Segawa Tomisaburo as Yadorigi, the Wife of Ogishi
Kurando* (Toshusai Sharaku) 57, **21.35**
Self-Portrait (Leyster) 91, **23.14**
Self-Portrait as Saint Paul (Rembrandt) 92, **23.15**
Sèvres porcelain 144, **26.3, 26.7**
Shaffer, Peter: *Amadeus* 164n
Shah Jahan 49–50, 52, 59
Shahjahanabad ("The Red Fort"), Delhi 49–50,
21.22, 21.23
Shakespeare, William 62, 66, 69
sharia law 44, 60
shawm 93
Shelley, Mary 111
Shikibu Murasaki, Lady: *The Tale of Genji* 113
shipbuilding 47, 70
silk manufacture 30, 46, 47
Sistine Chapel, Rome: *The Last Judgement*
(Michelangelo) 7–8, **20.4**
skepticism 84, 126
*Sketch for a Historical Picture of the Progress of the
Human Mind* (Condorcet) 109–10 (quoted)
slave ships 118, **25.2**
slavery 44, 102, 103, 106–7, 117–22, 136, **25.2**
slide rule 78
smallpox inoculations 47, 108
Smith, Adam 103–4
Wealth of Nations 104–5 (quoted)
social contract 98–9, 115
Social Contract, The (Rousseau) 133
sociology 102
sonata (sonata allegro) form 94, 96, 164–5, 166,
169, **26.33**
Soufflot, Jacques-Germain 150
Pantheon (Church of Sainte Geneviève), Paris
150–1, 153, **26.15**
Spain 4, 11, 70
painting 10, 35–6, 148 *see also* Greco, El
Spectator (periodical) 113
spinning jenny 117
Spinoza, Baruch 84
Spirit of the Laws, The (Montesquieu) 102